14

5-60

Yale Historical Publications

Miscellany, 101

Treasures among Men

The Fudai Daimyo in Tokugawa Japan

Harold Bolitho

New Haven and London: Yale University Press

1974

Library of Congress catalog card number: 73-86885
International standard book number: 0-300-01655-7

Designed by John O. C. McCrillis
and set in Baskerville type.
Printed in the United States of America by
The Vail-Ballou Press, Binghamton, New York.

Published in Great Britain, Europe, and Africa by
Yale University Press, Ltd., London.
Distributed in Latin America by Kaiman & Polon,
Inc., New York City; in Australasia and Southeast
Asia by John Wiley & Sons Australasia Pty. Ltd.,
Sydney; in India by UBS Publishers' Distributors Pvt.,
Ltd., Delhi; in Japan by John Weatherhill, Inc., Tokyo.

To the memory of my parents

Harold and Kathleen Sheila Bolitho

One day, a man of some consequence was planting rice seedlings, oblivious of his rank, with kimono tucked up, sleeves tied, a basket of seedlings on his back, and covered in mud. Tokugawa Hirotada, who chanced to pass by, saw him, and said "Isn't that Kondō?"

Seeing Kondō in such a condition, tears sprang to Hirotada's eyes. All his samurai were accustomed to working like this, although they tried to keep it from him.

"As you all know," Hirotada said, "I have no large fiefs to give you, and you are therefore driven to these extremities to support your wives and children. Were you newcomers [*shinsan*] I could not ask it of you, but you are all fudai of long standing, and love your lord. The fudai are treasures among men."

Adapted from Ōkubo Hikozaemon,
Mikawa monogatari

Contents

Preface

During the final three decades of the sixteenth century, after some two hundred years of chronic civil war, Japan began to take the first steps along the path leading from substantive anarchy toward a form of unified central government, and her progress, once begun, was rapid. The three famous unifiers of those years—Oda Nobunaga, Toyotomi Hideyoshi, and Tokugawa Ieyasu—each building upon the achievements of his predecessor, worked swiftly to give Japan once more, by the first years of the seventeenth century, both the sense and the reality of nationhood. Ieyasu, the final unifier, was able to establish a national administration (called the Bakufu, in imitation of the government founded in Kamakura by another warrior four hundred years before) at his personal seat of government in Edo—the modern Tokyo—which had far more claim to total hegemony over the islands of Japan than any earlier rule, even its Kamakura namesake. Gathering to itself powers never previously employed in Japan on a national scale, the Tokugawa Bakufu made use of them to impose two-and-a-half centuries of peace upon a nation of independent feudal barons.

A national government indeed, one might say, comparing the Tokugawa Bakufu with its forerunners and contrasting the Tokugawa peace with the centuries of bloodshed from which it had emerged. Yet it must be recognized that, significant as it was, the authority of the Bakufu was by no means complete. Despite its protestations, it was never to be so powerful that it could give Japan complete unity. The barons remained, their traditional prerogatives limited perhaps, but there nevertheless, their capacity for internecine warfare circumscribed, but not extinguished, since ultimately they were to rise again to overthrow the Bakufu. The Tokugawa Bakufu was strong, but never so strong that it could take the final step to national unification and dispense with the barons altogether; the feudal tie, by which land was given in exchange for obedience, remained to be reenacted symbolically each time a shogun or a baron died.

This book is an examination, albeit oblique, of the equilibrium
between central government and baronial independence, of the
balance between centrifugal and centripetal forces, as it was
during the Edo period, the years 1600–1868. It is observed mainly
through the fudai daimyo, a group of men who, while owing a
particular personal allegiance to the Tokugawa house, and serving as members of the national government, were also barons,
with the special responsibilities, privileges, and needs of provincial rulers. Their position was ambivalent—of the Bakufu, but
not of it; of the powerful barons, but also *not* of them. It is in
their shifting position between the two poles, the inward pull of
the Bakufu on one side, and the outward thrust of the barons,
or daimyo, on the other, and in their changing response to the
demands of central authority, that the ebb and flow of centralized
political power in Japan can be traced.

It has been my good fortune, in my work on this subject, to
be closely associated with three scholars who, perhaps more than
any others, have left indelible imprints on the study of Tokugawa
Japan. My debt to each is very great. The first is John Whitney
Hall, who supervised the Yale doctoral dissertation on which this
work is based and whose approach to the study of the local history of the Tokugawa period has profoundly influenced my own.
The second is Fujino Tamotsu, who guided my earliest reading
on the institutional history of Tokugawa Japan, and who since
then has been a generous and learned adviser. The third, Tsuji
Tatsuya, has given advice, criticism, and practical help on numerous occasions and in unstinting measure. There is little in
this work, whether theme, method, or bibliography, which does
not in some measure reflect my association with these men.

I owe warm thanks also to many others who have freely given
me time, encouragement, information, and criticism: in Tokyo,
Kanai Madoka, Abe Yoshio, Tsuda Hideo, and Kojima Shigeo;
in Tsuruoka, Saitō Shōichi; in Kokura, Yonezu Saburō; in New
Haven, James Crowley, Robert Bockman, and all the members
of the Hall seminar; in Melbourne, Jack Gregory, who first taught
me the history of Japan. I am grateful, too, for the patience and cooperation of the librarians and archivists of the Shiryō Hensanjo,
the Cabinet Library, the Ministry of Education Archives, and the
library of Tokyo Municipal University—all in Tokyo—the Ster-

ling Memorial Library at Yale, and the Harvard-Yenching Library. For financial assistance, I am indebted to the donors of the Saionji Memorial Scholarship, on which I first went to Japan, to the Myer Foundation, which enabled me to stay there for a vital third year, and to Yale University, which supported me throughout my course, initially on a graduate fellowship, and later, most generously, as Yale Fellow in East Asian Studies.

To my wife Anne, who has typed the manuscript in its various forms, advised, encouraged, and uncomplainingly set up house several times in three different countries, go the warmest thanks of all.

H.B.

Abbreviations

1. Introduction

The Bakufu did not arrive at its present predicament overnight; it is the result of decades of accumulated weakness.
Nishimura Shigeki, 1867 [1]

The Beginnings of Tokugawa Rule

Nobody could deny that the battle which took place on the grassy
upland of Sekigahara was a decisive military victory. The loose
confederation of warriors which fought beside Tokugawa Ieyasu
on that autumn day in 1600 had little difficulty in defeating the
even looser coalition confronting it. After chasing the western
army through the mist for seven hours, Ieyasu's eastern forces began to straggle back in midafternoon, bearing with them, so says
one official chronicle, more than 35,000 enemy heads as grim
tokens of their success (*TJ* 38 : 70).

This was a battle which had developed naturally, even inevitably, out of the situation of 1598. Toyotomi Hideyoshi, the second
of Japan's three unifiers, had died in that year, and his death had
plunged Japan back into uncertainty. Where a military chieftain
in his sixty-third year might have been expected to leave behind
him mature sons, cousins, and nephews to take up his burden,
Hideyoshi left only one son, Hideyori, a child of six. At once the
administrative and military machine that Hideyoshi had taken
over from Oda Nobunaga and had polished and perfected was
endangered. Hideyoshi himself had controlled it only with difficulty, so it was an impossible task for a child. On his deathbed
Hideyoshi extracted pledges of loyalty, on his son's behalf, from
vassals and allies, but it was unlikely that any such pledge wrung
from his ambitious and ruthless followers would long survive
him. Within a few months of Hideyoshi's death, his carefully
nurtured government was in fragments.

---

1. Quoted in Kojima Shigeo, "Bakuhan-sei hōkai-ki ni okeru kaimei-ha
kanryō no keisei," *Nihonshi ronkyū*, p. 457.
Unless otherwise indicated, all translations from the Japanese are my own.
All Japanese names appear according to customary Japanese usage, with
the family name preceding the individual's given name.

These fragments—by 1600, welded rather precariously into two opposing forces—met at Sekigahara, and victory fell to the group gathered around Tokugawa Ieyasu, once Hideyoshi's enemy, and later his strongest and least-trusted ally. The rival force had suffered two major defections in the course of the battle, and this, together with the obvious reluctance of some of its members to commit their troops to the thick of the fighting, led to its convincing defeat. Ishida Mitsunari, one of the nominal leaders, escaped the battlefield, only to be picked up six days later in the mountains of his old domain. His capture followed hard on that of Konishi Yukinaga, one of his confederates, and preceded by two days that of another, Ankokuji Ekei. All three were executed, after a decent interval, and their heads set up on the corners of Sanjō Bridge.[2] Of the prominent generals, Shimazu Yoshihiro, daimyo of Satsuma, hurried back to the safety of his southern domain, to make his grudging peace with the Tokugawa at a later date; Mōri Terumoto gave up his occupation of Osaka Castle, with some relief, in return for a promise (subsequently broken) that he would be permitted to keep his vast fief intact.

The victory at Sekigahara, then, had been a convincing one; but, even so, Tokugawa Ieyasu cannot have felt completely secure as he doffed his hood, put on a ceremonial helmet, and swaggered out to view the heads of those who had taken up arms against him (*TJ* 38 : 227). In the course of a long career, he had made and broken too many solemn promises, torn up too many pledges signed in blood to trust those extracted from his own current allies. His major supporters at Sekigahara—among them leaders of powerful warrior bands like Katō Kiyomasa, Fukushima Masanori, Asano Nagamasa, and Kuroda Nagamasa—still possessed independent bases of power. It was not to be supposed that they entertained no ambitions for themselves. Their word alone was hardly their bond, for they too had broken promises before, most recently that sworn in 1598 to the dying Hideyoshi. As a veteran of an age in which military alliances lasted only as long as discretion permitted, Ieyasu recognized how precarious it was to rely on men who were his peers, had been his rivals, and who had come to be his allies only within the last two years.

2. Imai Rintarō, *Ishida Mitsunari*, pp. 193–220.

Despite the ease of the victory at Sekigahara, despite the rout of those most openly his enemies, Ieyasu knew that his main difficulty would lie with his allies, and with the men who were even now moving to offer him tardy allegiance.

The potential vulnerability of Ieyasu, even after his greatest victory, is often overlooked by historians. Naturally enough, those chroniclers of the battle of Sekigahara who were contemporaries or near-contemporaries, or who shared in the later advantages of Tokugawa rule, all tended to emphasize the cataclysmic and decisive nature of the engagement. Before was nothing but chaos and bloodshed, and after, only peace and prosperity—so say the traditional accounts. One such description dubbed it "a great battle in which the fate of the nation was in the balance" (*TJ* 38 : 70 —*tenka wakeme no dai-gassen*), and this inflated phrase is echoed in the term *tenka no wakeme*, still in use among those Japanese historians who see Sekigahara as a watershed in Japanese history.[3] One scholar has claimed that, as a result of this battle, "the authority of Ieyasu began to shine like the sun breaking through dark clouds," while recently another has emphasized Ieyasu's consequent "supremacy," his ability thereby to "dominate the whole country."[4] Notwithstanding Ieyasu's nervous alliance with so many daimyo of questionable loyalty, and despite the continued presence of Hideyoshi's son as a potential focus for disaffection, the legend of Sekigahara is still a very potent one.

It is also misleading. If it is claimed that at Sekigahara Tokugawa Ieyasu had assured his complete mastery and authority, much of his subsequent caution is difficult to explain. His behavior between the victory at Sekigahara in 1600 and the victories against Toyotomi Hideyori in 1614–15 is inexplicable unless it is realized that Ieyasu still had considerable cause for unease, and uneasy he was. True, he had himself declared shogun in 1603, deriving from this ancient court title an appearance of legitimacy for the Bakufu, the government he was setting up in Edo. But he could place little reliance on the legitimacy obtained from a rubber-stamping court in Kyoto; legitimacy of this sort, since it was open to all comers, to anybody powerful enough to

3. See for example Kitajima Masamoto, *Edo jidai*, p. 11.
4. Kurita Motoji, *Edo jidai shi, jō*, p. 74; Conrad Totman, *Politics in the Tokugawa Bakufu, 1600–1843*, pp. 13, 33.

claim it, may have been a useful sword for the strong, but it was
no buckler for the weak. By declaring Ieyasu shogun in 1603 and
conferring the same title on Hidetada, his son, upon Ieyasu's retirement two years later, the Imperial Court no doubt confirmed
Tokugawa prominence. However, the appointment of Toyotomi
Hideyori to the even more venerable position of Minister of the
Right [5] in the same year was an ominous indication that, powerful as they were, the Tokugawa were by no means without rival.

Seen simply as a potential Young Pretender, Toyotomi Hideyori
was awkward enough, but as long as his only likely supporters
were those defeated at Sekigahara, the nascent Tokugawa rule
was in little danger. What did make the danger both acute and
immediate for the Tokugawa was not vanquished enemies, but
victorious allies, and Ieyasu was here at his most vulnerable. Instead of impressing his allies with his authority, he was constrained to treat them as equals; instead of overawing them, he
was compelled to placate them. Thus it is that we see the con-
queror of Sekigahara, after 1600, supposedly with all Japan at
his feet, in the anomalous position of having to distribute more
land to his hungry allies than he had actually won. He confiscated a total of 6,221,690 koku from the enemy at Sekigahara,[6]
but promptly gave out that much and more in fief increases—a
total of 6,511,000 koku.[7] Much of this went to his major confederates. Katō Kiyomasa had his already substantial domain at
Kumamoto doubled, as did Fukushima Masanori at Hiroshima.
Both Kuroda Nagamasa and Ikeda Terumasa had their holdings
trebled, giving them fiefs comparable to those of the other two.
Maeda Toshinaga was rewarded for what had been little more
than studied neutrality by having his enormous domain at
Kanazawa increased to over one million koku, confirming his position as the greatest of the daimyo.[8] Yet even after this generosity, Ieyasu still had to tread warily. He had good reason to
know that increased landholdings served only to sharpen the
appetite for more; after all, his own hunger had been whetted in

5. One of the three chief administrative posts in the ancient court hierarchy.

6. Fujino Tamotsu, *Bakuhan taisei shi no kenkyū*, p. 150.

7. Calculated from Nakamura Kōya, *Tokugawa Ieyasu monjo no kenkyū*,
2 : 814–20.

8. Ibid.

this way ever since 1560, when, as a petty provincial chieftain, he had begun his career of territorial expansion. By increasing the power and resources of those who had joined him at Sekigahara, Ieyasu could hardly expect to buy their quiescence, particularly when some of them still proclaimed sentimental ties with Toyotomi Hideyori.[9] It took Ieyasu over ten years of careful diplomacy to prepare the way for his assaults on Hideyori at Osaka in 1614–15, and, even then, with doubts about the intentions of generals like Katō Tadahiro, it was not without risk.[10]

Even his own personal vassals, the fudai daimyo, who are the subject of this work, provided Ieyasu with cause for concern. The rhetoric of the age, which they employed so readily, proclaimed their total loyalty to their master and their utter rejection of selfish motives, yet they, too, had to be rewarded for their services, receiving more than one million koku of the land which had been seized. The largest individual increase went to Ii Naomasa, whose earlier holding of 60,000 koku was trebled. Most of the others were granted smaller increases, usually less than 30,000 koku. But even here, amongst his most trusted, most dependent vassals, Ieyasu obviously had reason for anxiety. In 1614, just a few months before the Osaka winter campaign, Ieyasu confiscated the domain of Ōkubo Tadachika, a senior Bakufu official whose forebears had served the Tokugawa house since the late fifteenth century. The Ōkubo castle at Odawara was placed under guard, its outer walls torn down, and Tadachika himself packed off to close confinement in Ōmi.[11] While the precise motive is unclear, it must have been unusually compelling to prompt so drastic a step just when, with plans already afoot for an attack on Osaka, the Tokugawa needed every ounce of available support. Ieyasu mistrusted Tadachika's close contacts with the more powerful daimyo of the west country.[12] Nor did the anxiety stop here. In

9. Toyoda Takeshi has noted (in his essay "Eiyū to densetsu," *Rekishi to jimbutsu*, p. 21) that despite Tokugawa rule every tozama daimyo maintained in his domain a shrine to Hideyoshi, under the title *Hōkoku jinja*. Some enshrined statues of Hideyoshi or other memorabilia.

10. Yoshizumi Mieko, "Edo bakufu no kansatsu seido," *Nihon rekishi* 244 : 56.

11. Imaizumi Shōzō, *Nagaoka no rekishi*, 1 : 48.

12. Murakami Tadashi, "Shoki Bakufu seiji no dōkō—Ōkubo Iwami no kami Nagayasu jiken o chūshin ni," *Nihon rekishi* 205 : 26; Kodama Kōta and Kitajima Masamoto, eds., *Monogatari han shi*, 2 : 415.

the wake of the Ōkubo incident, Ieyasu was so concerned about
the loyalty of his own vassals that he demanded an oath of
allegiance, signed in blood, from the men he and his son, Hidetada, had selected to be the chief administrators of the Bakufu in
Edo. Of the nine clauses which made up this document, the third
read—"As Ōkubo Sagami no kami [i.e., Tadachika] has now incurred our displeasure, henceforth you must have no further contact with him or his son," an injunction which suggests Ieyasu's
reservations even about those closest to him.[13]

Victory over Toyotomi Hideyori in the Osaka winter and summer campaigns of 1614–15 was to place the Tokugawa in a much
safer position, although Ieyasu himself did not live to enjoy his
newfound security. In his seventy-fifth year, he contracted a chill
while out hawking and died within a year of Hideyori, the Young
Pretender of Osaka, who had so inhibited his drive for power. It
was Hidetada, Ieyasu's third son and titular shogun since 1605,
who now assumed the leadership of Japan with new assurance.
Despite rumors that Hideyori had escaped to Kyoto, that he had
not died at Osaka—rumors so pervasive in western Japan that
even the English merchant Richard Cocks came to hear of them
in his little trading post at Hirado [14]—Hideyori was dead, and
with him had vanished the only possible center around which
those discontented with the Tokugawa could assemble and for-
get their mutual differences. In this new, and comparatively relaxed situation, Tokugawa Hidetada, and his son Iemitsu after
him, could set about the real business of accumulating military
and political power for themselves, no longer having to share it
so scrupulously with others.

During the years 1616–51, these two rulers, with gathering
speed and confidence, steered the Edo Bakufu toward that guise
of feudal centralization and control under which it is best known
to us. In their hands, powers adopted only tentatively by Ieyasu
were broadened and strengthened, and they were to acquire prerogatives of a sort which the founder of the Bakufu had been
unable to contemplate.

By ambitious laws, particularly those gathered together in the

13. Nakamura, *Tokugawa Ieyasu monjo*, 3 : 821.
14. *Diary of Richard Cocks*, p. 12; Furukawa Koshōken, the geographer,
who traveled around Kyushu in 1783, wrote of rumors that Hideyori, escaping
to Satsuma, had found shelter there (*Saiyū zakki*, p. 98).

Buke shohatto (a set of Bakufu edicts regulating the behavior of daimyo) of 1615 and in the revised version of 1635, and also by the determined use of already existing administrative powers, the Tokugawa Bakufu turned to launch a frontal assault on those aspects of Japanese life which had hitherto inhibited the emergence of centralized control.

The list of powers and prerogatives this new government was to amass during the first half of the seventeenth century is indeed impressive. At the time of Iemitsu's death in 1651, there seemed few areas of activity where the power of the provincial barons had not been subordinated to the will of the Tokugawa Bakufu. One by one the daimyo had come to surrender all those independent privileges which had been so much a part of feudal Japan. Their tenure of their domains had become conditional, their freedom from external inspection had vanished, as had their traditional right to fortify their domains as they saw fit, and their fiscal immunity had been seriously impaired. The Tokugawa Bakufu had established its right to control foreign trade, and to control the major commercial centers together with the general machinery of interregional trade, coinage, and supplies of precious metals. No longer were daimyo free to conduct their own quarrels or their own foreign relations. In short, regional independence, encouraged by the topography of a land mountainous in the extreme and sanctified by an historical tradition which had never really known forceful centralized government, seemed to be breaking down under the first three Tokugawa shogun.

These advances in centralized government in early seventeenth century Japan are all well known, but they are sufficiently important to warrant a closer examination to see just what they represented.[15]

The Forms of Tokugawa Control

Of all the powers accumulated by the Edo Bakufu to assert its supremacy over the daimyo, the most potent and spectacular was that by which it could give and take land at will. It could crush

15. This catalog of Bakufu powers is so widely accepted that it has virtually become a standard feature of Japanese works on the Bakufu-han system. See Fujino, *Bakuhan*, pp. 171–310 passim; Kitajima Masamoto, *Edo Bakufu no kenryoku kōzō*, passim; Kurita, pp. 130–73; Kanai Madoka, *Hansei*, pp. 24–30,

a daimyo and his vassals, sending one to confinement or death, the others to lives of déclassé impoverishment, or it could move them all at will from one end of the Japanese islands to the other, building up other daimyo, other vassals, to replace them just as easily. Modern historians have seen this right as the cornerstone of Japanese feudal authority, "the basis of feudal landowner- ship," indisputable token of the shogun's "absolute authority over the daimyo." [16] Under the first three Tokugawa, the feudal tie which rewarded allegiance with a grant of land and punished disloyalty by taking it away was no empty formality. In the half century encompassing their reigns, some 213 daimyo were stripped of land, rank, and title by Bakufu attainders,[17] considered by one historian "the most severe of the Tokugawa family's measures of daimyo control." [18] During this same fifty years, 172 people were awarded fief increases to give them 10,000 koku and above, and so make them daimyo for the first time; at least another 206— daimyo already—were given further increases.[19] At the Bakufu's command, daimyo were moved from one part of the country to another on no fewer than 281 occasions.[20] In an age which mea- sured power and prestige in terms of how much land one held and how many fighting men that land could support, the early Bakufu, by giving and taking away so freely, made quite clear that it was the fount of all power and prestige.

To a large extent, after the massive punitive confiscations leveled at those vanquished at Sekigahara, the early attainders, reductions and fief movements were aimed at strengthening the Bakufu's hand against those it mistrusted. Ieyasu, for reasons al- ready outlined, was unable to turn on his nominal allies, but his son and grandson suffered less from these constraints. The purge of rival leaders began in 1619. In that year Fukushima Masanori, who had held the left flank of the van of the eastern army at Sekigahara, and indeed had unwittingly led the first engagement

16. Fujino, *Bakuhan*, p. 6.
17. Nakamura, *Ieyasu monjo*, 2 : 812, claims ninety after Sekigahara; Fujino Tamotsu, "Edo Bakufu," *Iwanami kōza Nihon rekishi* 10 : 25–27, claims 123 after 1602.
18. Fujino, *Bakuhan*, p. 192.
19. Ibid., pp. 154, 173, 180, 181, 236–37; the figure of 206 is calculated from pp. 718–24.
20. Ibid.

against the Ukita forces, was repaid in strange coin by having his 498,000 koku domain at Hiroshima confiscated. Accused of building new fortifications—that is, of presumptive rebellious intent—Masanori was given a small domain (45,000 koku) to maintain him, and was cast into close confinement for the remainder of his life.[21] Katō Kiyomasa, who had also fought on the Tokugawa side at Sekigahara, by dying in 1611, spared himself from witnessing the destruction of his line in 1632, when his son Tadahiro, deprived of his tenure of 520,000 koku at Kumamoto, was exiled to the Japan Sea coast.[22]

These, and many other similar acts of attainder were transparent attempts by the Tokugawa to rid themselves of uncomfortably powerful potential rivals. But, apart from this, the early Bakufu moved no less rapidly against those daimyo, irrespective of size and family history, who had proved themselves incapable of governing their domains in an orderly fashion. Peasant unrest, family squabbles, vassal vendettas, excessive taxation, disrespect towards Edo, failure to produce an heir—any one of these was sufficient to place in gravest jeopardy the position of any daimyo, be he enemy, ally, or Tokugawa retainer. No fudai daimyo, however devoted to the Tokugawa cause, could be confident of evading punishment warranted on any of these counts; even Sakai Tadakatsu, grandson of one of the Tokugawa "Four Guardian Kings," went in fear of a Bakufu reprisal in 1632 after there had been a mass exodus of peasants from his domain at Shōnai.[23]

To ferret out such offending daimyo, as well as to keep itself informed of conditions in their domains, the Bakufu began to send out inspectors, often without prior notice, to report on the internal stability of the various daimyo domains. The body of inspectors called *junkenshi*, in particular, formally established in 1633,[24] were the object of respectful attention from the han, the daimyo domains, for an unfavorable report could, and often did, incur the Bakufu's weightiest displeasure.[25] They were charged

21. Imai, p. 192; Imaizumi, 1 : 38, 42.
22. Tsuji Tatsuya, *Edo kaifu*, p. 357.
23. *Tsuruoka-shi shi*, 1 : 265.
24. Ibid.; *TK* 3 : 326-27.
25. Yoshizumi, "Kansatsu seido," p. 77.

with enquiring into such matters as the laws and legal procedures of the han, the eagerness with which domain authorities were discovering and extirpating evidences of the Christian religion, and the state of commerce, together with impositions on it (*TK* 3 : 328–29). Often their reports were full-scale enquiries, in which, apart from such matters as the dimensions of the castle, town firefighting facilities, and cases of notable filial piety, information was gathered on the population of the domain and the standard of living in the farming communities.[26] With such a mandate they were virtually certain to encounter cases of mismanagement or oppressive government demanding Bakufu intervention.

The *kunimetsuke*, or provincial censors, too, from their first appearance in 1609, and still more from their formal inception in the late 1620s, were another brake on daimyo independence. While the junkenshi specialized in whirlwind inspections, seldom taking longer than a fortnight, the kunimetsuke were sent by the Bakufu into certain han, where the daimyo was either very young or ill, and generally stayed there until such time as the Bakufu was satisfied that matters were being conducted according to its specifications. In either case, the Bakufu's intention was plainly to have its scrutiny of han internal affairs accepted as a fact of political life.[27]

Bakufu military predominance was another reality with which the daimyo had to live from the beginning of the Tokugawa period. This took the obvious form of overwhelming superiority in size of domain and number of forces. With its four million koku of crown land and its sixty thousand fighting men, the Tokugawa Bakufu was far larger than any of its likely opponents. Assuming, as they did, that the fudai domains were theirs to command as well, the Bakufu could draw on resources many times larger than those which any conceivable combination of opponents could possess. This in itself might have been thought to provide sufficient military security, but the Tokugawa did not stop there. In 1608 the daimyo of western Japan were ordered to turn over all their larger ships to the Bakufu, and this was rounded off with a flourish in the *Buke shohatto* of 1635, which

26. *Buzen sōsho,* 18 : 23ff.
27. Yoshizumi, "Kansatsu seido," pp. 53–60.

contained a prohibition against the construction of any vessel of a capacity of more than 500 koku (*TK* 1 : 64). The *Buke shohatto* of 1615 had explicitly condemned the existence of large castles as a "threat to the state"; it was forbidden to build new fortifications, and even repairs to existing works had to be approved by the Bakufu (*TK* 1 : 61). It was for his contravention of this law that Fukushima Masanori came to be punished four years later. Also in 1615 the "one castle per province" order was announced, calling upon the daimyo to destroy all fortresses in their domains, with the exception of that in which they resided.[28]

Not satisfied with compelling daimyo to tear down redundant castles inside their domains, and restricting their right to repair or augment those which remained, the Bakufu also forced them to contribute heavily to its own ambitious building program.

The first part of this involved the transformation of Edo Castle —hitherto an undistinguished fortress on the edge of a swamp— into a building more worthy of housing the shogun's person and government. In this the Tokugawa succeeded, with a flurry of large-scale building projects between 1602–36. When Ieyasu first entered his Kantō domain in 1590, the castle was in decay— so much so that, as one record notes," the thatched roof, caulked with mud, had leaked, and the matting had rotted." [29] Within a few short decades, assisted by the hapless daimyo, it was to become a gigantic castle, the splendor of which so impressed early European visitors.[30]

The second part of the Bakufu building program involved the construction of castles in other parts of Honshū. The first, begun in 1602, was Nijō Castle in Kyoto, a tangible intrusion of warrior power into the city of courtiers and monks. It was followed by castles at Hikone in 1604, Sumpu in 1606, Nagoya and Sasayama in 1609, Kameyama in 1610, and Takada in 1614, all of them built from materials, labor, and money provided by specified daimyo.[31] On top of this were demands for repairs to former Toyotomi strongholds, like those at Fushimi and Osaka, which the Bakufu intended to take over for its own use.

28. Kitajima, *Kenryoku*, p. 316.

29. *Ochibo shū*, p. 18.

30. See, for example, the comment of Rodrigo de Vivero y Velasco in Michael Cooper, *They Came to Japan*, p. 140.

31. Ōrui Noburu, *Nihon jōkaku zenshū*, 15 : passim.

No daimyo escaped these building activities, but the wealthier among them were called upon most often. Shimazu, Asano, Ikeda, Katō, Hosokawa, and Kuroda are names which appear with appalling frequency in the annals of this early building.[32] They provided the boats (Asano Yukinaga alone was responsible for 385) to transfer stones from the Izu Peninsula to Edo, paid for the quarrying of their quotas, and sent up huge armies of artisans, laborers, and officials to help on the construction.[33] In connection with their work on Edo Castle in 1606, for instance, the Mōri of Chōshū sent nearly two thousand men from their distant domain up to Edo. Then, as the allotted money ran out, Mōri Terumoto sent off a supplementary fifty kan of silver and promised to borrow more from the moneylenders of Kyoto and Sakai.[34] Date Masamune, working on Edo Castle in 1607, 1611, 1620, and 1629, and also bearing the brunt of the construction costs of Takada Castle in 1614, was in debt to the Daimonji-ya and Kikyō-ya, two of the Kyoto moneylending houses, well before he was finished.[35] If this seems excessive—and no doubt it was—it was not unusually so. During the same period, the Yamanouchi of Tosa were called upon to contribute to work on Edo Castle in 1605 and 1614, Sumpu Castle in 1607, Nagoya Castle in 1610, Kizu Castle in 1614, and on Osaka Castle on three occasions, in 1615, 1620, and 1625. Some idea of the burden involved can be gained from a contemporary estimate that during the Yamanouchi work on the walls of Osaka Castle in 1620, "each day, in addition to the peasant corvee, from two to three thousand day labourers had to be employed." [36] It is not surprising to learn that work on Edo Castle in 1635 cost Tōdō Takatsugu some 1,837 kan of silver.[37] Nor is it surprising that, by the 1620s, not only the Date, but many other substantial *tozama* daimyo were deeply in debt, among them the Shimazu, the Mōri, the Nabeshima, and the Yamanouchi.[38]

Plainly, the Edo Bakufu accomplished two major objectives

32. *Chiyoda-ku shi*, 1 : 414, 477.
33. Murai Masuo, *Edo-jō*, p. 49.
34. *Chiyoda-ku shi*, 1 : 426–27.
35. Kobayashi Seiji, *Date Masamune*, p. 184.
36. Sasaki Junnosuke, *Daimyō to hyakushō*, pp. 133–34.
37. *Chiyoda-ku shi*, 1 : 427.
38. Sasaki, *Daimyō*, pp. 132–33.

with its building program. First, it provided itself with a series of impressive fortifications in the strategically vital area between Kyoto and Edo without drawing on its own financial reserves. Second, by calling on the daimyo to bear all the expenses, the Bakufu helped keep poor the very people the castles were designed to intimidate, those against whom they were to afford protection.

However, the chief means of keeping the daimyo from dangerous affluence, and also the core of the Tokugawa Bakufu's system of military control, was the justly famous *sankin kōtai,* or alternate attendance system. After some years in which the daimyo were informally, but unmistakably, encouraged to spend part of their time in Edo and to send various members of their families there as permanent hostages, the sankin kōtai system became a firm obligation. The 1635 version of the *Buke shohatto* said, in its second clause: "It has been decided that daimyo and *shōmyō* are to alternate in residence at Edo; in the summer of each year, during the fourth month, they are to come to perform their duties" (*TK* 1 : 63). Initially this was to apply to tozama daimyo only, but in 1642 it was extended to cover fudai daimyo as well.[39] Of all the impositions shouldered by the daimyo, this was cumulatively the most costly. For the next 220 years almost every daimyo in Japan was to spend at least half of his life in Edo, a habit broken only briefly during the Kyōhō period. Their wives, and their children before maturity, lived permanently in Edo, in one or another of the several mansions which self-respect dictated that they maintain.

The results of this particular measure were profoundly important. To no small extent, the expenditures involved in maintaining several mansions (and rebuilding those destroyed by fire, in itself not the least of daimyo expenses), making long and stately journeys either to or from Edo once each year, buying and selling enough to sustain the large numbers of attendants at great distance from their homes was responsible for the expansion of commerce in the Tokugawa period. The same expenditure served to keep the daimyo in thrall to moneylenders. After vassal stipends, expenses related to sankin kōtai obligations accounted

39. Toshio George Tsukahira, *Feudal Control in Tokugawa Japan*, pp. 45–46.

for the greatest part of the expenditure of every domain. At Karatsu in North Kyushu, at the beginning of the nineteenth century, vassal stipends required almost two-thirds of the han income, and what was left over simply could not cover the 9,000 ryō needed for the sankin kōtai. More than one-third of this sum went toward the journey between Edo and Karatsu, a matter of thirty-four overnight stops. Not even at their most vindictive could direct Bakufu impositions begin to compare in cost with this sort of expense. In Chōshū, for example, from 1632 to 1636, the 24,000 koku demanded by direct Bakufu command pales into insignificance beside the massive amount of 330,000 koku spent in Edo, Osaka, and Kyoto on the sankin kōtai and matters related to it. Such burdens on the daimyo were likely to be discharged only at the expense of good government at home. The case of Fukuyama Han, where in 1815 the amount spent on the sankin kōtai—thirty percent of the total han expenditure—dwarfed the nine percent allotted to the expenses of han government, is all too common. On top of this, it is probable that a large part of vassal salaries also was eaten away by periods of enforced residence in Edo. As a measure which kept the daimyo in constant contact with Bakufu, provided living tokens of good faith, and kept them all paying out far more than they could afford, the sankin kōtai bore the earmarks of a successful measure of control.[40]

Linked with the sankin kōtai system was the attention the Bakufu gave to travelers; it had no wish to allow its permanent hostages—the wives and children of daimyo—to leave Edo. The establishment of a system of barriers, to be passed only with an official travel permit, attested to this. Instructions to barrier guards seemed to grow more elaborate with the passage of time. One of the earlier orders, of 1631, stated simply that "people with wounds, or women, or anybody else suspicious, are definitely not to pass [the barriers] without written permission," but by 1711, travelers were required to remove their hats, doors of palanquins were to be opened, corpses were not allowed to pass without

40. The information on Karatsu is to be found in *Karatsu-shi shi*, pp. 617–19, and also in Kitajima Masamoto, *Mizuno Tadakuni*, p. 57; for Chōshū, see Sasaki, *Daimyō*, pp. 134–35; for Fukuyama, see *Fukuyama-shi shi*, 1 : 498.

proper documents, and, in the case of daimyo, any irregularities were to be checked (*OKS* pp. 67, 72).

These manifestations of military control were accompanied by a policy of commercial control. Trade with foreign countries was brought under Bakufu supervision by the specially licensed merchants known as *ito-wappu*, a group which in 1604 was given a monopoly of goods (mainly raw silk) brought to Japan in foreign bottoms. Ultimately in the 1630s the Bakufu was to ban trade with Catholic countries and restrict the Dutch, English, and Chinese to Nagasaki; in the same years a series of edicts inhibited, and finally prohibited, overseas trading voyages by Japanese vessels. Nor was domestic trade neglected. If anything, the Bakufu was even more prompt in taking charge of the major Japanese commercial cities. In 1600, immediately after Sekigahara, the cities of Kyoto, Sakai, and Nagasaki were incorporated into the Tokugawa domain and placed under the supervision of Bakufu officials, and in 1619 the burgeoning city of Osaka finally joined them.[41]

The Tokugawa Bakufu was aware that it needed to establish itself beyond question as the overseer and coordinator of Japanese commercial life. The speed with which it asserted control over foreign trade and major market centers leaves little room for doubt on this point. It also hastened to make clear to the daimyo that there would be no tolerance of the regionalism and particularism which in preceding centuries had hampered the flow of goods from one part of the country to the other. The *Buke shohatto* of 1635 came out strongly on the side of free passage of goods throughout the country, whether through Bakufu or daimyo domain, with an order reading: "There shall be no interference with roads, highways, post towns, horses, boats or bridges; there must be no laws inhibiting traffic. Private barriers and new embargoes (*tsudome*) are prohibited" (*TK* 1 : 64).

In 1600, Japanese currency was in chaos; coins of Chinese, provincial and metropolitan provenance were in common, although not indiscriminate, use. A study of a remote northern domain (Akita) at the beginning of the Tokugawa period has revealed the circulation of no fewer than seventeen different kinds of gold, silver, and copper coin, some of them generally acceptable

41. Kitajima, *Kenryoku*, pp. 292, 296–99, 314.

throughout Japan, but many of them not. No government with any pretension to central power could possibly approve of such a cumbersome system, and the Tokugawa were prompt to grasp the prerogative of minting the nation's coins. They first minted gold and silver coins in 1601 and in 1606 produced their own copper coins; the use of all others was prohibited, initially a matter of some difficulty, but ultimately, as the daimyo were drawn one by one into activities in Edo and Osaka, the Bakufu's own coinage prevailed. In any case, since the Tokugawa had also taken charge of the nation's major sources of precious metals, there was little opportunity to mint coins privately. Each of the most productive of the Japanese gold and silver mines fell very quickly into Tokugawa hands. The Izu mine had been made part of Ieyasu's domain as early as 1590, and after the victory at Sekigahara he added to it the mines of Iwami (confiscated from the Mōri), Sado (confiscated from the Uesugi), and Ikuno. Iemitsu, who appropriated the Nobezawa silver mine in Dewa in 1634, as soon as it began to produce silver in large quantities, simply continued this trend.[42]

Finally, in this catalog of the prerogatives acquired by the early Bakufu, one must mention two essential to any centralized government. The first was the authority to settle disputes among the several daimyo, to which, the Bakufu first laid formal claim in the 1635 *Buke shohatto:* "The lords of all the provinces and domains are not to indulge in private quarrels, and must always behave with circumspection; however, when there are matters in dispute, the magistrate's office must be informed, and its decision is to be accepted" (*TK* 1 : 64). Whenever arguments arose between one han and another—as they often did over such issues as boundaries, water rights, and private disputes between members of one domain and those of another—they were to go to the Bakufu as a matter of course for its adjudication. The second of the indispensable Bakufu prerogatives was its control of foreign affairs. There was never very much doubt after Sekigahara that the shogun was the leading figure. By the time Iemitsu, the third

42. For Akita and its currency, see Fujino, *Bakuhan*, pp. 289–90. Information on the other aspects of currency and mining is from ibid., pp. 286–88, 290–91; from Kitajima, *Kenryoku*, pp. 302–03; and from Kobata Atsushi, *Nihon kōzan no rekishi*, p. 135.

shogun, issued the series of laws between 1633 and 1638 which effectively isolated Japan from all but the most limited of outside contact, there were no voices raised in overt protest at this most dramatic proof of the shogun's kingly powers. So tractable were the daimyo, and so readily persuaded of the justice of the Bakufu's position, that Chōshū, Fukuoka, Hirado, Karatsu, and Kokura Han, when a Chinese ship blundered into Karatsu Bay in 1644, spontaneously sent out ships to sink it without pausing to enquire as to its business.[43]

By almost any standards, the sum total of these prerogatives grasped by the early Bakufu is impressive. Through free use of attainders and fief transfers, the first three Tokugawa shogun came near to destroying the daimyo's independent possession of his domain; he could hold it only with Bakufu approval. No doubt there was an element of pious exaggeration in the statement of one early seventeenth century daimyo who informed his people, "Your daimyo is the lord of this province, but the rice-paddies and the fields belong to the Bakufu [kōgi]," [44] but it was very largely a recognition of the Bakufu's latent power. The unfettered use of inspectors did enormous damage to the principle of daimyo autonomy, and so did the twenty-first article of the 1635 *Buke shohatto,* which ordered that, "Throughout the country all matters are to be carried out in accordance with the laws of Edo." By forcing the daimyo into large extraordinary expenditures as well as recurrent ones through residence in Edo, the Tokugawa maneuvered them into a disadvantageous situation strategically, economically, and financially, and into a commercial world where it had some control, but the daimyo had none. They had also been deprived of the warrior's primal right, that of taking the law into his own hands, and of their capacity to speak for themselves in the crucial field of foreign relations.

This is undeniably a spectacular list of achievements, more so because no previous form of government in Japan had ever so successfully laid claim to such broad powers. Join to this the undisputed fact that the Tokugawa Bakufu endured far longer than any other ruling body in Japanese history, providing considerable prosperity and tranquillity for its people, and one has all the

43. *Karatsu-shi shi,* p. 570.
44. Quoted in Kitajima, *Kenryoku,* pp. 326–27.

ingredients necessary for a theory of Bakufu invincibility—invincibility, that is, until its final overturning. The popular view of the Edo Bakufu accepts this invincibility, emphasizing Bakufu omnipotence, ruthlessness, efficiency, and omniscience through an "elaborate system of espionage." Scholarly opinion, too, while less hasty to condemn the repressive aspects of such a government, is no less convinced of its authority. Some historians discern in the shogun a resemblance to the absolute monarchs of Europe, comparing the government over which he presided to the modern centralized state. Others, perhaps the majority, while more cautious, also note the proliferation of forms of state control under the Tokugawa, although they admit the limitations imposed by the continued survival of the daimyo domains. Such scholars, Japanese and foreign, see the Bakuhan system as a halfway house between feudal anarchy and monarchical absolutism, calling it *shūken-teki hōken sei*, centralized feudalism (or feudal monarchy, since the connotations are the same).[45]

There seems little reason to dispute this terminology, given the coexistence of elements of centralization and decentralization in Tokugawa Japan. Nevertheless, like all other pieces of historical shorthand, its very conciseness can be deceptive. Despite the convenience of such terms as "centralized feudalism" or "feudal monarchy" in describing the Bakuhan system, these scholars gloss over an area of considerable imprecision simply by suggesting a passive balance of forces which were, in fact, in constant tension and competition. Like the centaur, the concept of centralized feudalism is a plausible one, being composed of two elements each of

45. The espionage quotation is from Tsukahira, *Feudal Control*, p. 9, and a similar one is to be found in James Murdoch, *A History of Japan*, 3 : 77. References to similarities between the Japanese state and its ruler and European monarchies and their kings are to be seen in Sir George Sansom, *The Western World and Japan*, p. 182; Donald Keene, *The Japanese Discovery of Europe*, p. 125; Kanai, *Hansei*, p. 24; Nakai Nobuhiko, *Bakuhan shakai to shōhin ryūtsū*, p. 23; Kitajima Masamoto, ed., *Seiji shi*, 2., p. 5. Among those who write of Japan's centralized feudalism are Iwata Masakazu, *Okubo Toshimichi*, p. 12; S. N. Eisenstadt, *Modernization: Protest and Change*, p. 2; E. O. Reischauer, "Japanese Feudalism," in *Feudalism in History*, ed. Rushton Coulborn, p. 37; John W. Hall, *Government and Local Power in Japan, 500–1700*, pp. 346, 367–68; Fujino Tamotsu in *Fudai hansei no tenkai to Meiji ishin*, ed. Kimura Motoi and Sugimoto Toshio, p. 2; Tsuda Hideo, "Kansei kaikaku," *Iwanami kōza Nihon rekishi* 12 : 257.

which, in isolation, is quite familiar to us. Yet, unlike the centaur, which is most neatly half man and half horse, the balance of elements necessary to produce a static feudal monarchy is not easily obtained. Flux, not stasis, is its hallmark, and one of its two warring elements has always predominated over the other. In France and England, the balance was overturned when the monarch began to destroy the feudal order around him, making himself stronger at the expense of his barons. In Japan, there was a similar rejection of passive balance but in the opposite direction, toward a diminution of central powers with increasing baronial independence.

The Limitations of Tokugawa Control

In the years before its collapse, the Tokugawa Bakufu was to see all of its prerogatives, one after the other, successfully challenged by the daimyo. First went its right to the sole determination of foreign policy, openly abandoned in 1853 by a government so unsure of its authority that it felt obliged to canvass daimyo opinion on the most suitable response to make to Commodore Perry. Shortly after, its pretensions to arms control vanished, as daimyo were permitted to build ships free of the old restrictions, and this was followed later by the relaxation of the sankin kōtai system. In 1864, with the first Chōshū campaign, and in 1866 with the second, the Bakufu was to become involved in two successive wars to demonstrate its right to punish daimyo for disobedience; the first of these was only partially successful, and the second a disastrous failure.

The speed with which these signs of decay appeared after 1853, and the decisive impact they were to have on the Bakufu's capacity for survival, have often blinded historians to the existence of a far slower, far better established, cumulative decline of which they were the end product. As Nishimura Shigeki was to observe on the eve of the Bakufu's collapse, a very much longer process was at work—nothing less than "decades of accumulated weakness." [46] In almost every way, the Bakufu, on the eve of Tokugawa Iemitsu's death in 1651, was far stronger than that which awaited Commodore Perry's visit two hundred years later: the former seemed well on the way to centralized monarchy,

46. Kojima, "Kaimei-ha kanryō," p. 457.

while the latter was well on the way to ruin. The "decades of accumulated weakness" had virtually destroyed the Bakufu as a centralized government long before an official American foot was placed on Japanese soil. The first three Tokugawa shogun had acquired powers on an impressive scale, but this process was not to be maintained under their descendants, and many of the formidable powers already acquired were allowed to lapse. Of the prerogatives described in the preceding section, only a few were to survive in anything like the vigorous shape of the early years; the vast majority, once established, fell into disuse. Consequently, as Bodhidarma after nine years of meditation in the shade of a tree found his legs withered beyond all use, so the Bakufu was to discover that, through neglect of its prerogatives, it was unable to use them when its need was greatest.

The most durable of the Bakufu's powers over the daimyo was that reflected in the sankin kōtai, for it was to continue substantially unchanged until its abolition in 1862. It is true that, even from its inception, daimyo who had incurred unusual burdens were often excused all or part of their Edo duties. This was so in 1638, when those who had provided troops to suppress the Shimabara rising were released from attendance, and it was still the case in 1754, when Shimazu Shigetoshi saw his sankin obligation waived in return for contributions to an official engineering project.[47] Furthermore, during the years 1722–30 the mandatory term of residence was reduced from twelve to six months in each twenty-four months. For that matter, some daimyo were so fond of life in Edo that they lingered there past the obligatory period. It is surely significant that, of the twelve Makino daimyo of Nagaoka, all but two were buried in Edo. No matter where they died, the other ten, had they so wished, could have been preserved in brine and carried to Nagaoka for burial. The first Makino daimyo had done precisely that. It must surely argue some sentimental attachment to Edo on the part of those ten of his descendants who chose to stay there forever.[48]

There is other evidence to indicate that not all daimyo disliked their compulsory visits to the seat of the Bakufu. A letter

47. *Buzen sōsho*, 11 : 37; Yoshizumi Mieko, "Tetsudai bushin ni tsuite," *Gakushūin Daigaku Bungakubu kenkyū nempō*, 14 : 101.
48. Imaizumi, 1 : 53–55.

of complaint sent to the daimyo of Shōnai by his vassals in 1707 mentions, among other flaws in his character, his willingness to spend too much time there.[49] The sankin kōtai system may even have been self-perpetuating to some degree, carried on with daimyo consent. There seems to have been little to hinder any hostage who really wished to leave Edo. As a contemporary wrote of the Kurihashi barrier, just north of the city: "This barrier is in the charge of Lord Ina Hanzaemon, and here passersby are checked. Women travelers in particular are closely inspected. Yet, since it is situated in a broad plain, a detour of two or three ri in any direction will reveal many routes along which women may pass without scrutiny. Is this due to the benevolence of our government?"[50]

Nevertheless, none of this can diminish the fact that the sankin kōtai system lasted—despite the terrible toll it took of han finances—almost as long as did the Bakufu itself. Any discussion of the relative strength of the Bakufu in Tokugawa Japan must take this into account, just as it must the Bakufu's continuing role as mediator in daimyo disputes. Despite the waning of control over the daimyo, the forms of authority remained, and the survival of as symbolically potent a form as the sankin kōtai attests to a certain measure of feudal cohesion, despite all other evidence of fragmentation. Its continued existence alone renders it impossible to argue the utter collapse of the central government in the Tokugawa period, no matter how suggestive the evidence to the contrary.

Despite this, however, the singular failure in all other aspects of the Bakufu's machinery for daimyo control deserves recognition, delineation, and comment. The sankin kōtai may have existed with its significance unchanged throughout the bulk of the Tokugawa period, may have existed in fact far beyond the capacity of the Bakufu to enforce it—if it ever could—through such mechanical devices as barrier checks for women being smuggled out and weapons being smuggled in, but it must not distract us from recognizing that other centralized powers of the Bakufu were to be diminished to a greater or lesser degree as the Edo period progressed. The first two *Buke shohatto*—and the other

49. *Tsuruoka-shi shi*, 1 : 323.
50. *Tōyū zakki*, p. 4.

administrative commands as well—although seemingly awesome
enough in the range of powers they suggest, were only pieces
of paper. They simply defined the area of power to which the
Tokugawa laid claim. In no way do they show how far the
Bakufu, at any given time, was able to, or even wished to, set that
power to work. How far were they enforced?

First of all, what of the Bakufu's exclusive control of currency? True, it continued to use its minting prerogative, issuing
its own coins in its own time and for its own reasons. But from
as early as the mid-seventeenth century onward, it also began to
permit han to issue paper currency for circulation within their
own borders. The flow of *hansatsu*, as the notes were called, although interrupted briefly in the early eighteenth century, continued until the Bakumatsu, when there were some 1,700 different varieties in circulation in 244 domains, presenting a situation
even more complex than that which had greeted the Tokugawa
in 1600. The use of these notes, originally limited to the domain
of origin, was to spread much further, to the extent that some
han were forced to prohibit the circulation of the paper money
of other domains; Obama did this in 1820, for example. Still
more indicative of the Bakufu's loss of control is the fact that
its own currency was often put on the defensive. In many cases
han were so eager to promote their own paper currency that
they went so far as to prohibit the circulation of Bakufu notes
and coins. In Hikone, the former were banned in 1742 and the
latter in 1798.[51] No government intent on enforcing its authority
would derive much pleasure from defiance of this sort, and the
Bakufu's general complaisance casts doubt on how far it had
the power, or, more important, the will, to grapple with the problem. The original prohibition of hansatsu in 1707 was abandoned
in 1730. In 1759 it was announced that no more han would be
given permission to issue their own notes, and that certain sorts
of notes would be totally prohibited, the reason being that "if
this tendency [to freely circulate notes] increases it will be difficult to tell which is which later on," but all such measures were
without effect (*TJ* 46 : 740).

51. Figures for the Bakumatsu are from Endō Motoo and Ōmori Shirō, eds.,
Nihonshi handobukku, and from Takayanagi Mitsuhisa and Takeuchi Rizō,
eds., *Nihonshi jiten*. For Obama, see *Fukui-ken shi* Vol. 2, no. 2, p. 98, and
for Hikone, see *Hikone-shi shi*, 2 : 630.

The Bakufu's early control of mines also came to mean less as time went on. This was partly involuntary, since the significance of the mines acquired so early and so easily was to diminish markedly as their production decreased. Japan's output of gold and silver reached a peak in the early seventeenth century and began to fall away in a spectacular fashion from the 1660s onwards. It was one matter, for example, to own the Sado mines in the 1620s, when they were producing 5,000–6,000 kan of silver and 40,000–50,000 gold ryō annually, but quite another to do so in the 1640s, when they had stopped producing gold altogether, and still another in 1692, when their output of silver had slumped to an annual figure of 685 kan.[52] In any case, Tokugawa ownership and management of gold and silver mines seems to have been limited to the major mines only. There is no doubt that some domains maintained mines well established before Sekigahara, and others developed new ones, keeping the bulk of their produce themselves and paying only a portion of it to the Bakufu. In 1733 the Bakufu did declare itself interested in finding new mines, but as the declaration came in the form of instructions to *daikan,* the intendants of the Bakufu's own domains, there is reason to suspect that the old Bakufu right to gold and silver mines wherever they might be, was no longer asserted.[53]

Bakufu policy toward copper mines encourages this suspicion. Copper was relatively unimportant at the beginning of the Tokugawa period, but it grew rapidly in significance from the middle of the seventeenth century, when it came to replace the flagging gold and silver supplies as Japan's chief means of paying for her foreign trade at Nagasaki. By the 1660s copper was Japan's greatest single export, and was needed in such quantities both for this and for domestic use that the supply could not keep pace. Because of this, the Bakufu might reasonably have been expected to claim control of the copper mines as it once had with gold and silver mines, but this seldom was done. A thorough survey of copper mines was made in 1703, and it is presumably no accident that the following year the Bakufu confiscated the single most productive seam, running between Besshi and Tachikawa in Shikoku. But when other confiscations occurred, from time to

52. Kitajima, *Kenryoku,* p. 307; Kitajima, *Edo jidai,* p. 124; Kobata Atsushi, *Kinsei shakai,* p. 186.
53. *TJ* 41 : 219; for domain mines, see Kobata, *Kōzan,* pp. 135–36.

time, they were not nearly as significant. Of the fourteen richest copper mines in 1703, only the two in Shikoku were to come under Bakufu control; the rest, including the wealthy Ani mine in Akita and the Osarizawa mine in Nambu (which had 3,000 miners working on it in 1788) remained under the authority of the han. Throughout the eighteenth century there were a number of unsuccessful attempts to regulate the copper trade, to make sure the Nagasaki authorities always had enough for their needs. Apparently, wholesale confiscation of copper mines was no longer a feasible solution.[54]

Bakufu claims to control of national commerce were notoriously unsuccessful, but then so were the attempts of most daimyo to control the commercial life of their domains. The rise of local market centers away from both the provincial castle towns and the national markets of Osaka and Edo, together with the related rise of a new type of merchant, was the most important commercial development in Japan during the last century of Tokugawa rule, and it was one which proved resistant to control from Bakufu and daimyo alike. Nonetheless, in that area where Bakufu pretensions to national control conflicted most markedly with the demands of han-controlled commercial activity, the Bakufu lost out. Until 1859, for as long as the *Buke shohatto* was issued, the 1635 prohibition of private embargoes—*tsudome*—was repeated, but it had long since lost any meaning. In 1661, for example, Kaga had begun a series of edicts forbidding the export of commodities like fertilizer, soybeans, oil seeds, tobacco, and wax to other parts of Japan. It was also declared illegal to import into the domain rice and salt from other domains. A year later, Sendai issued a similar list of products which could not be sent outside the domain without express permission, and they also restricted the importing of rice, beans, the inferior grains, and iron.[55] There is nothing to suggest that the daimyo domains were prepared to pay overmuch attention to instructions which

54. Information on the Nambu mine is provided in *Tōyū zakki*, p. 211; the remainder is from Kobata, *Kōzan*, pp. 135, 179–80, 182–84, 195–202. See also *TJ* 45 : 793, 814, and *TJ* 47 : 113, 224.

55. For Sendai, see Sasaki, *Daimyō*, pp. 118–19; for Kaga, see Ōkubo Toshiaki, Kodama Kōta, Yauchi Kenji, and Inoue Mitsusada, eds., *Shiryō ni yoru Nihon no ayumi*, 3 : 253–54; for other domains, see Horie Yasuzō, *Kokusan shōrei to kokusan sembai*, pp. 44–49.

ran counter to their own commercial interests. Nor is there any compelling evidence of Bakufu readiness to enforce decrees on this issue. In times of famine, for example, it was quite common for daimyo to hoard their resources, denying foodstuffs even to those who needed them most. Any national government would surely have found this offensive, but the Bakufu, despite complaints, seems to have taken no strong measures against it (*TJ* 47 : 741, 748).

Tokugawa economic preponderance, seemingly so overwhelming in the beginning, was also to suffer as the years went by. Certainly the Bakufu still retained more than four times as much land as even the richest of the daimyo, however, it was far too fragmented to make a really efficient tax base; much of it, in fact, was so widely scattered that the Bakufu was forced to rely on nearby daimyo to provide the necessary administration. The 55,000 koku of Bakufu land adjacent to the Aizu domain, administered by that domain throughout the Edo period for reasons of convenience, had come to be regarded as a legitimate part of the Aizu fief by the early nineteenth century.[56]

Bakufu land was also undersurveyed (the last large-scale survey of the period was made in 1694–95), and what was surveyed produced nowhere near the taxation anticipated. Arai Hakuseki, when he gained access to the Edo accounts in 1707, calculated that the government received only one half of the taxes due to it (*OSK* p. 356). Furthermore, because of the fragmented nature of its domain, the Bakufu was denied what came to be one of the more significant sources of daimyo revenue. This was the system of han monopolies which emerged quite early and flowered from the beginning of the eighteenth century as daimyo after daimyo began to seek new sources of revenue. A total of sixty-two han were to develop their own monopolies, under various names, and the more successful of them were to see their financial cares considerably lessened thereby, but not so the Bakufu. The monopolies, although usually worked by merchants under license, depended on the authority of the daimyo for enforcement, and this was possible only in the heavily administered, well-defined

56. Kitajima, *Kenryoku*, p. 331; for Aizu, see Watanabe Sansei, "Bakuryō azukaridokoro ni okeru shihai no seikaku—Echigo-kuni Ojiya-machi no baai—," *Chihōshi kenkyū* 96 : 10–18

domains. Smuggling was the great enemy of the han monopolies, since local producers naturally preferred to sell their goods secretly elsewhere, at a competitive price, rather than to their daimyo at a price which he dictated; the looser the supervision, the easier such smuggling was. The Bakufu domains, in constant flux, and scattered throughout forty-seven of Tokugawa Japan's sixty-eight provinces, presented an insuperable barrier to the development of any efficient internal monopoly.[57]

In the nineteenth century, too, partly as a result of the growth of han monopolies and partly because of the rise of provincial market centers, the Bakufu's grip on the major Japanese markets came to lose a good deal of its meaning. Nowhere was this more pronounced than in Osaka, the city which the Bakufu had helped build up to be the fulcrum of national commerce. In 1842 Abe Masakura, the Osaka magistrate, wrote a report in which, after indicating a steady fall in the volume of commercial products entering Osaka, he proceeded to lay some of the blame for this at the feet of the daimyo. "The commercial produce hitherto sent to Osaka wholesalers by farmers and merchants," he wrote, "has of recent years been bought up by daimyo . . . [who have also] been buying up produce from other domains, claiming it to be from their own, and probably in not a few cases sending it off to wherever they please; . . . truly what they are trying to do is unbecoming to warriors." Abe's diagnosis of the situation was no doubt unsophisticated, but one cannot doubt the accuracy of his description. Some daimyo were buying up goods and selling them outside the traditional commercial centers, like Osaka, in order to obtain the best price possible, and Abe could point by name to some of the offenders, notably the daimyo of Himeji and Awa. There were others as well—Satsuma and Chōshū, of course, but also Hiroshima, Kii, Fukui, Owari, Akita, Yonezawa, Hikone, Nakatsu, and Oshi, to name but a few.[58] The real causes of Osaka's decline lie well beyond the compass of a discussion of Bakufu-daimyo relations; what is important to note here is that

57. Horie, *Kokusan shōrei*, pp. 13, 71; the figure of sixty-two is calculated from Takayanagi and Takeuchi, pp. 1150–52; See also chap. 2, n. 27, below.

58. Abe Masakura's report is to be found in *Ōsaka-shi shi*, vol. 5. Note in particular pp. 640–41, 648, 651, 665, 674. Kitajima, in *Mizuno Tadakuni*, p. 361, has indicated a doubt that the report was ever forwarded to the Bakufu.

in the nineteenth century some daimyo could move outside areas of central commercial control, ignoring the usage of the previous two hundred years. That they could do this with apparent impunity has serious implications for the Bakufu's claims to central authority; but it is even more damaging that by so doing they could win for themselves economic success at a time when the Bakufu was in considerable financial difficulty.

Equally serious is evidence suggesting that in some matters daimyo could ignore even the Bakufu's laws if they felt so inclined, although concrete examples are not plentiful. Historians have commented on the virtual unanimity of Bakufu and han edicts, and this does seem to have been the case. However, the apparent unanimity, I would suggest, is indicative of three things. The first is that, of the pertinent Bakufu edicts, the overwhelming majority were of a sort with which the daimyo could find agreement. Warnings against fires, Christians, beggars, prohibitions against mob action and the forceful presentation of petitions, bans on the sale of land, restrictions on the making of sake and the planting of tobacco on otherwise useful soil were all subjects close to the heart of daimyo and Bakufu alike. The second—to be the theme of a later chapter—is that as areas of potential conflict and competition between the Bakufu and daimyo emerged, the Bakufu failed to react with the assertive vigor of the early years. Finally, the third is that, as long as the Bakufu held the prerogative of attainder, no domain was likely to advertise its contempt. Any such resistance was concealed, perhaps as much by a Bakufu reluctant to invite confrontation as by daimyo unwilling to force it into a corner by any open display of defiance. Hence, han legal codes bear a strong resemblance to those of the Bakufu. Only occasionally does one encounter evidence suggestive of an undercurrent of opposition. The prohibition of embargoes, for example, mentioned above, provoked disobedience from daimyo as early as the mid-seventeenth century. Matsudaira Sadanobu's prohibition of unorthodox Confucianism in 1790 is another measure which was greeted with something less than enthusiasm by some daimyo; in both Hikone and Shōnai, for example, their local traditional heterodoxy was preserved unchanged.[59] Not until the nineteenth century, however, when in-

59. *Tsuruoka-shi shi*, 1 : 369.

creasing daimyo participation in commerce came into conflict
with Bakufu attempts to control it, did resistance become more
open. During the Tempō period (1830–44), when restrictions of
an ambitious and widely unpopular nature were introduced—
among them the prohibition of the *kabu nakama* and of han
monopolies—daimyo commonly disregarded them.[60]

This gradual loss of economic supremacy, striking enough, is
matched by an even more rapid and startling decline in Bakufu
strategic and military predominance. Ieyasu, Hidetada, and
Iemitsu had tried with some success to keep themselves stronger
than the daimyo, forcing them to build Bakufu fortifications at
their own expense, keeping close watch on their behavior, and
uprooting them from their domains when the occasion offered. It
was an impressive array of powers, but one which, in practice,
came to lose much of its meaning.

That there should have been a decline in the hectic rate of
impositions on the daimyo for projects like castle building need
come as no surprise. One would expect, given no more destruction of castles in war, and the emergence of no new enemies to
call for fortification in new areas, that the need for repairs and
building would decrease. One might also even expect that, once
the sankin kōtai system was established, the Bakufu would see
no more need for anxiety over the prosperity of its rivals. There
is more involved than this, however. In a country as accustomed
to natural disasters—earthquakes, typhoons, fires, and floods—
as Japan, and with a style of architecture vulnerable to them all,
castles did not usually stand for two hundred years without feel-
ing the ravages of time. This was the case with Edo Castle, where
the eighteenth and nineteenth centuries saw frequent repairs
and not a little rebuilding; yet the incidence of demands on individual daimyo slackened far more than the needs of Edo Castle
warranted. A reading of the Bakufu chronicles, the *Tokugawa
jikki*, between 1740 and 1780, for example, reveals at least ten
instances of repairs carried out without recourse to impositions.
The case of the Yamanouchi of Tosa, who contributed to the
construction of Edo Castle as often as any daimyo during the first
two decades of the seventeenth century, is symptomatic of this

60. Kitajima, *Mizuno Tadakuni*, p. 391; Tsuda Hideo, "Tempō no kaikaku," *Nihon rekishi kōza* 4 : 109–10.

relaxation; they are recorded as having contributed on just two occasions after 1650. A similar process can be seen at work in the castles ordered by the Bakufu for strategic locations in the provinces, like those of Hikone and Nagoya. These were originally built from daimyo contributions of money and labor and were no less affected by the accumulation of years, but repairs when necessary were not paid for by levies upon daimyo. Rather, contributions came from the Bakufu, as in 1767, when Hikone was given the loan of 5,000 ryō to rebuild part of the castle damaged by fire. When Nijō Palace was badly damaged by lightning in 1750, the Bakufu bore the cost of the repairs.[61]

Most symbolic of the decreasing demands on daimyo for castle building, however, is the fact that some needed repairs to Edo Castle were never carried out. The five-storied keep, the greatest in Japan, standing over 150 feet high, stood for only fifty years. Built in 1607, it fell victim to the great fire of 1657 which destroyed half the city, and was never rebuilt. The reason given— that in an age of peace the keep no longer had any military significance—rings plausibly enough in modern ears, but it must not be forgotten that in the provinces daimyo continued to rebuild the keeps of their own castles, almost invariably with some Bakufu assistance. Some daimyo went out of their way to make them more splendid than before; Nagoya, in 1752 replaced the clay tiles on the roof of its keep with bronze, and later added its famous golden dolphin finials.[62] Peace or no, it was not an age to overlook the potency of symbols of authority. That the Bakufu was willing to lend daimyo money to maintain their castle keeps, while neglecting its own, is a remarkable illustration of the increasingly modest position it came to hold.

It must be added that, to a limited extent, such early impositions on daimyo were replaced by others. Of these, the most important were contributions to civil engineering projects, which, from the early eighteenth century onward, required daimyo expenditures in areas quite remote from their own domains. They

61. For the years 1740–80, see *TJ* 46 : 466, 498, 502, 683; *TJ* 47 : 9, 37, 46, 69, 123, 296; the Tosa example is from Hirao Michio, *Tosa han*, pp. 246ff.; the Hikone example is from *TJ* 47 : 262, and the Nijō Palace example is from *TJ* 46 : 521.

62. Ōrui, *Nihon jōkaku*, vol. 15.

found this irksome, for it always involved them in more expense
than they liked, yet the incidence was not nearly as frequent, nor
the expenses so crippling, as in the castle-building decades. Okayama, one of the most heavily hit by these demands, contributed
to such projects on only nine occasions over 150 years. Furthermore, the Bakufu was ready to offer certain freedoms in return
for assistance, such as releasing Shimazu Shigetoshi, daimyo of
Satsuma, from his sankin kōtai obligation while he helped with
work on rivers in Ise, Mino, and Owari in 1754.[63]

Reflecting this new conciliation, there was a subtle change in
the military position of the Bakufu. The more independent of
the Sekigahara allies seemed no longer quite the objects of hostility and suspicion they had once been, no longer the major
butts of punitive demands for assistance. The Bakufu, too, lost
its early obsession with military preparedness. As early as 1723
it had come to rely on the support of neighboring daimyo in
suppressing peasant revolts in its domains in Echigo and Dewa,
on the Japan Sea coast. In 1734, such reliance was made explicit,
with a frank acknowledgment of its inability to preserve order in
its own domains where the peasants were notoriously restive. In
that year, any daimyo whose han abutted Bakufu land was autho-
rized to despatch troops at any sign of unrest. Action was to be
taken automatically, without Bakufu knowledge or permission.
Perhaps still more ominous was the relaxation, in 1853, of the
prohibition against the building of large ships, which had been
in effect since 1635.[64]

A dramatic parallel to this general loosening of economic and
military control is to be seen in the fate of the Bakufu's machinery for provincial inspection. Both the kunimetsuke and the
junkenshi had originally been used to impose the standards of
the Tokugawa Bakufu in Edo upon the domains, but the capacity of each to fulfill this function was eroded. In the case of
the kunimetsuke, the officials who took complete charge of a
domain for a period, it was lack of use which laid waste to their
importance. Before the beginning of the Kyōhō period in 1716,
the Bakufu employed them on seventy-one occasions, but in

63. Yoshizumi, "Tetsudai bushin," pp. 96ff.; Taniguchi Sumio, *Okayama han*, pp. 307ff.

64. Kitajima, *Edo jidai*, p. 159; Ōishi Shinzaburō, "Kyōhō kaikaku," *Iwanami kōza Nihon rekishi*, 11 : 295.

the succeeding 150 years they were to be used only eighteen times.[65]

The itinerant inspectors, the junkenshi, also suffered a decline which, while less obvious statistically—since they continued to be despatched to the provinces at regular intervals during the Tokugawa period whenever a new shogun was appointed—was hardly less striking. In their case, decline took the form of ritualization, a kind of petrification, affecting both their minatory potential and the accuracy of the information they obtained. There is ample evidence to support this conclusion in local archives,[66] but the most convincing proof is to be found in the travel diary of Furukawa Koshōken, a geographer and traveler who, in 1788, accompanied a party of three junkenshi in north eastern Japan. From his account there can be no doubt that the inspection tour was by this time very highly formalized. The junkenshi visited only those places laid down by tradition and saw only what their predecessors had seen. Much of their itinerary involved visits to shrines and temples, of marginal value in providing information necessary to centralized government. Many of the things they were shown there—at Suginomiya, a portable bookcase said to have belonged to Benkei, the near-legendary twelfth century priest; at Kotsunagi, an eleven-headed Kannon reputedly carved by Shōtoku Taishi, the seventh century protector of Buddhism; at Numakunai, a varied collection of phallic religious objects— although doubtless not without interest, were of still less importance. Wherever they went, the junkenshi were met by crowds of people (some clutching rosaries in superstitious awe), suggesting that their route was already well known. It should have been, since apparently a full years' notice had been given of their visit. Also, wherever they went, the junkenshi were accompanied by officials provided by the daimyo to make sure they saw no more than was convenient. Furukawa complains that most of the guides were ignorant, or at least feigned ignorance; near Ichikawa, one who had stolidly replied "zonji mōsazu" ("I don't know") to even the most casual questions was finally badgered into producing a letter from his superior, authorizing him to give certain replies to certain questions, and warning him to answer "zonji

65. Calculated from Yoshizumi, "Kansatsu seido," pp. 58–66.
66. For an example, see the records of Yonezawa Han. See Hanseishi Kenkyūkai, eds., *Hansei seiritsu shi no sōgō kenkyū—Yonezawa han*, pp. 107–10.

mōsazu" to anything else. It says something of the perception the
junkenshi had of the importance of their inspection that, as Furukawa records, on hearing this "everybody laughed heartily." The
entire tour, in fact, seems to have been something of a good-
natured game. Adding a Lewis Carroll overtone, answers to
questions, even when finally elicited, were often known to be
false by questioner and questioned alike. After having been informed by an official that there were around 1,700 houses in the
town of Morioka, Furukawa notes in his journal: "By tradition
this is an answer always given to the inspectors. In fact, there are
around three thousand houses." Instead of seeking out issues on
which to embarrass the daimyo, too, it seems that the junkenshi
were happy to avoid them. In Akita, for example, Furukawa
writes that it was known the peasants were so disgruntled with
a new tax that they wanted to lay a complaint against their
daimyo and were prevented from doing so only by the presence
of large numbers of domain officials. An aggressive, or even nor-
mally conscientious, group of inspectors could have chosen to
investigate the matter, but this party moved on.

From Furukawa's account, it is quite clear that the inspection
tour was a perfunctory one, a matter of form only. For the
daimyo it was a matter of some expense, since they had to provide the inspectors with guides, guards, adequate roads and
bridges, lodgings, and the occasional boat, but there was little
risk involved. The junkenshi could be relied upon to follow a
predictable course, in their travels as in their interrogations, and
to evade all confrontation not actively thrust upon them. It is
no surprise that the junkenshi sometimes felt they were not
being accorded the deference among the daimyo which their
position, and that of their government, demanded. Furukawa reflects this in his indignant account of a snub received from the
Sendai daimyo just outside Edo. "The inspectors are officials appointed to travel the land on the accession of the shogun, and
having the honor of his commission, they are entitled to the respect of all daimyo," he fumes, "but the daimyo of Sendai gave
us no greeting, and the samurai who accompanied him . . .
seemed extremely rude. . . . I cannot say whether it was more
indiscipline or discourtesy which made them shove ahead of us
like that." Quite clearly, like the kunimetsuke, the junkenshi

were no longer to be feared, and this undoubtedly had its effect on their original purpose, that of assuring that the standards of the central government were imposed upon the daimyo domains. The implications of this weakened inspections system for the Bakufu are equally obvious.[67]

If the inspection system, once feared by the daimyo for its mischief-making potential, had degenerated into such a flaccid state, it does no more than reflect a waning concern, on the part of the government directing it, with the pursuit of those aims for which that system had once seemed so essential. As the Tokugawa period progressed, the Bakufu seemed less interested in enforcing its wishes in the provinces, less eager to make sure offenders were punished with full rigor, less ready to acquire more land at the expense of others—less concerned, in short, to assert its primacy as a central government. The deterioration of the inspection system suggests this, and it is confirmed by the decreasing vigor with which the policy of fief confiscation was pursued. The power of attainder, to which Ieyasu, Hidetada, and Iemitsu had all given such single-minded attention, was the most important of the prerogatives of the central government and deserves the emphasis historians have placed upon it, yet the increasing reluctance of the Bakufu to invoke this, the ultimate weapon against the daimyo, demands no less emphasis. Certainly the first three shogun used it frequently and ruthlessly both to demonstrate and enhance their authority, but after the accession of Ietsuna, the fourth shogun, it began to fall into disuse.

From 1651 onward, for example, official sanction was given to deathbed adoptions—even to posthumous adoptions in some cases—something previously forbidden. On no fewer than fifty-eight occasions in the years 1600 to 1651 the absence of a formally recognized heir had led the Bakufu to confiscate the fiefs of dead daimyo; this figure represents almost half the total number of attainders of that period.[68] By permitting irregular adoptions, therefore, the Bakufu effectively consented to fight for more power, with one arm, its strongest, bound behind. The other arm, too, was soon to be used only sparingly. During the same

67. See *Tōyū zakki,* passim; for the specific incidents mentioned here, see pp. 103, 205, 216, 84–85, 7.
68. Kurita, pp. 283–86.

first half of the seventeenth century, various instances of daimyo
disobedience and maladministration had been the cause of at
least forty confiscations, but later such offenses generally came to
be greeted with little more than a reprimand. House arrest, for
example, was the only punishment imposed upon the daimyo of
Kokura Han in 1814, after a rather remarkable squabble during
which three hundred of his vassals migrated to another domain.
Many seventeenth century daimyo had seen their fiefs confiscated
for offenses far more trivial than this.[69]

With one arm bound and the other weakened, denying itself
the right to confiscate domains lacking a properly appointed heir,
and viewing defiance and inefficiency with new tolerance, it was
inevitable that the brisk rate of attainders maintained by the
early Tokugawa would decline. Where, between 1600 and 1716,
some 289 daimyo lost all or part of their domains, the remainder
of the Tokugawa period saw perhaps fewer than a score punished
in this way. This is astonishing neglect of an established prerogative, since one would anticipate that a government eager to
create, preserve, and increase its own eminence among a host of
petty nobles would place the greatest emphasis on this point.
Where the early Bakufu used land confiscated from daimyo to
augment the Tokugawa estates, in a fairly constant process, the
Bakufu during the latter part of the period actually permitted
Tokugawa landholdings to decline from 4,500,000 koku in 1732
to 4,190,200 by 1838.[70]

There was also a parallel relaxation in the exercise of a related prerogative, equally significant in a feudal context, that of
transferring the daimyo from one part of Japan to another at
the government's convenience. Prior to 1716, this form of coercive
power had been employed on 476 occasions, an annual average
of four cases; between 1716 and the fall of the Bakufu in 1868,
however, it was used only 107 times, an average of less than once
each year.[71]

So far had this particular prerogative declined, indeed, that
toward the end of the period it became unenforceable. In 1840

69. For confiscations because of lack of an heir, see ibid., pp. 288–91, and
also Tsuji, *Edo kaifu;* pp. 336–37. The case of the Kokura daimyo is contained in *Buzen sōsho,* 16 : 39–41.

70. Kitajima, *Kenryoku,* p. 331.

71. Fujino, *Bakuhan,* pp. 718ff.

the Bakufu announced a three-sided fief transfer, by which Matsudaira Narimori, daimyo of Kawagoe, was to be moved from his
rather poor domain near Edo over to a much more prosperous
fief at Shōnai. He would thus supplant Sakai Tadakata, daimyo
of Shōnai, who was to be taken from an area held in fief by his
forefathers for two hundred years and sent to Nagaoka, one hundred miles down the Japan Sea coast; his enfeoffment was to fall
from 140,000 koku to 70,000. Makino Tadamasa, daimyo of
Nagaoka (where his ancestors, too, had been since the early seventeenth century), displaced by this movement, would be given
Kawagoe.

In principle, there was nothing novel in the Bakufu's action.
The precedent had been solidly established in the course of many
early attainders, fief reductions, and daimyo movements, some of
them just as inequitable. The flagrant injustice was nothing new.
What was new was the way in which various groups reacted. Particularly in Shōnai, peasant displeasure was extreme. Possibly
protesting most of all the prospect of a new land survey and tax
increases which tended to follow on changes of daimyo family,
they held a series of mass meetings. They also sent representatives
into neighboring han to beg for intervention from the various
daimyo. Some went to Aizu, some fifty went over to Sendai, while
in the fourth month of 1841 four hardy Shōnai farmers presented
a petition to Tokugawa Nariaki, the daimyo of Mito. Still more
significant was the reaction of the daimyo. The twenty-three
daimyo of the *Ōhiroma,* the most prominent of the tozama
daimyo, sent a joint letter to the Bakufu, which carries some
startling implications for those who would assert the preponderance of Bakufu power, the continuation of its balance of terror,
and the eternal separation of tozama and fudai (the Shōnai Sakai
and the Nagaoka Makino being both old fudai families). What
the letter demanded was the reason; "As we have had no notification from you, and have not been given any information, we
humbly offer this communication. . . . Since Sakai Saemonjō
[i.e., Sakai Tadakata] comes from a line of hereditary officials,
why has he now been ordered to move and take over Nagaoka
Castle? We hereby inform you that we wish to be told." [72]

72. *Tsuruoka-shi shi,* 1 : 425–27; "Shōnai kemmon roku"; Kodama Kōta
and Kitajima Masamoto, eds., *Dai ni ki monogatari han shi,* 1 : 64.

The Bakufu could read the warning. In the seventh month of 1841, the order was revoked; but at what cost to Bakufu prestige, to its claims to daimyo control? Powers which in the early seventeenth century, had evoked no open hostility, by the early nineteenth century prompted so much opposition that there was no alternative but to abandon them.

A similar change took place in the Bakufu's right to speak for the nation in the field of foreign affairs. A government which in the 1630s could command total obedience to a strict policy of seclusion was unable to make a similar unilateral decision to abandon that policy in the crisis of the 1850s. No longer were all daimyo prepared to allow the Bakufu to speak for them in the matter of foreign policy. Of course the circumstances surrounding the two decisions, that to close and that to open, were totally different. The first was taken in the absence of any particular European opposition, the second had the urgency of Perry's demands and Harris' threats, bolstered by Dutch rumors and information about the Opium War. The peculiar cast of the diplomatic crisis of the 1850s was due to the military might of the nations pressing for entry; it was this which made it essential to have unanimity, and also a degree of military preparedness, whether for war or negotiation. Confrontation with militarily superior powers came at a time when the Bakufu was far less able to direct the daimyo to do anything unpalatable than it had been under Iemitsu. The magnitude of the Western threat was just one factor, the loss of Bakufu power another. At any time the response to the former might have been sufficient to shake the feudal monarchy system, but, coupled with the decay of the Bakufu's major powers, the threat Commodore Perry represented was substantial indeed.

Finally, in this record of impotence should be mentioned two essential prerogatives which were never established at all. One was the right to tax the daimyo—not just to levy irregular contributions for specific building or engineering projects, but the right to obtain regular assistance for the general expenses of government. In Western Europe, as the new monarchies emerged, it rapidly became a polite fiction that "the King should live of his own." The expenses of national government were far beyond the capacity of even the largest royal purse. In Japan, however, where the Bakufu took responsibility for many facets of national life, it did so largely without the assistance of the barons who owed it allegiance. True, in 1722, the eighth Tokugawa shogun, Yoshimune, introduced the *agemai-rei,* by which each daimyo had to give the Bakufu 100 koku for each 10,000 koku of fief. Yet this was done almost apologetically, and only after a full explanation of the circumstances. The lengthy preamble to the edict, and its conclusion—"Accordingly, though this is something unheard of in the past, all those with fiefs yielding 10,000 *koku* and above will be commanded to present rice. We take this shameful step since otherwise we have no alternative but to deprive several hundreds of our retainers of their allowances"—are too abject to sustain an interpretation of it as an assertion of autocratic power.[73] Even then, the agemai-rei was given a sugar-coating of sankin kōtai reduction, and it was promptly abolished in 1730 after proving generally unpopular.

The other major development which one might have expected, given the determined beginning made by the first three Tokugawa shogun, was the total abolition of the daimyo domain as an institution. At Iemitsu's death, this seemed not impossible; together with his father and grandfather, he had established a firm foundation for such an eventuality, both by expanding the Bakufu's own holdings and having free use of attainders and fief transfers. Seventy years after Iemitsu, however, not even as convinced a supporter of a stronger Bakufu as Ogyū Sorai could envisage a situation in which there would be no daimyo. He could only go so far as to suggest that "the incomes of daimyō which are more than 400,000 or 500,000 koku are excessively large for so small a country as Japan. . . . I would suggest 300,000 koku as the maximum income." [74] By regular forays upon the larger domains and gradual abolition of the smaller in favor of direct administration by government officials, the Bakufu might well have developed into a centralized monarchy. But, at some point in its accumulation of land, the Bakufu decided to call a halt; the daimyo institution was strong enough to keep on replenishing itself. When daimyo were attainted they were replaced by more daimyo, newly created if necessary, rather than by Ba-

73. Translated in Tsukahira, *Feudal Control,* pp. 117–18.
74. J. R. McEwan, *The Political Writings of Ogyu Sorai,* pp. 76–77.

kufu administrators who could be paid a salary and nothing more. As a result of such neglect of hard-won privileges, the slow path to centralized monarchy, followed by dynasties like the Tudors, was to evade the Tokugawa. Where the Tudors flourished, leaving a name synonymous with effective despotic government on a national scale, the Tokugawa grew progressively weaker and were finally overthrown. Although in 1601, the daimyo of Satsuma might consider the Tokugawa so secure that they could not possibly be overturned, "not even in a dream," it no longer appeared so to one of his remote descendants, who in 1867 was to play a leading part in the Tokugawa downfall.

The remarkable failure of Bakufu military, commercial, and political control has not escaped the notice of Japanese historians but much of its significance has. To Kurita Motoji, writing in the 1920s, there was an obvious softening of Bakufu control after the death of Iemitsu, the third shogun. However, he saw it as an entirely natural phenomenon, the product of a military stability which permitted the Bakufu the luxury of donning the velvet glove.[75] In this form, it fit in comfortably with his over-all view of the history of the Tokugawa period in which the sinews of control were alternately tightened and relaxed. To Kurita, the succession was basically a matter of Bakufu attitude, as he balanced the Confucian moralism of the three reform periods of Kyōhō, Kansei, and Tempō against the periods of alleged luxury and softened moral fiber which preceded and followed them, and this tended to obscure for him the cumulative decline in the elements of central control.

More recent historians, too, speak of the Bakufu's reaching a period of "stabilization" under Ietsuna, the fourth shogun, and while stressing the importance of the powers gained by the early Bakufu as means of national control, they regard reluctance to use them as a sign not of debility, but of strength.[76] By some curious logic, the failure of the later Bakufu to keep up the rate of attainders, reductions, and fief transfers established by the early Bakufu, for example, all powers which they rate very highly as signs of authority over the daimyo, does not signify to them a decline of authority, but rather a new stage of maturity and security.

75. Kurita, pp. 419ff.
76. Fujino, *Bakuhan*, pp. 311ff.

In this they are mistaken. Neither the enfeeblement nor the overthrow of the Tokugawa Bakufu seems completely natural. It is strange enough that the Tokugawa failed where the Tudors succeeded. But even more peculiar is the long period which intervened between the first traces of weakening and the final overthrow. In most important respects the power of the Shogun began to decline in the second half of the seventeenth century; there were later rallies, to be sure, but of a very limited and temporary kind. Yet the Bakufu survived for a further two hundred years, showing all the outward manifestations of effective government.

To contemporaries, there seemed no possible danger of a return to turbulence. At Matsushima in 1779, moved by the natural beauty before him, Furukawa Koshōken expressed this in an artless tribute to the government under which he lived. "Truly the country is governed in peace," he wrote, "the benevolent breezes from the shogun have reached every corner, and grass and trees bow to his virtue." [77] How could such tranquillity be produced for so long by a government capable of doing so little? How could a government no longer prepared to assert its absolute authority over the daimyo manage to preserve itself from their opposition?

How did the Tokugawa come to be overthrown? As we have seen, they relied specifically upon a balance of power to keep them in their position. The Tokugawa held over four million koku of crown land, and their various allies another twelve million koku, more than half of which was in the hands of the fudai daimyo. The total of land—and the armed men whose salaries that land paid—available to the Tokugawa to protect their hegemonial position was therefore in excess of sixteen million koku, against which the tozama daimyo could only muster nine million. [78] Yet despite this overwhelming supremacy on paper, when the crisis came in the 1860s, the balance of power failed to work in the anticipated way, and the Tokugawa were forced to rely on their own resources. How did this happen?

These questions cannot be answered without an examination of the role of the fudai daimyo, a group which has not previously

77. *Tōyū zakki*, p. 247.
78. See, for example, the figures in Conrad Totman, *Politics in the Tokugawa Bakufu*, p. 33.

been discussed at any length.[79] As the original vassals of the Tokugawa family before Ieyasu reached his pinnacle of success, the fudai daimyo rose to eminence behind him, leading his personal army and staffing his personal administration. Their descendants were to provide the Bakufu with its chief officials for over 200 years, and when factors like age, infancy, health, vitality, ability, and inclination took their toll of personal government by the shogun, so the fudai daimyo came increasingly to take over the functions of government.[80] The fudai daimyo, presiding over Bakufu policy, chose one sort of feudal monarchy over another. The decision for renewed feudal decentralization, rather than a gradual move towards centralized absolute monarchy, was theirs.

It has been almost a matter of faith with historians that the fudai daimyo were to the Bakufu what the rhetoric of the Tokugawa period made them proclaim themselves to be, the totally loyal, absolutely selfless servants of the Tokugawa house. Irimoto has said of them that they functioned in the Tokugawa period as the "faithful supporters of the Bakufu administration." Kitajima has agreed with this interpretation, pointing out that, since they all had small domains, they had no temptation to be anything else. Albert Craig has claimed that the most able fudai had, through their positions in government, "a positive sense of bureaucratic identification with the Bakufu" which "overshadowed their identity as daimyo of autonomous areas." Customarily, the fudai are seen as too engrossed in preserving their traditional role as Bakufu officials, and too obsessed with the rivalries of 1600 to think of undercutting Bakufu power or finding common cause with any but themselves.[81]

My reason for examining them is this. In answering the riddle of cumulative weakness, one must look first of all to Bakufu policy, and since that policy was for the bulk of the Tokugawa

79. Totman, who devoted a chapter to the subject of the fudai daimyo (or "vassal daimyo," to use his term) in *Politics in the Tokugawa Bakufu*, is the only Western scholar to have examined their role in any detail.

80. Ibid., chap. 10, for a description of this process.

81. The Irimoto quotation is to be found in Kimura and Sugimoto, p. 389; the Kitajima appraisal is in Kodama and Kitajima, *Monogatari han shi*, 2 : 15; for Albert Craig's assessment, see his *Choshu in the Meiji Restoration*, p. 17.

period determined and administered with the assistance of fudai daimyo, it must therefore have received their acquiescence. How could a group of men dedicated to the advancement of the Tokugawa house, men who had learned at their fathers' knees the sacredness of the obligations they bore the Tokugawa house, allow such enfeeblement? The collapse of the balance of power is even more directly dependent for its explanation upon the behavior of the fudai daimyo. Had they remained as steadfastly loyal to the Tokugawa in 1867 as their forefathers were in 1600, then the military supremacy of the Tokugawa would have remained unchallenged; instead, even this last bastion of loyal Tokugawa support was to crumble when the time came. Obviously, relations between the Tokugawa and their vassals had changed throughout the long years of the Tokugawa peace, and it is this weakening of loyalties in a society where loyalty was the supreme virtue that makes the fudai daimyo worth our attention.

2. Fudai Daimyo and Their Domains

When Tokugawa Ieyasu marched into the Kantō in 1590 to take up the possession of his new domain and to establish his government afresh in the ancient and crumbling fortress at Edo, he was accompanied by his band of vassals, his *kashindan*. Already, by 1590, he was the inheritor of a hundred years of territorial expansion. As Tokugawa lands had swelled, so had the ranks of Tokugawa dependents, and when Ieyasu crossed the mountains at Hakone and entered the broad, rich plain which was his new power base, he marched at the head of forty thousand men.

It was a heterogeneous group, in the sense that any army is— fighting men and coolies, military strategists and quartermasters, men who gave commands and those who accepted them, newcomers and men who had inherited their loyalties from fathers and grandfathers. But in other respects they shared much in common. Almost all of them came from that part of Japan—the eastern seaboard of central Honshū—where the Tokugawa had begun their rise to prominence. All had pledged allegiance to Tokugawa Ieyasu. In the case of the major military commanders, Ieyasu's vassals, they had done so directly and in person, offering their part in the feudal contract—loyalty and obedience—in return for the protection and patronage which was the other half of the bargain. In the case of the *baishin*, Ieyasu's rear vassals, the bond was indirect; their allegiance was to a military commander who in turn had sworn loyalty, on their behalf as on his own, to the head of the Tokugawa house. Should Ieyasu rise in influence and increase in prosperity, so would they all; if he fell, so too would they, master as well as man, general as well as groom.

This vassal band, much like those with which Ieyasu's other great warrior contemporaries had surrounded themselves, provided the central core of the fudai daimyo. These men, who are the subject of this work, assisted the Tokugawa house in grasping and holding power, but they ultimately impeded the intensification of that power. Without them there could have been no Tokugawa rule; without the constant support their presence implied there would have been no continuity in government; but so long as they remained, the Tokugawa Bakufu was to be denied access to the path which led from feudalism to absolute monarchy.

In the mid-sixteenth century, when Ieyasu's father had termed them "treasures among men," they were not yet daimyo, not yet feudal magnates, but their status was fudai, an adjective composed of two Chinese characters which, in conjunction, carry the meaning of "hereditary," or "through successive generations." Arai Hakuseki, who wrote of "fudai ai-tsutae no gokenin," or "vassals by hereditary succession," exemplifies the use of the term in the hands of Japanese of the Tokugawa period. In a feudal context, the fudai label carried such approbatory overtones as reliability, predictability, and unstinting and unswerving loyalty. Every daimyo house had amongst its vassals a fudai group which, by virtue of the antiquity and impeccability of its relationship with the daimyo, was accorded particular favors and privileges. These could include rights of special audience with the daimyo, almost invariably special access to his ear as trusted counselors, and sometimes certain material advantages. The "fudai no monodomo" for example, as observed by Furukawa Koshōken in the Sōma domain in 1777, were permitted to hold their own lands while other vassals less favored had to make do with a rice stipend from the domain granary.[1]

The term daimyo meant simply an eminent man, a territorial magnate. Throughout most of the history of its usage, it had no more precise meaning than this, but in the Tokugawa period it came to be applied to those warriors or descendants of warriors who held in fief land which each year produced an assessed 10,000 koku of rice or its equivalent in other produce. There were a handful of exceptions; for example, a few retainers of the greatest daimyo, who, while only vassals, held more land in fief than many daimyo, or the *gosankyō*, who, with no territorial base at all (being paid from the Tokugawa granary like any other vassals), were nevertheless considered daimyo by those about them.[2]

1. The statement attributed to Hirotada, Ieyasu's father, is from *Mikawa monogatari*, p. 281; for Arai Hakuseki, see *OSK* p. 377, and for Furukawa Koshōken, see *Tōyū zakki*, p. 269.

2. The *gosankyō* were the three collateral houses of Hitotsubashi, Tayasu, and Shimizu, which emerged in the eighteenth century from among the descendants of Tokugawa Yoshimune, the eighth shogun.

Yet for the overwhelming maority of cases, the equation of land-
holding with daimyo status held firm.

The Fudai Daimyo

It was in 1590 that the first examples of the confluence of these
two streams—the Tokugawa fudai, or hereditary vassals, and the
daimyo, or territorial magnates, appeared. In that year, Toku-
kawa Ieyasu was removed, by command of Toyotomi Hideyoshi,
his uneasy overlord, from his ancestral power base in the Tōkai
and despatched to the comparative isolation of the Kantō, beyond the mountains to the northeast. No matter how it was expressed, this was banishment, removal from the center of power
to the periphery, but Hideyoshi, reluctant to try the restraint of
his former enemy too far, awarded him a dramatically increased
enfeoffment. In place of his previous domain in the provinces of
Suruga,Tōtomi, Mikawa, Kai, and Shinano, Ieyasu was to control six provinces in eastern Japan.[3] He also came to assume
responsibility for numbers of local rōnin, unemployed samurai
who, having lost their masters in earlier battles, were eager to
find new employment. Some of these he was to absorb into his
own private household, while sharing others out among his
followers, as rear vassals.

His new enfeoffment, too, was hardly his alone. More land
represented, first of all, an added administrative burden, which,
under the unsettled military circumstances of the late sixteenth
century, he had little alternative but to share with his followers.
It also was regarded, by his vassals no less than by Ieyasu himself, as fresh spoils of war which the feudal contract compelled
him to distribute as rewards. Thus it is that, of the forty thousand men in his vassal band in 1590, more than forty entered the
Kantō to take up fiefs in excess of 10,000 koku. The revenue
from this land was to be theirs—subject to the demands which
Ieyasu, as their overlord, was entitled to make upon them—and
so was the responsibility for its administration. To this extent,
they were daimyo, yet, because they owed a prior commitment to

3. By convention, Ieyasu is said to have taken charge of the "eight Kantō
provinces" (Kan-hasshū), but in fact he held only six—Musashi, Izu, Sagami,
Kazusa, Shimoosa, and Kōzuke—according to Nakamura Kōya, Tokugawa-ke,
pp. 108–09.

Tokugawa Ieyasu, were still members of his vassal band, and held their fiefs through his grace and favor, they remained fudai vassals of the Tokugawa house.

From this original group of forty-odd fudai daimyo, the numbers increased gradually, keeping pace with the growing authority of the Tokugawa line. After Sekigahara, Ieyasu created a further twenty-eight, and by the end of his life, in 1616, there were ninety-one fudai daimyo. By 1690 their numbers had grown to 115, and, when Perry's ships appeared off the Japanese coast in 1853, there were 130. These fudai daimyo accounted for most, but not all, of the daimyo of Tokugawa Japan, of whom, by the end of the period, there were some 265; those remaining can be classified into two groups, which, like the fudai category, reflect their specific historical links with the Tokugawa house.[4]

The first, and most numerous of these, were the tozama daimyo, numbering more than a hundred, amongst them some of the most powerful individual daimyo in Japan. They included magnates like the Maeda, who held lands second in size only to those in the direct possession of the shogun, and also families like the Shimazu and the Date, who followed closely behind. Some of these tozama daimyo had opposed Tokugawa Ieyasu at Sekigahara, while others had supported him, but all had similar histories. Rising from the contending ruck of barons in the midsixteenth century, they had assimilated smaller neighboring rivals and had moved out to join the larger alliances then contesting the leadership of Japan. What distinguished the tozama from other daimyo was that, although they may have allied themselves with the Tokugawa from time to time, and many of them did at Sekigahara, it was as equals; the tozama had risen independently. For this reason, if for no other, tozama allegiance to the Bakufu, and acceptance of the order which the Tokugawa attempted to impose on Japan, has always been judged something less than wholehearted.

The *kamon*, or *ichimon* daimyo (sometimes known as the *shimpan*, or "related domains") form the last category of daimyo in this particular classification. The greatest members of this

4. Calculated from Fujino Tamotsu, *Bakuhan taisei shi no kenkyū*, pt. 1, tables 9, 14, and pt. 2, table 1; and from Kanai Madoka, *Hansei*, pp. 60–73; see Appendix below.

group, both in prestige and enfeoffment, were the so-called "three houses" (*gosanke*), lines established by Tokugawa Ieyasu's three younger sons, at Kii (555,000 koku), Owari (619,000 koku), and Mito (350,000 kuku); but there were others—the Fukui Matsudaira, for example, with a fief assessed at 320,000 koku, and the Matsudaira of Aizu and Matsue, with 230,000 and 186,000 koku, respectively. In 1853 there were twenty-four such daimyo. Many were substantial lords, accorded the respect due to those sharing the blood of the founder of Tokugawa preeminence, yet they were treated with reserve and caution by the main Tokugawa line, to whom their participation in the legitimacy conferred by blood, even if at a distance, rendered them a potential threat.[5]

By contrast with the tozama and kamon daimyo, the fudai daimyo were both more numerous and more dependent. They had none of the pronounced aspects of independence and autonomy of the tozama daimyo, nor did they share shimpan claims to special privilege; accordingly, their fiefs were among the smallest held by the barons of Tokugawa Japan. The Ii, who held 350,000 koku in their domain just across Lake Biwa from Kyoto, and ranked eleventh among Japanese daimyo in terms of magnitude, were by far the largest of the fudai daimyo. The rest had more modest domains, ranging from 150,000 koku down to the formal minimum of 10,000. The average fudai fief in 1853 was about 44,000 koku, while the median was 30,000. In the early eighteenth century, in many ways the golden age of the Tokugawa system, before shifts in the foundations had revealed themselves as cracks in the façade, the fudai daimyo accounted for some 5,450,467 koku, as compared with 3,260,000 koku held by the *sanke* and ichimon, and 9,798,670 by the tozama.[6]

From this brief description it would be easy to conclude that the fudai daimyo were a group sharing common ties, common family histories, and common reasons for gratitude to the Toku-

5. T. G. Tsukahira, *Feudal Control in Tokugawa Japan*, pp. 140–73; Conrad Totman, *Politics in the Tokugawa Bakufu*, chap. 6.

6. Earlier figures calculated from Tokyo Daigaku Shiryō Hensanjo, eds., *Dokushi biyō*, pp. 475ff. The later figures are from Tsukahira, pp. 140–73, although the list contained there, taken from a bukan, is not beyond dispute. I know of no such list which is.

gawa house, and indeed there is a general tendency amongst historians to treat them rather as an undifferentiated company. But it must not obscure the fact that the lines between the groups were not very clearly defined. At their outer extremities, fudai and tozama shaded into each other. Indeed, contemporaries were often uncertain about the precise status of some families. The Tozawa of Dewa were generally classified as fudai by the *bukan*, the warriors' social register; Arai Hakuseki, on the other hand, ranked them among the tozama in his *Hankampu*. Similar doubts existed from time to time about the status of such families as the Sengoku, Satake, Sanada, and Niwa, among others, reflecting the fact that the fudai were by no means homogeneous. (see app. for a table of fudai daimyo).[7]

At the center of the fudai daimyo were the Mikawa fudai, those who had been vassals of the Tokugawa family in the province of Mikawa at the end of the fifteenth, and beginning of the sixteenth, centuries. In this group were those with the longest ties with the Tokugawa, amongst them such names as Sakai, Ōkubo, Abe, Honda, and Sakakibara—all the so-called *mombatsu* (pedigreed) fudai. The Sakai family, from which sprang the three main lines at Himeji, Shōnai, and Obama, had been linked to the Tokugawa since a common fifteenth century ancestor. The Honda had been Tokugawa vassals and allies since the mid-fifteenth century, as had the Abe and the Aoyama. There were also a great many less-distinguished families whose ties with the Tokugawa house were similarly lengthy. The Watanabe and Uemura, for example, both of which houses held a good deal less than the median 30,000 koku during the Edo period had been Tokugawa vassals since the later fifteenth century.[8]

7. For the Tozawa, see Kodama Kōta and Kitajima Masamoto, eds. *Monogatari han shi*, 3 : 13. There is still considerable disagreement among historians on the precise limits of the fudai category. The Niwa of Nihonmatsu, the Wakizaka, and the Kobori, all classified as fudai by Kanai, in *Hansei*, pp. 60–73, are held to be tozama by the compilers of *Dokushi biyō*. Similarly, Kanai's "quasi-fudai" category includes families like the Sōma, Akita, Endō, and Arima which the *Dokushi biyō* holds to have been tozama. Throughout this work I have followed the classification, even more exclusive, employed in Takayanagi Mitsuhisa and Takeuchi Rizō, eds., *Nihonshi jiten*.

8. See their genealogies in *KCS*.

Yet not all Mikawa fudai had histories of such long associations with the Tokugawa. Others were to develop them only during the sixteenth century. The Toda, for example, formerly Imagawa vassals, entered the service of Matsudaira Kiyoyasu, Ieyasu's grandfather. Still others, including some of the most famous, allied themselves to the Tokugawa only during Ieyasu's lifetime. The Makino, for instance, were Imagawa vassals until a volte-face in 1565, when they pledged an undying allegiance to Ieyasu, whom, until then, they had been trying to kill. The Okudaira joined Ieyasu in 1561, then defected to Takeda Shingen, one of his opponents. They rejoined Ieyasu in 1573, when he needed them too badly to bother about their blemished records. The Ogasawara, also, did not become Tokugawa vassals until the 1580s, and Ii Naomasa, rewarded in 1590 with the largest of the individual fiefs among the Tokugawa *kashin*, came from a family of Imagawa vassals, and joined Ieyasu only in 1575, a scant fifteen years before he was given 120,000 koku in the Kantō.[9]

Many fudai had still more recent ties with the Tokugawa. Mizuno Katsushige, who, together with his descendants, was to hold Fukuyama han with 100,000 koku from 1619 until 1700, when failure to produce a satisfactory heir earned them a reduction to 10,000 koku and a transfer to Yūki, joined Ieyasu only after the death of Toyotomi Hideyoshi, whose vassal he had been. Kutsuki Mototsuna had been successively an Oda and a Toyotomi vassal before a last minute defection at Sekigahara sent him into the Tokugawa kashindan. Still another group of fudai daimyo did not come from notably soldierly backgrounds, becoming first fudai and then daimo by a more personal route. Inaba Masakatsu, for example, was brought into the Tokugawa orbit by his mother Kasuga no Tsubone, Iemitsu's wet nurse, and made use of this circumstance to build himself up to daimyo rank and fudai status in 1624. Yanagisawa Yoshiyasu (1658–1714), whose handsome private garden still stands in the Tokyo suburbs, was so useful as a confidant to Tsunayoshi, the fifth Tokugawa shogun, that during his career he increased his enfeoffment from 530 koku to 151,200, transforming himself and his posterity into fudai daimyo.[10]

Differing in their historical origins, the fudai daimyo differed too in the size and location of their domains. In the early Tokugawa period, these differences reflected not the antiquity or impeccability of their ties with the Tokugawa house, but, rather the functions of these daimyo within its vassal band. As we have seen, Ii Naomasa, a newcomer in 1575, was by 1590 the possessor of the largest fief amongst them; his son Naotaka preserved this position of superiority, having, by his death in 1659, doubled the size of his inheritance to 300,000 koku, twice as much as his nearest fudai rivals. A later increase of 50,000 koku brought the Ii domain at Hikone to the size it was to maintain throughout all but the last years of the Tokugawa period. The castle of Hikone was built by forced contributions on a site which Ieyasu himself selected. Ieyasu also took a personal interest in augmenting the number of Ii vassals, assigning large numbers of rōnin, or unemployed samurai, to service with them.

This generosity was no reward for long and faithful service. Rather, it reflected two things. Ii Naomasa had won for himself the position of leader of the Tokugawa forces, and it was in this capacity that he served at Sekigahara; Naotaka succeeded him, fighting with distinction at Osaka—and nudging aside a sickly elder brother in the process. It was this prominent position in the Tokugawa army that assured the Ii of their second claim to power, a large domain in a strategically important area. Hikone was seen, by contemporaries, as a "bulwark against Western and Central Japan," for it overlooked Kyoto, the Imperial city, by tradition the most politically sensitive part of Japan. The Ii, as well as providing for the military security of their own domain, were to keep a general watch over the course of events within Kyoto. Given the importance of the position, it would have been foolish to create a small han there. Given the military skill and experience of the Ii, as well as the size of their original vassal band, it would have been wasteful of human resources to send them elsewhere.[11]

10. Tejima Masuo, *Aki Bingo ryōkoku idaijin den*, pp. 76–77; KCS; Saitama-ken shi, 5 : 495–96.

11. *Hikone-shi shi*, 1 : 349ff., 415ff.

Admittedly the Ii were exceptional, both in the size of their domain and the speed with which they came into possession of it, yet they do serve as exemplars of one of the principles by which the Tokugawa later came to send fudai daimyo out to the remoter areas. Under Hidetada and Iemitsu, as increased military stability made possible gambles to win still more stability, the larger and more martial of the fudai came to be moved out to positions of some military importance. In 1617, Honda Tadamasa, son of Honda Tadakatsu (one of the four Tokugawa generals known as "the Four Guardian Kings") was sent down to Himeji, a domain straddling the route western daimyo would take to Kyoto or Edo, and given 200,000 koku. With a similar objective, in 1632, Iemitsu sent Ogasawara Tadazane to Kokura in North Kyushu, which was, as the family chronicle put it, "a vital part of the West country," giving him 150,000 koku, together with strict instructions that if he noticed "anything unusual, in any respect whatsoever," he was to "report it with all speed." At the same time, his nephew and brother, Ogasawara Nagatsugu and Ogasawara Tadatomo, were sent to adjacent areas, the former to Nakatsu with 80,000 koku, and the latter to Kimura, in the neighboring province of Bungo, with 40,000. Both were given instructions to work together under Tadazane's lead.[12]

In this way the more prominent fudai daimyo were sent out to the larger and more distant domains. Their military responsibilities were weighty, and the demands these movements made upon their vassals and their dependents, building new castles or refurbishing old ones, surveying their new domains, reorganizing their financial structures—were no less so.

The lesser fudai, in contrast, tended to be given domains closer to the Kantō, the core of Tokugawa military strength. The Bakufu began to reserve its Kantō domains for the men who acted as its officials, men of administrative ability and clerkly skills, without the taste, the capacity, the resources, or the background for war. Of the senior Bakufu officials appointed between Ieyasu's death in 1616 and the death of Tokugawa Iemitsu, the third shogun, in 1651, only four amongst twenty came from domains located outside the Kantō. Of these four, three were

12. *Kuwana-shi shi*, 1 : 175; *KCS*; *Fukuoka-ken shi*, vol. 3, pt. 2, p. 29.

within easy reach, with domains in the nearby province of Tōtomi. Naturally, as befitted their less exalted positions and their less exacting military obligations, the enfeoffments of these career officials tended to be smaller; of those appointed in these same years to the post of Senior Councilor, which was to become the highest regular office within the Bakufu, only three out of seventeen men had enfeoffments of more than 100,000 koku, while over half had 60,000 koku or less.[13] The Tokugawa in the early seventeenth century kept their strongest vassals at the perimeter of their power base and entrusted the performance of routine tasks to lesser vassals. In this they acted in obedience to the principle, forged over generations of civil war, which dictated that considerations of strategy should take precedence over those of civil administration.

Nor did the Bakufu make any effort to keep the fudai domains concentrated in one massive block. With the exception of those inside the areas of most complete Tokugawa control—the Kantō, the Tōkai coastal area, Osaka and the land around it—the fudai were generally distributed throughout Japan according to a formally unannounced, yet readily perceived, principle. A contemporary expressed it this way: "The provincial castle towns have been given to fudai intermingled amongst tozama daimyo; I believe this to have been carefully planned since the time of the God-Lord [Ieyasu]." He proceeded to indicate a pertinent example in northern Kyushu, where two fudai domains—Karatsu and Shimabara—interlocked with Saga, Ōmura, and Matsuura (which were all tozama domains) "like the fangs of a dog." [14] On this principle it was unthinkable that fudai fiefs should be kept in monolithic isolation from the rest of Japan. Certainly the closest concentration was in the Kantō and the coastal strip leading down to Kyoto and Osaka, but a significant number of fudai daimyo held domains outside these areas. By 1732, in fact, as against thirty-eight fudai domains in the Kantō and as many again in the Tōkai and around Kyoto, Nara, and Osaka, there were fifty-one fudai fiefs dispersed elsewhere about the Japanese islands. The traditional view of the fudai daimyo, which would have them almost exclusively a Kantō-Tōkai group, is a distor-

13. Calculated from Takayanagi and Takeuchi, and from KCS.
14. "Hiyōroku."

tion. Not only were they possessors of diverse historical antecedents, with markedly differing degrees of attachment to the
Tokugawa house, and different functions within it, but they also
varied just as much from each other in the geographical distribution of their fiefs.

Kitajima Masamoto, who has written more on the political and
institutional history of the Tokugawa period than any other
scholar, has claimed of the fudai daimyo that in a sense they were
not really daimyo at all, that their responsibilities as Tokugawa
vassals outweighed their concern for their role as territorial magnates. In comparison with the larger tozama daimyo, he observes,
"their consciousness of their fiefs was less developed; they were
very much aware that they were simply guardians of subordinate
castles . . . of the chief fortress at Edo." Elsewhere he has
claimed that the fudai daimyo very rapidly became "a group of
[Tokugawa] family officials with bureaucratic special features,"
and that this absorbed their energies and enthusiasm. Other
historians, too, have identified among the fudai daimyo this same
deficiency, a lack of a sense of personal possession of, and identification with, their domains. This is usually attributed to several
elements, as for example, fudai domains were often fragmented
geographically, therefore preventing any identification between
the daimyo and the land from which he derived his income.
Frequent fief movements, by which fudai families were constantly
shuttled from one part of Japan to another, are held to have inhibited this still further. In any case, the argument runs, their attention was focused primarily on the Tokugawa house and its
organ of government, the Bakufu, since successful competition
within this particular world afforded the fudai daimyo his only
satisfaction and offered him his only prospect of material advancement.[15]

The latter point will be taken up for examination in another
chapter, but here it is worth examining the first two elements of
this particular stereotype: fudai domains were more fragmented
than other daimyo fiefs, and fudai daimyo were moved from fief

15. The Kitajima quotations are from Kodama and Kitajima, *Monogatari
han shi*, 2 : 15, and Kitajima, *Mizuno Tadakuni*, p. 103. On the importance
of constant movement, see also *Monogatari han shi*, 2 : 18.

to fief with such frequency that they could develop no sense of permanence in relation to any particular part of the country.

The relatively small Sakura domain, not far from Edo, would seem to illustrate the sort of fragmentation from which many fudai domains are said to have suffered.[16] Under the latter Hotta, who held Sakura in fief from 1746 onward, only sixty percent of the domain income was provided by land in the vicinity of Sakura castle, the seat of the Hotta family administration. The remaining forty percent came from land held elsewhere, most of it some hundreds of miles away in the province of Dewa, and therefore not subject to quite the same degree of control or efficient administration as that portion which lay directly beneath the Hotta daimyo's gaze. Other fudai domains provide still more extreme examples of such fragmentation. The diminutive Shimodate fief, held by the Ishikawa house, for example, relied for almost half of its assessed income on lands lying some three hundred miles from its administrative center. When Abe Masaharu held the Iwatsuki domain in 1664, less than one-third of his enfeoffment lay inside his home province. In some cases, the landholdings of fudai daimyo were even further diversified as a consequence of accepting certain official posts within the Bakufu, posts which obliged the incumbent to take up land near Osaka in exchange for part of his fief during his term of office.[17]

Yet such extreme examples of fief fragmentation are by no means common, not even for Kantō domains, where the phenomenon was admittedly more marked than among fudai domains elsewhere. In 1664, while Abe Masaharu's fief at Iwatsuki was divided in the manner described above, other fudai daimyo in the Kantō fared considerably better. Andō Shigekata, for example, daimyo of Takasaki, further up the plain toward the mountains, held over 52,000 of his 60,000 koku enfeoffment within the one province, while Abe Tadaaki, daimyo of Oshi, had ninety percent of his holdings in Musashi. Outside the Kantō, the more closely unified fudai domain was the rule rather

16. Totman, *Tokugawa Bakufu*, pp. 158–60, offers Sakura as an example of the scattered landholdings allegedly common to the fiefs of the "bureaucratic daimyo."

17. Osaka Rekishi Gakkai, eds., *Hōken shakai no mura to machi*, p. 443; *Saitama-ken shi*, 5 : 58–59.

than the exception, as numerous examples testify. Matsudaira Nobunori, one such case, when moved in 1712 from a fragmented domain at Koga, in the Kantō, to Yoshida, near the present city of Toyohashi, found four-fifths of his domain there. A subsequent move back along the coast to Hamamatsu gave him a domain with some seven-eighths of its holdings unified. In Okazaki in 1762, the Mizuno held their entire enfeoffment in the area, and Matsudaira Yasuyoshi, who later followed them there, held ninety percent of his domain in the same locality. Unified domains, while far from unknown in the Kantō, were quite common in the Tōkai, and were the general rule in the more distant parts of Japan. At Fukuyama, near Hiroshima, the Abe held their whole enfeoffment in one block, as did the Ogasawara at Kokura, and in this they followed the common pattern of fudai fiefs outside the Kantō-Tōkai region.[18]

The claim, then, that the extreme fragmentation of their domains made it impossible for fudai daimyo to see themselves as feudal barons, is without substantial basis in fact. There is even less to be said for the assertion with which it is usually accompanied; namely, that they were also moved very regularly, that, as one authority has it, "being moved around was a common characteristic," making still more difficult their identification with any particular domain. It is certainly true, as Fujino Tamotsu has noted, that only eight fudai domains in the 1630s were occupied by families destined to hold them without interruption until 1868. The rest, particularly in the early part of the seventeenth century, when the Bakufu moved daimyo with considerable frequency, seemed in a constant state of flux, like the Ogyū Matsudaira, who found themselves in ten different fiefs between 1638 and 1764. Whatever the purpose behind such movements, there can be no doubt that the effect was to impede the emergence of any close identification between the fudai daimyo and particular tracts of land. While asserting the Bakufu's power to give and take land from its fudai at will, these movements also encouraged the fudai to keep their attention directed away from

18. For the Kantō, see *Gumma-ken shi,* 2 : 91–93, and *Saitama-ken shi,* 5 : 48–51; for the Tōkai see "(Mikawa Toyohashi) Ōkōchi kafu," and *Aichi-ken shi,* 2 : 130–31; for elsewhere, see *Fukuyama-shi shi,* 2 : 490, and *Buzen sōsho,* 18 : 25.

the transitory—their domains—to the permanent, the Bakufu and their relations with it. After all, there was no point in lavishing enthusiasm on the governance of a domain from which one could be removed at any time. No daimyo could be sure that his children would gain by his efforts in any particular domain; if he found favor with the Bakufu, on the other hand, he could expect increments which would be passed on to his heirs, no matter where he was sent.[19]

If this constant moving of daimyo in the early period was a matter of conscious policy—as I think it was—it was certainly not continued. As described in the previous chapter, the movements fell away in the early eighteenth century and were not revived in any great numbers. Although the years between 1603 and 1716 had seen 374 examples of fudai daimyo being shifted from one domain to another, the following 150 years saw such transfers on only 106 occasions. It comes as no surprise, therefore, to observe that by 1732, some seventy-five fudai families, sixty percent of the total, had settled into the domains they were to hold until the Bakufu fell in 1868. Even the Ogyū Matsudaira settled down in their permanent domain at Nishio in 1764. Many subsequent fief changes would appear to have taken place at the request of one of the parties involved, rather than springing from any official impulse to perpetuate fudai daimyo mobility, and so secure continued dependence and subservience.[20]

Stability and security of tenure thus saw a spectacular increase for the fudai daimyo as the Tokugawa period wore on. Where few in 1650 could have predicted with any confidence that they and their descendants would remain forever in their current domains, the situation one hundred years later was quite different. By 1750, movement of daimyo had become the exception, not the rule. The impact of this policy can only have been to strengthen one element of the fudai daimyo dualism at the expense of the other, to reinforce the landed gentleman at the expense of the Tokugawa vassal. Once he could assume continued tenure for himself and his heirs, once his position ceased to be dependent upon his good standing as Bakufu official or Tokugawa

19. Fujino Tamotsu, "Kongo no hansei-shi kenkyū no kadai," *Chihōshi kenkyū*, 44 : 10. The quotation is from p. 3.

20. Calculated from Tokyo Daigaku Shiryō Hensanjo, eds., *Dokushi biyō*.

favorite, then the fudai daimyo took a significant step away from
his original position as a personal vassal of the Tokugawa house.
His interests lay now in the stability, integrity, and prosperity of
his domain, and, in the pursuit of those interests, it was more
than likely the landed gentleman, the beneficiary of feudal decentralization, would disregard the duties of the Tokugawa
vassal. The needs of a centralizing government, whose servants
the fudai daimyo were, and the responsibilities of increasingly
autonomous local magnates (within whose ranks the fudai daimyo
were beginning to find themselves in the eighteenth century) were
incompatible.

The Fudai Domains

To explain just how this group of leading Tokugawa vassals
could come to find interests in common with the other daimyo of
Tokugawa Japan, often men against whose ancestors their own
forebears had once struggled, plotted, and fought, it is essential
to look more closely at the domains over which they presided and
at their responsibilities within them. As vassals of the Tokugawa
house, likely to be moved elsewhere at a moment's notice, what
was required of them within their domains was simply the maintenance of order. They were expected to devote their energies and
enthusiasm to the broader concerns of governing Japan, as servants of the Bakufu, and advancing the cause of the Tokugawa
house. Beside these duties, the cares of their domains, although
not to be neglected, were ephemeral. As daimyo, however, largely
freed from the uncertainties of constant movement, forced no
longer to compete for office to avert fief movement or fief reduction, there was every incentive to pay more care to the administration of their domains and, by careful management, to increase their wealth and the prosperity of those people, samurai
and commoners, dependent on them.

Each of the daimyo domains of the Tokugawa period had its
assigned *kokudaka* set down officially in the title deed which,
throughout the Tokugawa period, was bestowed on each successive daimyo in a formal ceremony at the castle in Edo. Conferred
by the shogun, this document testified to the daimyo that a certain number of villages, productive of a certain amount of rice
annually, were to be assigned to his charge. The kokudaka was

this amount of rice, from which tax could be taken at a rate decided upon by the daimyo within certain traditional limitations. No matter where the domain, no matter what other articles of value it was capable of producing, the major part of its income was derived from this most basic of taxes. Every daimyo had to make certain of securing his appointed share of the rice crop, and every daimyo, wherever feasible, had a vested interest in increasing the area of land under cultivation, and therefore increasing the amount of the harvest upon which he could call to meet his needs. Throughout the seventeenth century, in particular, this took the form of land reclamation projects, carried out either at the express order of the daimyo or with his consent and cooperation. So much success did these reclamation schemes have that, according to one calculation, the area of land under cultivation in Japan actually doubled during the Tokugawa period.[21]

Some of the most impressive examples of such gains belong to the tozama, particularly to those with large domains adjacent to the sea. The techniques of coastal reclamation were sufficiently advanced to allow projects like that initiated by the daimyo of Okayama, Ikeda Mitsumasa, which by 1664 had resulted in a ten percent increase in a domain already large. With the fudai daimyo, since they all had much smaller domains, the scale of the results was correspondingly lower, in absolute terms, but the impact was, if anything, greater, and it has been suggested that fudai daimyo in general increased the productive capability of their domains through reclamation projects to a greater degree than did tozama. By 1686 most fudai domains were able to show an increase in their real productivity over their formal kokudaka. Nagaoka Han, held by the Makino family, is quite typical of the enthusiastic attitude of fudai daimyo domains to land reclamation. In 1677 the domain authorities issued a proclamation containing the following clause: "In areas where there is land susceptible for reclamation, the village adjacent is to inform us of it; if this is not done, and an applicant should appear from elsewhere, then upon official inspection, according to the circumstances, the land is to be divided between them." By encouragement of this kind, they had succeeded in transforming their formal enfeoffment of 74,023 koku into a real productivity of

21. Kobata Atsushi, Kinsei shakai, p. 216.

129,190 koku before the end of the seventeenth century. By the end of the Tokugawa period, land reclamation had almost doubled the original Makino grant.[22]

Such increases, common as they were during the Tokugawa period, were never formally recognized by the Bakufu to the extent that they were included in the official fief registers. The result was a polite fiction, in which every daimyo was formally enfeoffed with an amount of land far less in fact than that from which he actually took his taxation. All participated in this fiction, the shogun who conferred the fief, the officials who stood behind him (many of them daimyo themselves), and the several daimyo who were the recipients. As they took part in the scramble for land reclamation no less eagerly or effectively than the tozama, so did the fudai daimyo also acquiesce in the fiction. They need not have done so, since land not formally bestowed upon them by the shogun could always have been restored to the Bakufu. Indeed, they should not have done so, for, on occasion, the Bakufu had enunciated the principle that all the unreclaimed land in Japan, all the land not specifically given out in fief, remained the property of the Tokugawa house. But they did not surrender the advantage they had won as feudal barons simply to gratify the ancient pulse of loyalty, and in this matter of reclaimed lands, as in so many others, their position was indistinguishable from that of the tozama.

The rice tax, although the most important source of income for the majority of daimyo, was by no means the only traditional object of taxation. Every baron had at his command an arsenal of miscellaneous taxes which, under the title *komononari*, could be adapted to embrace the most diverse articles. Fudai daimyo domains applied these just as freely as any tozama domain or shimpan. At Hikone, the fief of the Ii family, for example, komononari was levied on products such as soybeans, sweet potatoes, noodles, lumber, bamboo groves, and fish from both fresh and salt water, as well as on the nets used to catch them; even reed-gatherers paid a tax. At Karatsu Han, tea, paper, mul-

22. For fudai increases in *jitsudaka*, see Ōishi Shinzaburō, "Genroku, Kyōhō-ki no keizai dankai," in *Nihon keizai-shi taikei*, ed. Furushima Toshio, 4 : 55; Kanai, *Hansei*, pp. 60–73; *Nagaoka-shi shi*, pp. 103–09; Imaizumi Shōzō, *Nagaoka no rekishi*, 2 : 67.

berries, lumber, and silk floss were all liable to such taxation. Once products were sold and became commercial goods, they were often subject to a further tax of a different sort, the *unjōkin*. At Hikone this was levied on, amongst other things, tea, ships, and fish snares, while at Fukuyama, a fudai daimyo domain on the Inland Sea, it was demanded of some nineteen different commodities, including cotton, tobacco, fertilizer, salt fish, oil, coal, tea, and any sake imported from other parts of the country. Tradesmen, too, did not escape the daimyo net; at Hikone, taxes were demanded of carpenters, blacksmiths, tatami makers, tile makers, plasterers and launderers, and at Karatsu, in northwest Kyushu, both whalers and colliers received similar attention.[23]

This wide range of traditional taxes, acceptable to, and used by, all daimyo in Tokugawa Japan, while at first adequate to their needs, came to be less and less effective at meeting domain expenses as the Tokugawa period progressed. Long before the end of the seventeenth century most domains had begun to feel the press of economic circumstances, ichimon, fudai, and tozama alike, and had responded in a limited number of ways. It was possible to increase taxation, but farmers were very sensitive on this matter, and revolts were not uncommon. The only other avenues open were confiscations or forced loans from vassals (applied almost universally from the beginning of the eighteenth century onward) and loans from merchants within the domain, and in the commercial centers at Edo, Osaka, and Kyoto. This, too, became universal. In no cases, however, were these traditional measures more than a temporary palliative. Despite frequent incursions upon vassal stipends, and what could be forced out of local merchants, or wheedled out of those in Kyoto or Osaka, the daimyo of Tokugawa Japan marched deeper and deeper into debt.

Naturally, since they held the largest domains, the tozama daimyo could boast of the largest debts; in the year 1834, for example, Satsuma Han owed five million ryō, and Sendai seven hundred thousand, while the expenditure of Tosa was outstripping its income by twenty-five percent, and the daimyo of Izumi

23. *Hikone-shi shi*, 1 : 607–09; *Karatsu-shi shi*, pp. 620, 652–53; *Fukuyama-shi shi*, 2 : 489.

was repaying a debt the interest of which amounted to ten times the principal.[24] The fudai daimyo, although inhibited by the size of their domains from the expansive borrowing of the tozama, were nevertheless subject to the same pressures and lost no time enmeshing themselves in debts from which few were to emerge convincingly. Between 1822 and 1833, Sakura Han managed to build up its debts from a trivial 835 ryō to a more appropriate 24,637 ryō, and then discovered its credit was good for no more. In Fukuyama Han, from his modest vantage point of mere financial crisis, Abe Masakiyo in 1824 thus glumly surveyed his family's history of financial disaster: "In the 1750s and '60s our house was simply unable to pay its way, and at that time our vassals could not even afford to use lamps. However, by the time of Lord Shōtokuin [i.e. Abe Masamoto, daimyo between 1769–1803] things became more stable, and regulations were applied, so that by the 1780s conditions became a little easier. But even then we had a debt of 800,000 ryō." Himeji Han, by 1821, was in debt to the extent of 730,000 ryō.[25]

As we have seen, the daimyo, through taxes like komononari and unjōkin, were already attentive to the miscellaneous products and varied commercial activities of their domains. Increasing and chronic indebtedness was to intensify this attention as the period progressed. The original aim of securing for the daimyo a share of the economic life of his fief was to remain as a motive for encouraging local production, but there were other considerations. Increased production would lead to sales in the market centers of Osaka, Edo, and Kyoto, and so bring more money into the domain. Diversification was encouraged too, out of a simple mercantilism, as may be seen in this advice of a samurai to his daimyo in 1791: "If we make use of goods we ourselves have produced, we will profit, because the money exchanged for them will not go elsewhere." [26] Official encouragement for the production of commercial goods, accompanied by protective measures of various kinds, was common to most domains, large or small, fudai or

24. Tanaka Akira, *Bakumatsu no hansei kaikaku*, p. 126; Matsuyoshi Sadao, *Kanemochi daimyō binbō daimyō*, p. 12.

25. Kimura Motoi and Sugimoto Toshio, eds. *Fudai hansei no tenkai to Meiji ishin*, p. 22; *Fukuyama-shi shi*, 2 : 934; Horie Yasuzō, *Kinsei Nihon no keizai seisaku*, p. 294.

26. Horie Yasuzō, *Kokusan shōrei to kokusan sembai*, p. 42.

tozama, as one possible escape from a situation becoming progressively more desperate. In some cases it passed beyond mere protection and encouragement, to assume the form of an official monopoly, in which domain officials participated, together with local merchants, in the collection and sale—outside the domain —of commercial goods.

From at least the middle of the eighteenth century onward, and increasingly after the beginning of the nineteenth century, domain after domain began to compel peasants to sell their most popular products to designated merchants or officials, who would then transport the goods to the national markets. There, they would dispose of the goods for much more than they had paid. To a samurai class which had been raised to despise commerce, this was no doubt distasteful in theory, but its practical advantages were undeniable. As ruler of the domain, the daimyo could force his peasants to sell—at a price which he could dictate, and in return for paper money (hansatsu) which he printed at his discretion—products which could be sold outside the domain for the hard cash he found so necessary.

A total of sixty-two domains were to develop formal monopolies of this type during the Tokugawa period. The majority of them were tozama and ichimon domains, and amongst these are to be found the most commonly cited examples of domain monopolies: the Satsuma sugar monopoly, Aizu wax and lacquer, Uwajima paper, Tokushima indigo, and so forth. But some fudai, at least, were equally alive to the advantages of such activity, and no fewer than twelve domains developed formal monopolies of their own. Here, as in the less formal encouragement to commerce of which all domains were guilty, the response of fudai domains, and the success it obtained, were likely to be affected not so much by their special ties with the Tokugawa family, nor by their favored position in the Bakufu administration, as by a whole host of vastly more material considerations, such as the locations of their domains and their suitability for special products.[27]

27. Takayanagi and Takeuchi, pp. 1150–52. Of the sixty-three domains cited, one (Maebashi) falls outside the debate, since it did not develop its silk monopoly until after the Bakufu had been overthrown. The fudai domains among them are: Tsuruoka, Sakura, Kanō, Hachiman, Ueda, Hikone, Obama, Kameyama, Shingū, Himeji, Fukuyama, and Funai.

Once again, if the fudai daimyo were prevented by background, experience, higher allegiance, and Bakufu policy from becoming too engrossed in the affairs of their domains, little sign of it is to be found in their commercial policies. Ii Naotaka, for example, the Hikone daimyo in the early part of the seventeenth century, spent twenty-five years at Edo without paying a single visit to his domain, yet it is recorded that whenever he received a report from Hikone he would always enquire after the price of Takamiya cloth, a fabric for the production of which Hikone was famous. From this period onward the domain both fostered and controlled the Takamiya cloth industry, deciding on such matters as the standard of measurement. In 1799, Hikone set up its *kokusankata*, an organization to coordinate and control the sale of Hikone products outside the domain, and, in its first five years, this brought in a profit of 8,227 ryō, rapidly becoming the focus of domain industry. By the 1750s the kokusankata had taken over control of the manufacture and sale of a certain sort of cloth known as Nagahama crepe (*chirimen*) in return for protecting the sale of the material in Kyoto, thereby receiving a substantial profit. This activity was opposed by Kyoto weavers and by various Bakufu officials as well. In 1830, during the period when many domains were indulging in a scramble over monopolies of commercial products, Hikone finally declared a monopoly of Takamiya cloth; material leaving the domain for sale paid a tax and was given a stamp permitting its export. Buyers from elsewhere were refused permission to enter, but by contrast Hikone buyers were encouraged to buy up the production of adjacent areas. So far was Hikone Han prepared to go in its pursuit of monopoly that it decreed arbitrarily that cloth dealers in the entire region, even those in neighboring domains, had to obtain its official license.[28]

As by far the largest of the fudai han, Hikone might well be expected to have developed an interest in monopolies no less enthusiastic than that of those tozama han it rivaled in size and productivity. Yet the development of fudai interest in commerce by way of direct control and monopoly of domain products was by no means merely a function of size. Himeji, to the west of

28. *Hikone-shi shi,* 1 : 637; 2 : 28, 49, 60–63, 399.

Osaka, was indicated by Abe Masakura in his 1842 report to the Bakufu as a particular offender in this regard. He mentions that "all the cotton produced in Himeji, in Harima, has been bought up by the daimyo" (a monopoly, incidentally, which brought in an estimated 600,000 ryō per year at its peak), that it has a monopoly of hides and salt and also on a special sort of building stone called "dragon mountain stones," noting sourly in this latter connection that Himeji's public-spirited response to the Osaka fire of 1837 was to increase the price of its stones.[29]

It might be complained here that Himeji Han, with its formal enfeoffment of 150,000 koku and its position in one of the most economically advanced areas of Tokugawa Japan, was hardly more typical of fudai domains in general than was Hikone. What then of still smaller domains? Fukuyama Han, a domain of 110,000 koku under the Abe, was famous for its monopoly on the rush matting used to cover tatami, the soft straw mats which are even now the usual form—and were then the exclusive form—of floor covering in Japan. In 1711, the year after Abe Masakuni moved into Fukuyama, he prohibited the unauthorized export of the rush matting, "whether by land or sea," and ordered that it be brought first into the castle town to pay the special rates charged on it. By the early nineteenth century the domain had opened up a trade center to encourage the use of its rush matting in Edo. Fukuyama, too, was interested in controlling the destination of its cotton production, which was handled in the same way. In 1784 it attempted a formal monopoly of its cotton, which continued until 1831, when it was turned over to the control of local merchants. Karatsu Han, at 60,000 koku, just half the formal size of Fukuyama, had monopolies in paper mulberries (which was a raw material for the manufacture of paper), wax trees (haze, or sumac), dried medicines, and sea slugs. Suwa, with 30,000 koku, was interested in promoting silk production, and Funai—near the present city of Ōita in North Kyushu—which, with its kokudaka of 21,000 koku, was even smaller than the median fudai han, encouraged the planting of wax trees and established a monopoly at the end of the eighteenth century. By

29. Kodama and Kitajima, *Dai ni ki monogatari han shi,* 5 : 452; *Osaka-shi shi,* 5 : 667.

1804, it too, like Fukuyama, had declared a monopoly of rush matting.[30]

Size, then, was no barrier to fudai participation in commercial enterprise. Nor necessarily was the matter of the shape of the domain, whether unitary or fragmentary; for example, Nakatsu under the Okudaira, with only a little over half of its 100,000 koku in Nakatsu, North Kyushu, and much of the remainder across the Inland Sea near Hiroshima, was no less interested in commerce than many larger domains.[31] Much of the evidence suggesting that the fiefs of fudai daimyo were ineligible, because of their small size and lack of cohesiveness, to join in the chase after prosperity is taken from the Kantō domains, which were by no means typical.

There is no doubt that on the whole the Kantō fiefs lagged behind their fudai brothers—and behind all others as well—in the development of an independent commercial life. Many of them, like Tsuchiura, would seem to have developed no commercial interests, no monopolies at all. Others, like Sakura Han, with its coal, made feeble attempts to enter the race, only to be sucked into the Bakufu orbit. Proximity to Edo, not the size or configuration of the domain, was responsible for the general lack of independent commercial development among Kantō domains. Mito Han, for example, the largest domain of the Kantō area, despite advantages of size, shape, and special relationship to the main Tokugawa line, encountered quite as much difficulty in establishing a monopoly of its *konnyaku* produce as Sakura did with its coal monopoly.[32]

In any case, absence of a formally established monopoly cannot be taken to indicate disinterest in the prosperity of the fief. No domain could be indifferent to the sale of its goods, whether it monopolized them or not. Of those which, in the early nineteenth century, began to bypass Osaka in the search for more advantageous markets elsewhere, some were held by fudai daimyo, whose special ties to the Tokugawa and their government should

30. *Fukuyama-shi shi*, 2 : 586–87, 696–700; *Karatsu-shi shi*, p. 620; Nakabe Yoshiko, "Bunsei Tempō-ki hansei kaikaku to Osaka shōnin shihon (ge)—Bungo Funai han to Kōnoike Izuke," *Hyōgo shigaku*, 18 : 3–4.

31. Kuroya Naofusa, *Nakatsu han shi*, pp. 312, 328-29.

32. For Sakura coal, see Kimura and Sugimoto, pp. 78–81; for Mito *konnyaku*, see Kitajima, *Mizuno Tadakuni*, p. 364.

have precluded this. Of these fudai domains, some, like Hikone and Himeji, did have official monopolies, but others who participated in this contempt of traditional practice—among them Oshi, Nakatsu, Sagara, and Bitchū Matsuyama—had none.[33] Nor could any fudai domain, regardless of its history of loyalty, neglect measures which elsewhere had led to increased efficiency. Hansatsu, for example, the paper currency widely developed and used in Japan from the eighteenth century onward, were seized upon by fudai domains with no less enthusiasm merely because of the implicit violence done to the preeminence of the Bakufu's own currency. At the very least, sixty fudai domains began to print their own hansatsu as the period progressed, and one, if not more, was prepared to prohibit the use of Bakufu currency within its confines.[34]

Every domain in Tokugawa Japan considered its commercial life a matter of the utmost importance. The expenses involved in sustaining a large class of samurai, who drew their stipends whether or not they were usefully employed, the cost of the sankin kōtai and the conspicuous consumption which was so much a part of it, and the occasional crushing blows from natural disasters or enforced participation in Bakufu projects all placed pressure on traditional sources of income. There were limits to what could be achieved by economizing. The only way to escape the situation lay in augmenting revenue by more efficient use of traditional resources or by an aggressive search for new ones, and every daimyo was caught up in this simply because of his obligation to his domain and those who lived in it.

The fudai daimyo, as we have seen, were no less enmeshed in this situation than were the tozama or the kamon daimyo. Their domains may have been smaller and more fragmented, their security of tenure more questionable, but nevertheless their needs as daimyo were sufficient to involve them, whether they wished it or not. On this issue of the commercial and economic management of their domains, therefore, more than on any other, the

---

33. Kitajima, *Mizuno Tadakuni*, pp. 363–64.
34. Chihōshi Kenkyū Kyōgi-kai, eds., *Chihōshi kenkyū hikkei*, pp. 163–68. Since this list excludes all domains under 30,000 koku, it is far from complete. It should also be noted that some domains did not begin to use hansatsu until after the Restoration.

dualism inherent in the concept of the fudai daimyo could be expected to come to the surface. The Bakufu itself, as the Tokugawa period progressed, had little cause for satisfaction with its own economic position, and, given the finite resources of a country shut off from the rest of the world, it was inevitable that it should come into direct competition with the daimyo as it too began to cast around for new sources of income. Which of the two elements forming a fudai daimyo would predominate in this event? Would the Tokugawa vassal submit to the needs of the shogun, his overlord, at the expense of his independence, or would he instead affirm that independence even if it involved the denial of traditional loyalties?

The evidence suggests that in fudai domains, whenever the obligations of the daimyo came into conflict with the obligations of the Tokugawa vassal, the considerations of the domain were paramount. Despite repeated Bakufu injunctions to free trade, fudai daimyo did not scruple at forbidding the entry of merchants from other domains into their own, or at banning or placing high taxes upon the sale of products from elsewhere with the intention of keeping money within the han.[35] The search for mercantilist self-sufficiency and for products which could be sold at the national markets led most domains to neglect the various Bakufu prohibitions on the use of good paddies for such commercial crops as sugarcane and indigo.[36] In search of greater returns, as we have seen, fudai domains, from Hikone (350,000 koku) to Sagara (10,000 koku), did not feel constrained to remain within the confines of the traditional market system. Obviously, for many fudai domains, inherited loyalties had little appeal when their expression was likely to entail poverty and debt. In situations of national crisis, too, the fudai daimyo seemed content to cast his vote for independence; widespread famine saw families as prominent as the Abe of Fukuyama, the Sakai of Obama, and the Mizuno of Hamamatsu turning their backs on the national need by prohibiting the export of foodstuffs from their domains.[37]

35. Under the Mizuno, Hamamatsu prohibited the entry of merchants from other domains and also prohibited the importing of sake. At Fukuyama under the Abe, from the early eighteenth century onward, imported sake and dried fish were both subject to a special duty.

36. Takahashi Kamekichi, *Tokugawa hōken keizai no kenkyū*, p. 142.

37. *Fukuyama-shi shi*, 2 : 690; *Fukui-ken shi*, vol. 2, pt. 2, p. 99.

The Vassal Bands

Even if such *sauve qui peut* realism was personally distasteful to the fudai daimyo, the pressure upon him of the domain and its needs gave him little opportunity to resist. Individually, some may have felt prompted by feudal loyalty and obligation into a palpable expression of abnegation, but the mechanics of domain organization worked to inhibit this. Every daimyo in Tokugawa Japan was under certain pressures which made it difficult for him to take individual action; in many cases, if he resisted, the tranquillity of his fief would suffer, and some sign of Bakufu disapprobation ensue. One such pressure was merchant influence upon the domain, which had a considerable impact on the direction taken by the daimyo in his efforts to escape from financial problems. Another pressure, and by far the most important, was the influence vassals had upon their daimyo. An examination of this is essential for an understanding of the fudai daimyo and his role in the Edo period. Ironically enough, the early Tokugawa, by assigning rear vassals to their fudai, making the daimyo responsible for their well-being, and punishing any signs of disharmony between the daimyo and his vassals, served to institutionalize one of the most potent forces which in later years was to dilute the significance of the personal tie between the Tokugawa and their fudai.

From at least as early as the beginning of the eighteenth century, daimyo were turning to merchants for help in their financial difficulties. While merchants inside the domain had no alternative but to lend money to their ruler, those in the great commercial centers of Osaka, Kyoto, and Edo had the privilege—often exercised—of refusing. In either case, however, the daimyo surrendered more than a mere promise to repay. Inevitably, this resulted in closer relations with merchants and closer dependence upon them, with an increased readiness to listen to their advice on the economic life of the domain. If the merchants depended on han prosperity for repayment, so did the daimyo depend on merchant affluence for further loans when necessary. No further reason for cooperation could be needed. A common enough phenomenon in the Edo period, this kind of collaboration did not spare the fudai domains. The case of the Homma family in

Shōnai Han is a well-known fudai example of this process. There, the domain government did much of its borrowing from the Homma, a family of local merchants with wide-ranging commercial interests. In 1749 Homma Shōgorō was given samurai rank, with an annual stipend and the right of New Year audience with the daimyo, in return for lending a quantity of rice. His son, Shirōzaburō, increased both his stipend and his samurai rank by gifts of 4,000 ryō in the 1760s, and, in 1767, he began to participate in the Shōnai Han administration. In 1775 he was called upon to organize the domain finances, a role later to be repeated by one of his descendants in 1815.[38]

If merchant influence was not usually as participatory as this, it was nevertheless present in other forms. In Nakatsu Han, loans from local merchants led to their being awarded special privileges in the conduct of local commerce. In Fukuyama Han, as in many others, merchants were customarily given commercial privileges in return for acting as official tax collectors, and in Funai Han, an Osaka merchant house which had underwritten an issue of hansatsu there in 1826 took to writing frequent letters of advice. Most domain monopolies and other business ventures were in fact presided over by merchants, without whose expertise they would have been inoperable.[39]

Such alliances between the domain and the merchants inevitably served to circumscribe the course of action open to the fudai daimyo; merchant suggestions for economic improvement were not likely to be inhibited unduly by possible conflict with Bakufu policy. Standing as they did outside the feudal framework, the merchants could scarcely be expected to sympathize with a bond of loyalty from which samurai society rather pointedly excluded them. But what then of the still more powerful pressures exerted upon the daimyo by his own vassals? With them, the bond of loyalty was eulogized as the supreme human relationship; as they claimed to be bound by it to their daimyo, so one might anticipate their respect for a comparable bond

38. *Tsuruoka-shi shi,* 1 : 337–48, 376.
39. Shindō Mitsuyuki, "Hansei kaikaku no kenkyū—jōkamachi shōgyō no kiki o tsūjite mita Nakatsu han hōken kōzō no hōkai katei—," *Keizaigaku kenkyū,* vol. 2, pt. 2, pp. 98–99; *Fukuyama-shi shi,* 2 : 537; Nakabe, "Bunsei Tempō-ki," p. 5; Horie, *Kokusan shōrei,* p. 134.

between their daimyo and his overlord, the shogun. Did the vassals of the fudai daimyo encourage him toward, or away from,
the ideal of selfless service?

On this point, at least, one could reasonably expect a divergent
response between fudai and tozama domains. After all, the vassal
bands of each group had been formed under markedly different
sets of circumstances. Almost without exception, those of the
fudai daimyo were amassed considerably later than those of the
tozama, amongst whom the Shimazu, Date, Mōri, and Uesugi, for
example, had all been prominent daimyo with vassals of their
own since the thirteenth and fourteenth centuries. They had
acquired their vassals at a time when they were needed for fighting, forging then bonds of mutual dependence which later proved
difficult to set aside. On the whole, tozama vassals entered the
Edo period with a set of well-established individual rights, the
products of an age when their daimyo needed them just as much
as they needed him. This accounts for much of the difficulty
which some tozama had with their kashindan in the early Tokugawa period. While the majority of daimyo came to assemble
their vassals into permanent residence in the castle town, some,
like the Shimazu, were unable to. The Shimazu vassals were not
gathered together in Kagoshima, but remained semi-independent
local warriors, living in areas which they administered personally,
with vassals of their own, throughout the Edo period. The same
was so of Sendai Han, where a form of miniature sankin kōtai
was in use.[40] When vassals were in possession of relatively strong
rights, like these, they were sensitive of such possession and
moved quickly to repulse any threat to them from the daimyo.
In many cases this led to large-scale internal dissensions known as
oie-sōdō (disturbances in the lord's household). Of the most
famous such feuds of the Edo period, the greater majority took
place within tozama kashindan, such as those of the Date, Ikeda,
Nabeshima, Ikoma, Maeda, and Tsugaru.

With the fudai daimyo, however, as so very few had been of
any consequence much before 1590, it might be imagined that
such problems of adjustment would have been minimized. The
typical fudai daimyo kashindan was formed after Sekigahara, and

40. Saitō Toshio, "Sendai han no kashindan kōsei—seiritsu-ki no kōsatsu,"
Nihon rekishi 219 : 62–64.

kept on growing, absorbing new members, until well into the second half of the seventeenth century, at which time both koku-daka increases and attainders came to a stop.

When Ii Naomasa moved into his domain at Hikone during the year 1603, his kashindan consisted of something over a hundred men, of whom seventy-four had previously been vassals of the Takeda, a formerly powerful northern daimyo family, and forty-three were rōnin, masterless samurai from various parts of the Kantō, who had been assigned to Naomasa at the order of Tokugawa Ieyasu. During the next thirty years, as the Ii found their kokudaka increased from 180,000 to 350,000, and found a corresponding rise in the number of vassals they were expected, if not obliged, to maintain, they began to recruit more members. The majority of these came from the areas into which the Ii had moved, particularly from Ōmi, where they absorbed many former vassals of the Ishida, Sasaki, and Asai.[41] Plainly this house would seem to have had little to fear from its vassal band, for most of the men were taken on as it suited the convenience of the Ii family. Instead of a feudal bond emphasizing the mutual de-pendence of the parties involved, and their vulnerability without each other, ties formed in the seventeenth century were much more one-sided. No longer shared, the sense of vulnerability lay wholly on the shoulders of the vassal, in need of employment far more desperately than his daimyo, in an age of peace, needed to employ him.

Other fudai han also began with very small kashindan. The 203 vassals who accompanied Makino Tadashige to Nagaoka in 1618, for instance, increased to 662 by 1862; not many of these were able to boast of long historical association with the Makino house. The Sakai, with a far longer history as petty feudal barons than most fudai families, went to Shōnai with an established vassal band of their own, but, even so, by the time Tadakatsu died in 1647 there were some 192 newcomers, mostly rōnin from the disbanded Mogami kashindan. Mizuno Tadayoshi, daimyo of various domains in the Mikawa area between 1620 and 1676, obviously did some active recruiting of vassals. There is a record of his asking one of his more recent acquisitions, a former Echizen samurai, to recommend from his former companions any

41. *Hikone-shi shi*, 1 : 418-21.

he thought suitable for his new master's band. An armchair admirer of military skills and bravery, he collected many rōnin who had fought well for the government forces at Shimabara. He also absorbed some of the former vassals of the Ryūzōji, once a prominent Kyushu daimyo house, and some from the Terasawa, who had been purged after the Shimabara battle. This sort of tendency was even more pronounced among the newer fudai daimyo. The Tsuchiya family, for instance, which had begun very humbly in the Edo period, slowly built up from scratch a kashindan of which the most senior recorded vassal family was that of the Hayakawa, the leading *karō* (senior counselor), who had been with them since around the beginning of the Tokugawa period.[42]

With this sort of history and background, the fudai kashindan tended to be smaller and weaker than those developed over a much longer time by the tozama. As the prospect of actual warfare receded, and as Bakufu demands for the maintenance of large groups of fighting men fell away, the fudai daimyo could build up their kashindan as they needed to at their leisure, and in moderate numbers as they could afford them. The tozama, however, were saddled with much larger vassal bands they had built up for use in a period of warfare, and were to find, once peace arrived, that they had more than they needed or could afford. The problem was still more acute in tozama han which had suffered a reduction in size. In Chōshū, for example, the Mōri tried to maintain as many as they could of the vassals left over from the days of their glory. In Yonezawa Han, where the Bakufu first confiscated 900,000 koku of their domain, leaving them with 300,000 koku, later to be cut further, the Uesugi tried to reduce the numbers in their kashindan but still found themselves with over 7,000 vassals being supported by a kokudaka of 150,000. Fudai daimyo with domains of a similar size were much more favorably placed. The Sakakibara of Takada, in Echigo, who also had 150,000 koku, maintained on this fewer than 2,000 kashin. The Sakai of Himeji, another fudai family with the same kokudaka, had a kashindan of just over 2,000. The smaller fudai han had an even better ratio. At Tsuchiura, the Tsuchiya held 95,000

---

42. *Nagaoka-shi shi*, p. 125; *Tsuruoka-shi shi*, 1 : 252–53; "Hiyōroku"; "(Tsuchiura han) Shoshi nempu."

koku and, as far as I have been able to determine, only 719 vassals.[43]

There was a similar divergence in the pattern of vassal stipends. The Edo period saw in the majority of domains a move toward depriving vassals of their associations with particular pieces of land and assembling them all in the castle town, where they were paid salaries from the domain granaries. Their former rights of collecting their own taxes from specific areas, and dispensing administration and justice, were taken over by the han.

In many cases this was a slow process. Some of the older tozama domains indeed escaped it altogether, as vassals resisted all attempts to deprive them of traditional ties with land and people. In such cases—not uncommon in northeastern and southwestern Japan—the authority of the daimyo was largely limited to the castle town. Once outside, he had to work at secondhand, through his vassals, in the administration of the domain. Not only was he cut off from direct authority over many of his subjects, but he was also deprived of any of the advantages accruing to land reclamation, the benefits of which went to his vassals.[44]

In the case of most fudai houses, however, their frequent early movements around Japan, and their lack of well-established and entrenched vassal bands, minimized the problem for them. At Nagaoka Han the vassals were transferred from a fief system to a rice salary system of payment, at their own request, a few years after they were moved there. Obviously, the fief system was one they were not accustomed to, and they complained of its inequalities, observing that "some parts of the domain have frequent droughts or floods, and therefore the income from them is low in some years; under such conditions we find it difficult to continue." [45] At the beginning of the Sakai family's tenure of Shōnai Han, vassals were actually given pieces of land to provide for their maintenance, but within the space of a few years they all came to be paid from the domain granary; a certain identification of some vassals to particular tracts of land was maintained, but it

43. Hanseishi Kenkyūkai, eds., *Hansei seiritsu*, p. 369; the figures for Tsuchiura are calculated from "(Tsuchiura han) Tsuchiura sumai goke-chū sekijun," and " (Tsuchiura han) Edo sumai goke-chū sekijun."

44. Some examples of *jikata chigyō* are to be found in *Tōyū zakki*, pp. 260, 269.

45. *Nagaoka-shi*, p. 127; Imaizumi, 1 : 220–21.

carried no rights with it, being merely a polite counterfeit of a fief system. The same was true of Hikone, where in 1618 the han appropriated all rights over the fief areas, although here, too, a sort of fictitious link persisted. In the majority of fudai han, not even this vestige of enfeoffment remained. Most of them followed the pattern of the Tōkai fudai fiefs, which knew only payment of vassal salaries from the domain granary.[46]

Yet despite all the dissimilarities which set the vassal bands of fudai daimyo apart from those of their tozama peers, the condition of their internal power struggles during the Tokugawa period was remarkably uniform. There is nothing to suggest that in fudai domains, the vassal bands, regardless of differences in numbers, subinfeudation patterns, and date of formation, proved any more amenable to daimyo control than in tozama domains. Fudai domains did avoid the worst excesses of the oie-sōdō, but they were by no means free from them. While the Honda were at Kōriyama, for instance, in the 1670s, they were involved in an internal struggle of some magnitude. A disputed succession, with the han government split into factions, each supporting a claimant, culminated in two suspected poisonings and led to the Honda domain being split into two parts. Similarly, a succession dispute in Suwa Han in the late eighteenth century masked a faction struggle within the han government and only just escaped causing the sort of scandal the Honda incident had. A rather spectacular difference of opinion between opposing factions within the Ogasawara kashindan in Kokura Han at the beginning of the nineteenth century prompted some of the leading vassals and 300 of their supporters to abandon the domain and move to a neighboring fief for shelter. At issue was the right to counsel the daimyo. It was a gesture which had its effect— they were brought back in triumph, having made their point, and the leader of the opposing faction was forced into retirement.[47]

These were the sensational exceptions. Far more usual was a

46. *Tsuruoka-shi shi*, 1 : 258–59; *Hikone-shi shi*, 1 : 473–74; *Aichi-ken shi*, 2 : 358, n. 3.

47. Kodama and Kitajima, *Monogatari han shi*, 5 : 248–51; Kodama and Kitajima, *Dai ni ki monogatari han shi*, 3 : 389–90 and 7 : 40–41; *Buzen sōsho*, 16 : 39–41.

sort of gentle seesawing between vassal factions, or even more commonly, between the daimyo and his vassals, a situation which usually resulted in one group coming to his support. At stake was the arbitrary power of the daimyo, tolerable enough, perhaps, in the hands of a mature and capable man, but menacing if the daimyo were a child, a fool, or a wastrel. In civil wars, such rulers could not survive for long, but under the Tokugawa peace, itself an embodiment of the hereditary system, their positions were guaranteed and perpetuated. Able or incompetent, cautious or spendthrift, just or unjust, the daimyo of Tokugawa Japan were immune to frontal assault by those dependent upon them. They were not so secure, however, from more subtle inroads upon their power, in the form of a system of counsel, by senior advisers from amongst their vassals.

No less readily than other han, fudai domains also came to adopt a form of conciliar government in which the daimyo, although he could on occasions assert his position, took a decreasingly active part. Indeed, one of the classic justifications of this kind of control of a daimyo by his vassals comes to us from just such a fudai domain (Nagaoka) and from a remarkably early period—in this case the mid-seventeenth century. The office of karō, or counselor, although not absolutely hereditary, was usually limited to a handful of vassal families in a domain; the occasion for this particular justification comes in a letter from one karō to a colleague recently selected for the post.

> Those families which have customarily held the office of karō are familiar with the domain laws, and they pass this knowledge on to their children and grandchildren. . . . As long as these descendants of karō become karō themselves, then the laws will be kept without deviation. . . . But if the guidance of tradition should be set aside, and all left to the discretion of the daimyo . . . he can appoint any clever man who panders to his wishes. The importance of karō lies not in their wisdom or ability, but in the fact that they are the repositories of the law.[48]

One could ask for no more explicit statement of vassal distrust of the unbridled power of the man they were pledged to serve unto death. The daimyo emerges from this letter as a man in

48. Imaizumi 1 : 172.

whose discretion it is unwise to rely, who must be restrained by impersonal advisers rather than by the scheming men he really prefers. Not all vassals would have agreed with the elitism which reserved the privilege of counsel to so few families, but all would have approved of a process of decision-making less capricious than that restricted to one man.

Such pressure was constant upon the daimyo of Tokugawa Japan, and there is perhaps no clearer way of demonstrating this than by selecting as an example one fudai daimyo family and charting through it the course of the eternal tug-of-war between the daimyo and his vassals. The Mizuno line which ultimately was to produce the nineteenth century Bakufu reformer Tadakuni was in many ways typical of the fudai han in the path it followed. Like other fudai families, it began in the Edo period with a strong personal government. The first two Mizuno daimyo of the Tokugawa period, Tadamoto and Tadayoshi, were nothing if not the administrators of their domains. The formal record of Tadayoshi's life in the archives compiled by his descendants speaks thus of his interest in government. "In the time of the Lord Tesshō [this being his *hōmyō*, his posthumous Buddhist name] little use was made of the senior officials in any matter whatsoever. Generally the ordinary samurai were ordered to carry out his demands; he would even draw up such things as guard rosters himself, and have them copied by clerks. Those who served as his personal companions were all minor vassals." This, however, served only to sow the seeds of rancor and faction among the vassals, for the conflict of generations was not unknown in the Tokugawa period, and in a domain setting such conflict was often productive of political dissension. In the case of the Mizuno, "relations between the Lord Tesshō and his son, Lord Tsu-un [Tadaharu, daimyo of Okazaki Han from 1676–92] were somehow uneasy, and so some despicable samurai, unable to find favor with the father, found employment with the son."

The tension within the vassal band over the daimyo's use of personal advisers of low rank, rather than the han senior officials, was to continue. The memoirs of just such a slighted official tell the story.

> When the Lord Kōryū [posthumous name for Tadayuki, daimyo of Okazaki between 1699–1731] went to Kyoto [i.e.,

when he was made Kyoto Deputy in 1714], a man called
Ushio Shirōzaemon Kintane was appointed the first Grand
Chamberlain. His rank was equivalent to that of *toshiyori*
[the second most senior position in the han administrative
hierarchy] and it was his duty to look after official matters
. . . although he did not seal official documents. . . . Well,
there is no precedent for such a thing as a Grand Chamberlain; to rank them equal to the toshiyori in the order of
officials is to diminish the post of toshiyori; . . . if those
personal companions have power it can lead to trouble.

The office died out, and for a time relations between the
Mizuno daimyo and his vassals appeared equable, by which it
can probably be assumed that the control of the government
was in the hands of the latter. When Tadatoki, the seventh
daimyo came to office in 1737, he was a boy of thirteen. "Since
the reign of his father, there were signs that the leading vassals
had become proud and selfish," claims the official chronicle,
setting the scene for what one modern historian has described as
a tragedy.[49] Whatever the provocation, as Tadatoki came of age,
he too developed his own group of confidants and began a program of reforms. In 1746 he forced two of the han counselors to
resign, and then retire, and they were followed in 1747 by another. On the first day of the new year in 1749, indisputably the
social peak of the domain year, three of Tadatoki's senior counselors failed to attend at the castle to give him their formal greet-
ings. On the second day, no senior counselors came to the castle
at all. Having found out the reason—feigned ill health—Tadatoki sent messengers to try to persuade them to attend. The
chronicles of his family give an account of one such attempt:
"When on the third occasion a messenger was sent to Mizuno
Motochika, it was with the request—'if you are sick, you may
come in a palanquin, but whatever the case you must come
quickly and offer your services,' yet audaciously he did not
come." Then followed a war of nerves, which Tadatoki lost. On
the seventh day of the new year, the daimyo went in person to
visit one of the counselors he had dismissed, and on the nine-

49. Kitajima Masamoto, "Meikun no higeki," in *Kokumin seikatsu-shi
kenkyū,* ed. Itō Tasaburō, vol. 1.

teenth day he visited Mizuno Motochika, who had refused the command to visit him. Two days later, Tadatoki dismissed six of his personal companions, and shortly after reinstated one of the fallen counselors. His rebellion had been broken in a way which made his forced retirement in 1752 and subsequent death mere grace notes to the episode.

Naturally enough, this outburst was followed by a period of reconciliation, helped by the fact that the ninth daimyo, Tadakane, being adopted into the family from the Asano, took a generally more conciliatory and passive position in the han government. According to the chronicle, "everything was left to the senior counselors," and once more they "began to grow haughty," and "give proof of autocratic powers." In 1805, however, Mizuno Tadaakira became daimyo and threw down the gage by demanding that he be informed of everything pertinent to the government of his domain. On the face of it, a reasonable request, but nevertheless it prompted a visit from the leading counselor, Nihonmatsu Yoshikane, who said in reproof, "It was the custom of your predecessor to entrust the details of han government to his senior counselors." In his reply—'I shall not be bound by precedent"—Tadaakira was declaring an intention to conduct his own government, which he shortly made good by dismissing Nihonmatsu, then by demanding, in 1807, that each of his officials swear a personal oath of loyalty to him on their appointment, and finally by insisting that reports from the domain censors, the *metsuke,* be submitted directly to him. On his retirement in 1812 he urged his son Tadakuni to rely on the advice and information of his metsuke rather than that of his karō.[50]

Mizuno Tadakuni, although he restored his father's old enemy Nihonmatsu to office, was plainly just as headstrong as Tadaakira had been. Setting himself on a path for an official career in the Bakufu, Tadakuni was at first encouraged by his vassals, who thought there might be some money in it, but they soon realized it would cost much more than they had anticipated. When his vassals began to demur, Tadakuni overrode them; in the face of considerable hostility, he had himself transferred from his domain at Karatsu to a much less affluent one at Hamamatsu. Later, in 1833, a counselor who outspokenly protested against

50. Kitajima, *Mizuno Tadakuni,* pp. 91–92, 95.

Tadakuni's increasing expenditure was thrust into prison, and, in the 1840s, despite hostility within his domain, he launched an expensive coastal defense project.[51]

The example of the Mizuno family's struggles with its kashin is useful in suggesting several common features of relations between daimyo and vassals. Tadakuni's example, as mentioned above, shows, as Tadatoki's does not, that in the last resort the active fudai daimyo was the supreme political power within his domain. The only recourse open to the vassals of such a daimyo was the one which Nihonmatsu took after the move to Hamamatsu; that is, remonstrative suicide. Tadatoki's case, however, shows that the vassals, if they stood firm, could make things very unpleasant for the daimyo, and could often render the han government unworkable. Still, the petition, or the remonstrance, was a far more frequent weapon. Finally, another instructive feature of the Mizuno case is this. At times when the daimyo was a minor, like Tadatoki, or sick, or when, like Tadakane, he was adopted and was therefore diffident about joining a contest into which he had not been born, or when, like Tadamitsu, Tadateru, and Tadayori, the daimyo just did not concern himself with "the details of han government," it did not matter. The daimyo was not forced to active participation in government; birth had placed him in his seat, and decreed that each year he would live as befitted the head of a domain. The vassals, however, in season and out of season, under conciliatory daimyo as well as abrasive ones, were forced to compete for more power, for more and more control of han affairs.

Every domain, fudai or tozama, was far more than the personal plaything of one man, far more than a gift bestowed on one individual in the provinces by another in Edo. More than just the daimyo and his family, the han was the sole means of livelihood of all the daimyo's vassals. On its success or failure, on its prosperity or poverty, on its very existence, hung the fortunes of the kashin, and of their families as well. The way to service under other masters had been denied them, and there was no other form of employment they could countenance or the world they knew could provide.

51. Most of the above is based on "Hiyōroku," with additional information from Kitajima, *Mizuno Tadakuni*, pp. 154–55, 165, 456.

The personal decision of one man, taken for personal reasons —like Mizuno Tadakuni's decision to request a transfer of his fief—could cause massive reverberations on the lives of his vassals. The personal impulse of one man in the capital to give a gift, to offer men or money for a service, or to present himself for an official position may have affected himself no less than any one of his vassals, but the loss, the expense, the risk meant to the daimyo only greater or lesser degrees of opulence, and in any case, the choice was his. To the vassals, however, large and small, the consequences of any such actions presented themselves in a form both stronger and more immediate, for they were reflected in the size of their stipends. The Mizuno, for example, had been in financial difficulties since the end of the seventeenth century, and so, naturally, were their vassals. This was revealed by an order of 1701 excusing those with less than 150 koku from maintaining horses. Salaries were cut by twenty to thirty percent in 1763 to help cope with the expenses of moving from Okazaki to Karatsu, and the 1760s and 1770s saw vassals ordered to borrow from the han granary to supplement their inadequate salaries. From 1783 onward, hardly a year went by without seeing a decree to the effect that salaries would not be paid in full. In 1806, for example, it was ordained that for the next five years vassals would receive only sixty percent of their stipends.[52]

The Mizuno were by no means alone in their financial problems. In Shōnai Han, the Sakai made their first onslaught on vassal stipends in 1690, with a twenty percent reduction which was to be renewed every year for the next hundred years. The only exceptions were in 1699–1704 and 1708–1711, when vassal restiveness caused the Sakai to turn to the Osaka moneylenders instead, and in 1741, when a particularly bad crisis caused stipends to be stopped altogether; they were replaced by a dole of one litre of rice per man per day, with a minimum of money for expenses. This was repeated in 1752. Of all fudai han, it was probably Hikone which most nearly approached financial health, yet even there samurai stipends were cut on numerous occasions.[53]

The reasons for the general financial crisis in the han are com-

52. "Hiyōroku."
53. *Tsuruoka-shi shi*, 1 : 321–46; *Hikone-shi shi*, 1 : 517.

plex and lie far beyond the scope of this work. What needs to be noted, however, is the fact that a crisis existed and it affected the daimyo's vassals far more closely than it affected the daimyo's person. Han finances perpetually trembled on the edge of collapse. A daimyo's personal habits, for example, could make all the difference between a favorable and unfavorable financial position. The costs of Bakufu office, to which, in general, fudai daimyo alone were liable, were considerable. As Mizuno Tadakuni said in an apologetic letter to his vassals: "Fudai daimyo in particular have unpredictable expenses, far beyond those of tozama daimyo." Even a personal hobby, like Hotta Masayoshi's passion for hawking, could involve, as his samurai biographer noted reproachfully, "miscellaneous expenses which were not inconsiderable," and, in this particular case, it led directly to a stipend reduction for his vassals. A similar reduction took place in Nakatsu Han under Ogasawara Nagamaru, allegedly because he indulged in his own hobby, apparently the collecting of pretty girls, with more enthusiasm than discretion.[54]

The daimyo, therefore, invited the attention and solicitous advice of his vassals, whether he wished for it or not. The feudal contract may have demanded their selfless service and quiet obedience, but far more powerful obligations to themselves and their dependents dictated otherwise. They were committed to controlling the daimyo as his counselors, and if they failed in this (which was in itself rather unlikely, given that the daimyo spent at least half his career away from his domain and perforce left many decisions in their hands), then there were other alternatives. Remonstrative suicide, already mentioned, was one, and remonstrative petitions another. Shōnai Han, for example, provides two instances of the latter, one in 1707, the other in 1745. In the first of these, the daimyo was taken to task for his devotion to a particular form of religious ritual and was then requested to eat more frugally (with a limit of one soup and three vegetables at dinner), not to dress so extravagantly, not to spend so much time in Edo, and to reduce the costs of his private household.[55]

On the whole, the vassals were successful in restraining their

54. Kitajima, *Mizuno Tadakuni*, pp. 147–48; "Hotta kafu"; Kuroya, 1 : 42.
55. *Tsuruoka-shi shi*, 1 : 323.

daimyo, providing pressures which could never be ignored, and sometimes supplanting him in all but title. Ernest Satow, as a young man in Japan in the 1860s, could observe that "the *daimiō* . . . was a nobody; he possessed not even as much power as a constitutional sovereign of the modern type, and his intellect . . . was nearly always far below par." The fudai daimyo was no exception to this process of etiolation, a fact of cardinal importance for this argument. It is possible, although not likely, that fudai daimyo throughout the whole Tokugawa period maintained toward the Tokugawa house sentiments of personal loyalty powerful enough to blot out all thoughts of personal interest. After all, his domain was seldom the birthplace of the daimyo, rarely the place he spent his youth, often not even the site of his ancestral graves. Edo filled those roles for him, and it was here that he met his friends and carried on his social and cultural life. His domain was often backward, getting there was frequently troublesome, and living there was usually dull and attended by a whole host of minor discomforts, as exemplified by the kamon daimyo of Aizu, over sixty miles from the sea, who "could rarely eat fresh fish when in residence." [56]

If the daimyo could afford to be dispassionate about his domain, however, his vassals most certainly could not. They were born there, and when they died they joined their ancestors, who were buried there. Few vassals spent much time in Edo, so, for most of them, the domain was the only life they knew, the focus of all their ambitions, and above all, limited though it was, the sole source of their security. It was pressure from these vassals that kept even the fudai daimyo wedded to the interests of his domain. The vassals provided him with guardians, teachers, advisers, and assistants, and it took a particularly forceful and dedicated man to do his own will rather than theirs. Under such circumstances, the personal loyalties of the daimyo, unless shared by the vassals, would be unlikely to receive more than rhetorical expression.

It was unlikely that such loyalties could be shared. In fact, even to the vassals of fudai domains, the Tokugawa Bakufu must have seemed quite as capricious and menacing as their daimyo. Irreg-

56. Sir Ernest Satow, *A Diplomat in Japan*, p. 38; for the daimyo of Aizu, see *Tōyū zakki*, p. 28.

ular Bakufu impositions could make all the difference between
the prosperity or poverty of a domain, as at Shōnai, where, in
1741, vassals were forced on to the dole as a result of the cost of
repairing the Nikko Mausolea two years before.[57]

Fief transfers, the prerogative of the Bakufu, were also generally unpopular, for they cost money on both the domain and
personal levels. No local merchant was eager to advance money
to a daimyo who was about to cut his ties with the area completely. In such cases there was even less prospect of repayment
than with one whose continued residence was assured. Consequently, the domain government was forced upon its own resources to pay for the move, and the burden was thrown in turn
upon the vassals, whose stipends were often cut. In 1763, when
the Mizuno were transferred from Okazaki to Hamamatsu, the
vassals seemed to feel more strongly about the move than did the
daimyo, and were ready to draw up petitions to the Bakufu to
have the order rescinded. After all, the daimyo may have been
losing the tombs of those of his ancestors who were not buried in
Edo, but his vassals were also losing ancestral tombs, and twenty
to thirty percent of their stipends into the bargain, to cover
general moving costs. Their personal expenses in this were their
own responsibility and, since, like their daimyo, they found their
local credit irreparably damaged, they frequently were forced to
sell household goods to pay for their removal.[58] The most regular
imposition of all, the sankin kōtai, was recognized by vassals for
what it was—in the words of a counselor to the Mizuno daimyo
of Karatsu, "the major item in a daimyo's expenditure." [59]

There is little reason, then, in the general financial difficulties
of the late Tokugawa period, to imagine that the vassals of fudai
daimyo would have encouraged their masters in any act of loyalty
detrimental to the economic stability of their domain. Nor is
there evidence to support any such belief. What there is would
seem to suggest the opposite. Nishimura Shigeki, for example, as
counselor to Hotta Masayoshi, the daimyo of Sakura Han, submitted to him in 1857 a position paper, which, amongst other
things, urged the abolition of "those laws by which domains and

57. *Tsuruoka-shi shi,* 1 : 336.
58. For example, see *Gyōda-shi shi,* 2 : 102.
59. Kitajima, *Mizuno Tadakuni,* p. 61.

land holdings may be transferred." Later, in 1863, when the Bakufu finally abandoned the sankin kōtai system, the same man applauded it but complained that it came too late.[60] These sentiments, since they are applied to those two aspects of Bakufu authority which had the greatest adverse impact on the financial health of the domains, are quite understandable.

They also indicate the failure of the fudai daimyo to fill the dual role which had been envisaged for them, that of local administrators who upheld and strengthened the central government. The fudai daimyo who entered the Tokugawa period were vastly different from those of their descendants who left it in 1868. Nearly three hundred years of peace is a long time to rely on the personal loyalties born of shared dangers, and it proved much too long for these bonds to withstand the tensions imposed by the fudai daimyo dualism. By allowing their vassals to assume responsibilities for men and land, by punishing any neglect of these responsibilities, by permitting them security of tenure, by countenancing the emergence of fudai daimyo who were young, sick, or stupid, and then further by forcing these daimyo into semipermanent absenteeism, so that their own vassals could win control of them, the Tokugawa house unwittingly encouraged the fudai daimyo to work against it.

Conclusion

We have seen that the fudai daimyo were formed by the blending of two distinct elements: the vassals of the Tokugawa house on the one hand, and the local magnates of Japan's high feudalism on the other. It should be recognized, however, that these were strangely incompatible elements in a class from which successive Tokugawa Shogun were expected to find military support and administrative guidance. Centralized feudalism, as a form of government, allowed no neat and permanent stabilization, and neither did the marriage of two similar and equally incongruous elements in the institution of the fudai daimyo. Where the hereditary vassal was dependent and subservient, constantly in the shadow of his master, the feudal baron saw his major responsibility in the efficient management of his own domain; where the fudai was free of all obligation save that to his lord,

60. Kojima, "Kaimei-ha kanryō," pp. 454–55.

the daimyo was encumbered with duties to his vassals and to the people of his domain. How was this dissonance resolved? What role could a man bearing this institutionalized conflict within himself play in a government which, suspended between feudalism and absolutism, was obliged to move towards one or the other? It is from this division of loyalty that the fudai daimyo as a group derive their fascination, and, in the context of flagging centralized power, described in the previous chapter, that they derive their own special historical significance.

Apart from introducing the fudai daimyo and his domain, and establishing the precarious balance of the two elements of which he was composed, I have tried, in this chapter, to bring out three things which I feel have received little scholarly attention. In each case I have done no more than apply, in an unfamiliar area, information well known to every Japanese historian and historian of Japan.

First, I have tried to show how difficult it is to speak of the fudai daimyo as a group, particularly as a group representing common interests or attitudes. In their history, their relations with the Tokugawa house, the location, extent, and configuration of their domains, and their historical attachment to them, they differed from each other to such an extent as to render group activity for a common interest implausible. In a later chapter, I shall be dealing with a common crisis to see if, in fact, there was any unanimity in their response to it.

Second, I have tried to show that in some important respects many fudai daimyo had reason to find common cause with tozama daimyo; they shared common financial problems, and the commercial development of Tokugawa Japan offered them all opportunities, which were seized by those who had the chance to do so. In other respects, certain of the Bakufu's powers, particularly those of financial impositions, attainder, and fief transfer, represented threats which affected large daimyo as well as small, fudai daimyo as well as tozama. Whether there were other factors which might have served to keep fudai and tozama daimyo from ever making common cause is a subject I leave for the next chapter.

Finally, I hope to have demonstrated that the general transfer of power, whether total or merely partial, into the hands of vassal counselors makes it even less likely that fudai daimyo

would be able to give practical expression to the feudal sentiments of loyalty and selfless service. The sentiments were expressed often enough, and sometimes may even have been felt,
but one can search in vain for instances of practical expression.
There is no reason to assume that, for vassals, the loyalties of
Sekigahara were quite so significant at second hand.

3. Fudai Daimyo and Tozama Daimyo

> The distinction between the fudai and tozama daimyo is now merely a matter of name, for there is no real difference between them.
>
> Ogyū Sorai, 1722 [1]

Despite the gulf in origins and allegiance which separated them, fudai and tozama daimyo had much on which they could make common cause. As daimyo, responsible for the well-being of vassals and subjects, they were all equally uneasy with their financial vulnerability, all equally reluctant to accept certain elements of centralized control, and, increasingly, were all drawn to commercial activities of one sort or another. The narrow divisiveness of the Sekigahara labels could be transcended on any one of these issues. Still, those labels remained. The connotations of the terms fudai and tozama underwent a conspicuous change, but they nevertheless continued part of the Tokugawa political lexicon.

When the Tokugawa period began, the fudai daimyo were cossetted and nurtured by gifts of men and lands, by assignment to locations of vital importance, and by participation in the process through which Bakufu policy was created. Ii Naotaka, in writing in his testament of Tokugawa "favours received over many generations," even allowing for obligatory hyperbole, still spoke for the fudai daimyo of his generation.[2] Yet, although such rhetorical acknowledgements persisted, the facts sustaining any sense of particular privilege were soon to disappear. Only in one aspect was privilege preserved, the almost complete exclusion of all but fudai daimyo from higher Bakufu office; the consequence of this will be examined in the following chapter. For the rest, the erosion of a separate fudai identity was virtually complete. The Tokugawa balance of power, relying upon the successful institutionalization of personal loyalties, required of the fudai daimyo a sense of group identity and particularity to withstand latent tozama challenge. Once the fudai daimyo, or the vassals

1. J. R. McEwan, *The Political Writings of Ogyū Sorai,* p. 75.
2. *Hikone-shi shi,* 1 : 429.

ruling in his name, ceased to value those historical conditions which set him apart from other daimyo, then there remained nothing to forbid making common cause with those who, even though once enemies, now shared so many of the same preoccupations. This achieved, the Tokugawa balance of power would lie in ruins. The preservation of a specific fudai identity, although a matter of great importance for the Tokugawa Bakufu, was to prove beyond it.

The ebbing of fudai identity did not pass unnoticed. In 1622 it was given eloquent and moving expression by Ōkubo Hikozaemon, a man in his seventieth year who, while no daimyo, was a member of a notable fudai family. During his long life, he had witnessed and assisted the surge of Tokugawa success, but then, in 1613, with the journey nearly done, he had seen his nephew Tadachika, the head of his house, attainted, and the Ōkubo fortunes destroyed. All of this is recounted in his *Mikawa monogatari,* a chronicle of the Tokugawa rise and the part taken in it by the fudai families. Ostensibly written for the edification of his children, to apprise them of the loyalty of their ancestors to successive leaders of the Tokugawa house, it nevertheless contains sufficient caveats to leave the impression that Hikozaemon was in fact addressing himself to a wider fudai audience. "If this manuscript should be read by those of lengthy fudai lineage," he warns at one point, "do not think that I have exaggerated my own family's part. That is not so. I did not write this to have others read it. . . . I have given instructions that this should not pass outside the confines of the family, and others are not to see it."[3]

Plainly, in writing this chronicle, Hikozaemon felt that his children—to say nothing of all the other fudai houses for whom it was not written—needed to be reminded of the glories of their heritage. The need was for encouragement as much as for instruction, to maintain morale as much as to requite filial piety, for it is clear that by 1622 Hikozaemon was disturbed by the position of the fudai. They were no longer cherished by the Tokugawa house which had once relied upon them, and Hikozaemon therefore found it necessary to exhort continued loyalty, even if more neglect were to follow, even if, the ultimate insult, "you

3. *Mikawa monogatari,* pp. 435–36.

should be set in charge of the shogun's sandals or the shogun's horse, yet you must not leave to take another master." [4] The more the *Mikawa monogatari* calls attention to the historic role of the fudai, the clearer can be discerned a world where this was no longer important.

Almost a hundred years after Ōkubo Hikozaemon committed his memories and his fears to paper, there was to be another expression of regret at the passing of the personal relationship between the fudai daimyo and the Tokugawa house. This time it did not come from below, but from above, and in contrast to Hikozaemon's pessimism, it contained both an implicit apology for past slights and the hope of renewed favors in the future. In 1716 the newly designated shogun, Yoshimune, called the leading collateral houses and the fudai daimyo to him for an audience during which he impressed upon them the warmth of his regard. This was followed the next year by a further, and even more unusual, expression of solicitude when, to quote the Bakufu's official record, "on the twenty-third day [of the twelfth month] the fudai group were summoned to attend the palace. They were given an audience with the shogun in the *Kuroki shoin* [one of the chambers in Edo castle]. After a particularly cordial reception, the shogun despatched them to a feast of cranes, caught by his own hawks, and to a convivial party; they all thanked him and withdrew to the feast." Later, in 1721, in the first flush of his reform program, Yoshimune once again called the fudai before him. This time, while noting their special relationship to him and the warmth of his affection for them, he proceeded to upbraid them for their shortcomings and urged them to set an example to the tozama (*TJ* 45 : 9, 97, 248–49).

Neither of these examples of nostalgia for past ties is particularly important. Hikozaemon's protest remained the only one of its kind, perhaps because in 1622 most fudai daimyo were too preoccupied with learning their new roles to pay much attention to the complaints of any member of the Ōkubo house. Similarly, Yoshimune's gestures, since they were never pursued in any more tangible form, served merely as a grace note to a tune already familiar to all. Their significance for this argument lies in what they reveal about the relations between fudai and tozama.

4. Ibid., p. 427.

The *Mikawa monogatari* is not a complaint about the blurring of the distinction between the traditional vassals of the Tokugawa house and its enemies; the fudai are being replaced in the affections of the Tokugawa, Hikozaemon says, by newcomers, and it is this which rankles so badly. Equally, Yoshimune's tacit apologies in 1716 and 1717 are an atonement for thirty years of neglect, during which fudai daimyo had been removed from their positions of influence in Bakufu government and replaced by new men like Yanagisawa Yoshiyasu, Manabe Akifusa, and Arai Hakuseki.[5] Neither case shows any concern for the comparative standing of fudai and tozama; each is dominated by the consciousness of a more immediate threat, that of being supplanted by more recent favorites. It is jealousy of their proximity to the locus of power which occasions each of these assertions of fudai particularity, not any consciousness of lasting differences between them and the tozama.

Indeed, it is questionable how far the traditional barrier between fudai and tozama had managed to survive into the Edo period at all. To the Confucian scholar Ogyū Sorai, as he wrote his memorial to the shogun, Yoshimune, in 1722, it seemed as though the difference between daimyo had outlived all usefulness and no longer corresponded to reality. "The distinction between the fudai and tozama daimyo is now merely a matter of name," he wrote, "for there is no real difference between them . . . now both fudai and tozama are closely related, and, having been reared in Edo, both regard the city as their home."[6] From the context in which he wrote, it is clear that he was considering the matter from a military standpoint, and in this he was quite correct; the chasm between the two groups of daimyo was narrowing. After the Osaka campaigns, military pressures subsided, and this, while encouraging a new amicability between the daimyo, also began to corrode that sense of fudai uniqueness and privilege which their ties with the Tokugawa had hitherto fostered. Fudai daimyo may have retained a certain ceremonial identity—as when they accompanied the shogun to worship at Momijiyama Shrine, or when, together with the Imperial representatives from Kyoto, they had the privilege of first audience

5. Tsuji Tatsuya, *Kyōhō kaikaku no kenkyū*, pp. 98ff.
6. McEwan, pp. 75–76.

with each new shogun—but otherwise there was little discrimination.

In many respects this had been the case from the very beginning of the Edo period. The more powerful tozama were the only daimyo ever to receive gifts of the Matsudaira name or of Tokugawa daughters as brides for themselves or their heirs. At all levels there seems to have been a good deal more fraternization than is usually taken to be the case. In 1647, Shimazu Mitsuhisa, the tozama daimyo of Satsuma, felt no constraint about inviting the shogun, Iemitsu, and such fudai daimyo as Ogasawara Tadazane to watch his hunting dogs show their form at Ōji. Daimyo pitted their sumo wrestlers against one another throughout the Tokugawa period without reference to positions taken at or before Sekigahara.[7] Neither reason nor evidence suggest that tozama and fudai sat and glared at each other for 250 years. It has been claimed that some tozama domains, like Chōshū, for example, maintained an implacable sense of grievance toward the Tokugawa, coupled with an iron determination to do something about it, but one suspects that this was a retrospective belligerence, developed after, rather than before, the Restoration.[8] All indications suggest that, for the greater part of the Edo period, the tozama were as eminently placable as the Bakufu and the fudai were placatory. They visited each other, exchanged gifts, and even played politics together when in good health, and when ill they sent each other favorite physicians. They were even known to do business to their mutual advantage, as in the case of the fudai Ogasawara of Kokura, who had a regular arrangement whereby port facilities at Kokura were rented to the tozama Arima of Kurume.[9]

Certainly it is difficult to see any indication in the relations between tozama and the Bakufu of the reserve which second-class citizenship would have fostered. Ikeda Mitsumasa, tozama daimyo of Okayama, felt sufficiently secure to write a searing attack on the way in which the Bakufu functioned under Sakai

7. Wakamori Tarō, *Sumō ima mukashi*, pp. 43–46; *Buzen sōsho*, 11 : 45.
8. Albert M. Craig, *Choshu in the Meiji Restoration*, pp. 19–25.
9. *Buzen sōsho*, 12 : 132; 16 : 6. There is evidence that both Matsudaira Sadanobu and Tokugawa Nariaki numbered fudai and tozama daimyo among their supporters. See Imaizumi Shōzō, *Nagaoka no rekishi*, 1 : 91, and *Mito han shiryō (bekki jō)*, pp. 18–21.

Tadakiyo. His tozama status seems not to have curbed his criticisms, nor, in his complaint of growing daimyo impoverishment, did he speak for tozama alone.[10] One hundred fifty years later there was to be an equal lack of restraint among the tozama signatories of the 1841 letter. In asking the reasons for the Shōnai-Nagaoka-Kawagoe fief transfers of that year, the daimyo of the Ōbiroma were not merely defending their own exclusive rights. They took action to protect two fudai daimyo, plainly in the belief that the general rights of daimyo, whether fudai or tozama, were more important than the perpetuation of differences between them.

The truth was, as Ogyū Sorai had claimed, that, save in the most formal sense, the status difference between tozama and fudai had been extinguished. In the *Bukan,* the popular yearbooks providing information about daimyo and *hatamoto,* it is true that the status of the daimyo was customarily included, albeit with no great concern for accuracy. The order of precedence for daimyo, however, on the whole reflected not the length or intimacy of their degree of contact with the Tokugawa house, but rather, a more certain token of prominence, the magnitude of their formal enfeoffments, and in this the compilers did no more than reflect the general disinterest in the fudai-tozama divisions.

Intermarriage

One of the surest manifestations of this neglect, on the part of Bakufu and daimyo alike, appears in the matter of daimyo marriages. In 1615 the first *Buke shohatto* specifically gave notice of the official intention to regulate all marriages between daimyo families, arguing that otherwise enemies could build up marriage alliances to threaten Tokugawa control. This clause was repeated in all subsequent versions of the edicts, and Bakufu approval was necessary whenever the child of a daimyo family married or was given in marriage. In this alone the Bakufu possessed machinery by which the special characteristics of the fudai could be affirmed. Had there been any attempt to keep the concept of fudai lineage alive, by preventing the dissipation of a sense of common identity, one would expect it to appear at its strongest

10. Taniguchi Sumio, *Ikeda Mitsumasa,* pp. 65–69.

in the matter of daimyo marriages and adoptions. A society in which fudai married women from other fudai families and adopted their heirs exclusively from fudai households would certainly have been the perpetuation both of the wedge between fudai and tozama and of a strong sense of fudai solidarity. If any elite had been intended, this would have served to bring it into being and to preserve it inviolate from tozama taint. Yet this was not done.

Instead, there was frequent intermarriage throughout the Edo period, with the precedent being set by the Tokugawa themselves. Ieyasu's son Tadateru married Date Masamune's daughter, while his daughter Ichihime (before her premature death) was betrothed to one of Masamune's sons. When Ieyasu ran out of children he could use for marriage alliances, he borrowed them. Both Kuroda Nagamasa and Fukushima Masanori married girls Ieyasu had adopted for just that purpose. One of Hidetada's daughters married the hapless Toyotomi Hideyori, another married the daimyo of Kaga, Maeda Toshitsune. Similarly, the fudai, during the early period, did not hesitate to intermarry with tozama families. To take the most prominent example, Ii Naotaka married the daughter of Hachisuka Iemasa, tozama daimyo of the province of Awa, who at that time had a kokudaka no less than that of the Ii themselves.[11]

These marriages of the early years of the Bakufu are usually judged pacificatory in intention, and it may be that they were so in effect, as well. Yet the marriage of fudai with tozama families was not confined to the first two decades of the Tokugawa period; rather, it continued without interruption throughout the following two centuries. Fudai families could welcome the daughters of tozama, and send their own off to tozama houses, without the slightest imputation of disloyalty. An analysis of the daimyo marriages recorded in the *Dokai kōshūki*, compiled in 1690, shows that marriage across status lines had become a commonplace. Using only those cases where daimyo had married women from other daimyo households, and, in the case of more than one marriage, taking only the first alliance, one finds the following results: of seventy-eight fudai daimyo, forty-six, somewhat more than half, had allied themselves to other fudai

11. *Hikone-shi shi,* 1 : 452.

families; four had married women from ichimon families, while twenty-eight, rather more than a third, had selected brides from tozama houses. Turning to the seventy-nine tozama daimyo whose consorts had come from other daimyo households, one discovers an even more thorough amalgamation: thirteen had looked to ichimon houses for wives, thirty-four to other tozama, and no fewer than thirty-two had moved across the Sekigahara barrier to take brides from fudai houses.[12] There was, then, no stigma attached to marriage alliances with tozama families in the general sense. Similarly, there is no evidence of more specific prohibitions. The marriage policies of the ichimon families attest to this quite eloquently. Of seventeen separate alliances, weddings and betrothals, contracted between daimyo of the Hisamatsu Matsudaira house during the Tokugawa period, ten were with tozama families, among them the most illustrious—Shimazu, Maeda, Date, Kuroda, Hachisuka, and Asano—while of the remaining seven only two involved fudai families. Hoshina Masayuki, one of the leading powers in the Bakufu after the death of Iemitsu in 1651, used his children to ally himself with some of the greatest tozama families, including the Maeda of Kaga, the richest daimyo in Japan. In the eighteenth century there are instances of a Tayasu girl marrying a Nabeshima, a Hitotsubashi girl marrying a Shimazu, and a Hitotsubashi taking a Kyōgoku girl as his bride.[13] Far from any stigma being attached to marriage with tozama families, there was obviously some cachet involved. Hoshina Masayuki—and the eighteenth century *sankyō* families too, for that matter—was in a position where he could obtain for his children virtually the marriage alliances he wanted, and he clearly wanted alliances with daimyo of substance. It is in these marriages that one can discern a clue to the real nature of prestige among the daimyo of

12. Calculated from *Dokai kōshūki*. In determining which daimyo were tozama and which fudai, I have adhered to the pattern set by Takayanagi Mitsuhisa and Takeuchi Rizō, eds., *Nihonshi jiten*. Using this categorization, there were 115 fudai daimyo and 110 tozama daimyo in 1690; of these, thirty-nine had no recorded consorts, while fifteen, adopted by daimyo, had married girls from their adopted families. A further thirteen marriages did not involve other daimyo houses at all. The remaining marriages are as analyzed above.

13. *TJ* 47 : 102, 108, 258; Shibusawa Eiichi, *Rakuō kō den*, app.

Tokugawa Japan; it was not the antiquity of one's ancestral ties with the Tokugawa family, nor was it one's eligibility for Bakufu office, but rather, it was the amount of one's kokudaka which made for prestige. Kokudaka was as important in determining eligibility for marriage as it was in determining one's position in the *Bukan*.

In the case of what might be called 'primary' marriages, those in which the heir apparent of a daimyo was married, or in which his daughters married the heirs apparent of other daimyo, there was a marked tendency to ally with families of roughly comparable formal enfeoffment, so this automatically condemned many fudai families to marriages with other fudai. After all, there were rather more of them in the 10,000–50,000 koku range than there were tozama. Any example, however, shows that alliances with tozama were not exceptional.

The Mizuno family, which served as an illustration of fudai daimyo-kashin relations in the previous chapter, may here serve as an example of middle-ranking fudai daimyo marriages, although, with their 50,000–60,000 koku, they were actually slightly above the average.

Tadayoshi, the first of the Mizuno to find a wife during the Edo period, was married in 1625 to the daughter of Inoue Masanari. As he had already been a daimyo for five years, he was a fair match for the daughter of Inoue, another fudai (daimyo of Yokosuka, with 52,000 koku), who was at that time a prominent Bakufu administrator. Tadaharu, Tadayoshi's son, was to marry the daughter of Maeda Toshitsugu in 1660. This was, of course, an alliance with a tozama family, one of the branches of the great Kaga domain. Toshitsugu was, in 1660, the daimyo of Toyama, with 100,000 koku, while Tadaharu was heir apparent to a domain of 50,000 koku at Okazaki. It was a good match for them both, although not a spectacular one for either. Tadaharu's son, Tadamitsu, was to marry, in 1683, when he had become the heir apparent to the domain of 50,000 koku at Okazaki, the daughter of Honda Tadahira, who was daimyo of Utsunomiya with 110,000 koku. This was the standard sort of middling fudai alliance.

The next daimyo, Tadayuki, made a rather exceptional marriage. Born the fourth son of Tadaharu in 1969, he was adopted by a related family of Mizuno, who were Bakufu hatamoto, and seemed destined for a career as a low-ranking member of this class, with a little over 2,000 koku. During this time, he married a girl from a nondaimyo family, and so, after working his way up through the Bakufu ranks to a prominent position in the brigade of guards, he was already married when the illness and death of his elder brother Tadamori catapulted him back into the succession of the main line in 1699.

Tadayuki's son, Tadateru, seems to have been in poor health as a child. After the termination of an engagement to an equally sickly girl (the daughter of Naitō Kii), who died before the wedding took place, he married the daughter of a hatamoto in 1713. This may seem a strange alliance for a man who was not only heir apparent to 50,000 koku, but the son of a Junior Councilor as well. It must be remembered, however, that, while Tadateru was in poor health, his father was still a robust forty-four. However, the son did live to inherit his father's domain, increased to 60,000 koku by Tadayuki's successful career in Bakufu office, only to die seven years later, at the age of forty-six, leaving as heir his eldest son Tadatoki, aged twelve.

Tadatoki's youthful succession to the position of daimyo, while it assured him of difficulties in his later attempts to control his vassals, was no doubt also responsible for obtaining a good match for him. In 1742, when he had been daimyo for five years, Tadatoki married the daughter of Honda Tadayoshi, the Senior Councilor, daimyo of Koga, with 50,000 koku. From Honda's point of view, as a Bakufu official, he could probably have wedded his daughter to the heir apparent of a larger domain, but in a period where early death did not spare daimyo families, he may well have felt that the security of an alliance with an incumbent daimyo would compensate for any possible decrease in kokudaka.

The next Mizuno daimyo was adopted from a related branch, and he married Tadatoki's daughter in accordance with the usual practice which dictated that, if a daimyo had no daughter for an adopted son to marry, he could adopt one. Tadakane, his successor, was also adopted, this time from the family of Asano Munetsune, daimyo of Hiroshima, whose second son he was. This adoption of an heir from a prominent tozama family, like the Asano, was not unusual among daimyo of any category.

Providing for younger sons was a perennial problem, and even the most prominent and wealthy of daimyo could be expected to welcome such a solution. Tadakane, too, married the daughter of his adopted father.

Tadakane's son Tadaakira was to take as his wife the daughter of Asano Shigeaki, daimyo of Hiroshima. This marriage, linking a fudai domain of 60,000 koku with a tozama domain of 426,000 koku, was a most unusual one, and quite incomprehensible, unless one gives attention to the personal ties binding people of the same blood, even if they should go by different names. Tadakane had been born into the Asano family (Asano Shigeaki was his elder brother), so it was in affirmation of blood ties that Tadakane should request, and his brother permit, the marriage of their children.

The product of that union was Mizuno Tadakuni, the Bakufu reformer of the early 1840s, and with him the Mizuno marriage pattern reverted to normal, for, in 1811, he was to marry the daughter of Sakai Tadanobu, fudai daimyo of Obama (103,558 koku). It was a good match for the Mizuno house, since the Obama Sakai had a secure position among the most prominent fudai households; it was equally advantageous to Tadakuni personally, because his new father-in-law was the Bakufu's Kyoto Deputy, and within a few years was to become Senior Councilor. The years in which Sakai Tadanobu held the latter office, 1815–28, surely not entirely coincidentally, were to see Tadakuni promoted through the posts of Superintendent of Shrines and Temples, and Keeper of Osaka Castle, to Kyoto Deputy, just a step away from Senior Councilor himself. For the Sakai, though not a spectacular match, it was tolerable.

Tadakuni's son, Tadakiyo, who became daimyo upon his father's retirement in disgrace in 1845, was to marry in 1852, the year after his father's death. His consort was the sister of Inoue Masanao, the fudai daimyo of Hamamatsu who, in terms of family history and enfeoffment (60,000 koku), was in every way an equal. The match could also be interpreted as an affirmation of political sympathies, since both bride and groom were the offspring of men who had been close political associates during the Tempō reforms, Mizuno Tadakuni as leader, and Inoue Masaharu, an appointee, as Senior Councilor.

So much, then, for the marriages of the Mizuno daimyo; what sort of marriages did they arrange for their daughters, and what sort of adoptions for younger sons? Of the sixteen Mizuno daughters to survive in an age of relentless infant mortality, two were to marry vassals from the Mizuno household, eight were to marry fudai daimyo, and the remaining six married tozama. All but two of the fourteen alliances with daimyo involved the lords of small to middling domains. During the Tokugawa period, the successive Mizuno daimyo also sent out twelve younger sons for adoption; two of these were forced on Mizuno vassals, five were taken by hatamoto, and the other five were adopted by daimyo, of whom four were fudai, and one kamon. Not one of the five daimyo houses concerned had an enfeoffment of more than 15,000 koku, but, given the difficulty in disposing of younger sons, a place in the succession to any daimyo domain, no matter how small, was a matter of some congratulation.[14]

This brief glance at the marriages and adoptions of one representative fudai family shows quite clearly the absence of any stigma, formal or otherwise, against alliances with tozama families; had there been such an impediment, the marriages with the Maeda, Asano, Katagiri, Arima, and Kyōgoku, and also the Asano adoption, would have been impossible. Certainly the majority of Mizuno marriages were the result of arrangements with fudai families of roughly comparable enfeoffment, but the exceptions are sufficient to suggest that this was not due to deliberate exclusion of tozama; it was, rather, the parity of size of the enfeoffments of the contracting parties, not their family histories or their supposed standing in the eyes of the shogun, which determined this imbalance. As there was an overwhelming preponderance of fudai among daimyo with small fiefs, it was only to be expected that they should look mainly to each other for marriage partners. A similar principle dictated the adoption of younger sons out of the family, since those fortunate enough to find positions in daimyo houses could expect to do so only at the lower ranks of the scale, and it was here that the fudai daimyo were most numerous.

14. The foregoing is taken largely from "Hiyōroku," with additional material from the "(Kazusa Tsurumai) Inoue kafu," "(Wakasa Obama) Sakai kafu," and Tokyo Daigaku Shiryō Hensanjo, eds., Dokushi biyō.

If the lower to middle fudai families showed no particular hesitation in allying themselves with tozama families, the larger fudai showed even less, perhaps because their opportunities were greater. Of the seven marriages of daimyo of the Obama Sakai family (103,558 koku) that can be traced, three were to the daughters of tozama daimyo. Of their own daughters, out of a total of fifteen recorded marriages, five were with tozama. The Sakai from Himeji did just as well. There, although only one daimyo is recorded as taking a bride from a tozama family, nine Sakai girls were married to tozama daimyo.[15]

The mingling of fudai and tozama becomes even more explicit with an examination of the marriages of a tozama family. To take as an example the Arima, a small tozama family, who held 50,000 koku at Maruoka in Echizen, is even more informative than to examine the marriages of one of the monster tozama han, where protocol limited the number of possible partners to the shogunal house, the great tozama and sanke houses, and the court nobility. The Arima daimyo, in nine first marriages, obtained eight fudai brides for themselves; their daughters, in fifteen alliances with daimyo families, married twelve fudai.[16]

The list of fudai-tozama marriages and adoptions could be prolonged indefinitely, but to conclude this section, allow me to cite the case of the Abe of Fukuyama. This particular branch of the Abe was descended from Abe Shigetsugu, the Bakufu official of the early seventeenth century. From the mid-eighteenth century onward, his descendants compiled a record of Bakufu office-holding unsurpassed among fudai families. From Abe Masatomi (1700–69) onward, not one of the Fukuyama Abe daimyo failed to hold Bakufu office at some stage of his career. If there was ever any Bakufu hostility to tozama daimyo and suspicion of contacts with them, one would expect to see it reflected in a discriminating approach to the pedigrees of those who sought and obtained Bakufu office. There most surely can have been no such antipathy. Of the six successive daimyo of Fuku-

15. "(Wakasa Obama) Sakai kafu"; "(Harima Himeji) Sakai kafu."
16. It should be noted that the historians differ on the precise status of the Arima. Kanai Madoka, in *Hansei*, p. 65, lists them as quasi-fudai, while Fujino Tamotsu, in *Bakuhan taisei shi no kenkyū*, p. 720, has included them among the tozama. In this, as in all other cases, I follow the lead of Takayanagi and Takeuchi, which sets them among the tozama.

yama who ruled between the Abe entry into Fukuyama in 1710 and the incumbency of Masahiro (the Bakufu official to whom fell the duty of negotiating with Commodore Perry in 1853), no fewer than five found brides from among the daughters of tozama daimyo, and they were substantial ones: Yamanouchi of Tosa, Shimazu of Satsuma, Nabeshima of Saga, Tsugaru of Hirosaki in northern Japan, and Niwa of Nihonmatsu.[17]

The record of the Abe of Fukuyama, if slightly unusual in the intensity of its marriages with tozama, is at least expressive of one aspect of the effects of fudai-tozama intermarriage, which has been the subject of this section. No less so than among other fudai daimyo, Bakufu officeholders were accustomed to finding brides for their sons and grooms for their daughters among a group of feudal lords whom theory declared to be the object of official suspicion and disfavor. Just as one cannot suspect these men of having willingly sought out unfavorable marriage alliances, or of selecting for their sons brides from any suspect quarter, so one cannot imagine the perpetuation of any discriminatory policy from a group of Bakufu officials who may have been born of tozama mothers or may have looked towards tozama to provide them with favorable marriages for their children. How could one persuade Abe Masasuke, for example, whose mother was a Shimazu, whose wife was a Niwa, and whose daughter-in-law was a Tsugaru, that the tozama constituted a threat to the Bakufu's hold over Japan which Masasuke, as a Senior Councilor, should not hesitate to suppress? The spirit of fudai sodality, given form in the hostilities of incessant civil war, evaporated in the warmth of the Tokugawa peace, and its disappearance was presaged by free intermarriage. To a government established by force, explicitly dependent upon the prolongation of traditional antagonisms for a favorable balance of power, this should have been cause for alarm. That it was not is due to the increasing role the fudai daimyo themselves played in the administration of Bakufu policy. They could not be expected to enforce, as officials, discriminatory distinctions which had long ceased to have any meaning for them as individuals.

It may be objected that the peculiarities of Japanese family life—particularly in daimyo families during the Edo period,

17. *Fukuyama-shi shi*, 2 : passim.

where concubinage, sexual segregation, parental and fraternal absenteeism were the rule, where marriages were contracted on behalf of children by those older and wiser than either of the two people most deeply concerned, where husbands spent half of their married lives away from their legal wives, where the responsibilities of adoption were far more awesome than anything with which the West is familiar—make these family ties less significant than they would be in the modern world. All of this is true, and must mitigate against attributing to the Japanese of the Tokugawa period quite the degree of personal attachment to one's family which with us is preserved despite marriage and adoption. To admit this, however, is still not to claim that the daughters and sons of daimyo entered marriage and adoption without any backward glance whatsoever. They came, not as tabulae rasae, ready to have inscribed upon them whatever the new family decreed, but as the possessors of links with people, places, and customs. Ties of affection and obligation continued to exist after marriage and adoption, and the Bakufu was aware of this fact. On occasion it acknowledged such ties, as, for example, when it sent a message of condolence to the daimyo of Owari in 1732 on the death of his real brother, Matsudaira Yoshitaka, daimyo of Takasu. Yoshitaka, born into the Owari household, had been adopted in 1706 by Matsudaira Yoshiyuki, but obviously the fraternal bond had survived to this extent, that the Bakufu took formal cognizance of it. On occasion, too, the Bakufu not only acknowledged such ties, but made specific use of them. In 1619, when formal notification of attainder was served on the tozama, Fukushima Masanori, by two messengers, one of them was the fudai daimyo, Makino Tadashige. Although to the casual eye simply another juxtaposition of fudai and tozama, it was in fact a meeting between brothers-in-law, for Tokugawa Ieyasu had adopted Makino Tadashige's sister for the purpose of giving her to Fukushima in marriage. The Bakufu's purpose in sending Makino on this particularly sensitive errand was not to affront the tozama daimyo with the presence of a traditional enemy, but to mollify him with a brother-in-law. A comparable approach was used in the attainder of the tozama, Katō Tadahiro, in 1632, when the duty of taking charge of the Katō stronghold at Kumamoto, although once again assigned to a fudai daimyo, happened to fall upon Katō's uncle, Mizuno Katsushige. In making use of the uncle, the Bakufu hoped to preclude the possibility of armed resistance from the nephew. In 1649, too, when the tozama, Hosokawa, died, leaving a very young successor, the fudai, Ogasawara Tadazane, was commanded to supervise the administration of the Hosokawa domain. While superficially another assertion of the special status of the fudai, it was a far more subtle and benevolent move, for the young daimyo was Tadazane's own grandson.[18]

Bakufu Policy

If the difference between fudai and tozama had become merely one of name, as Ogyū Sorai had suggested, one could expect to see this reflected in the official policy of the Bakufu. After all, throughout the greater part of the Tokugawa period that policy was formulated by fudai daimyo, chiefly through the position of Senior Councilor, and their decisions could be expected to mirror the waning of the old distinctions. This is precisely the case. Where the customary interpretation of the fudai daimyo as the staunch defenders of the Tokugawa house against the unruly tozama leads one to anticipate evidence of Bakufu discrimination in favor of one group against the other, all that is to be found is a remarkable impartiality.

This is to be seen, first of all, in the Bakufu's diminished concern for the strategic role of the fudai domains. Originally, as we have seen, the early Tokugawa sent their strongest and most capable vassals into fiefs of particular strategic importance, usually to positions on communications routes or on the borders of tozama domains. From these situations, they were charged with the surveillance of movements whether through their own domains or in those of their untrustworthy neighbors. In the cold-war atmosphere of the first years of the seventeenth century, such fudai daimyo played an essential part in assuring the stability of the Tokugawa regime; they were handpicked, and, if their successors proved too ill or too young to fulfill their onerous military obligations, the Bakufu did not hesitate to replace them with men more capable. This did not continue, and as

18. *TJ* 45 : 599–600; Imaizumi, 1 : 38–43; *Fukuyama-shi shi,* 2 : 46; *Buzen sōsho,* 11 : 46.

daimyo movements slackened throughout Japan from the eighteenth century onward, so too did occupation of strategic domains stagnate. Security of tenure then gave rise to circumstances in which fudai could form close alliances with the very daimyo they were supposed to be watching. The Ogasawara of Kokura, for example, in an area regarded as "the key to the West," had close ties with both the Kuroda and the Hosokawa, their tozama neighbors. The Okudaira, of Nakatsu, another important North Kyushu domain abutting on the Inland Sea, adopted an heir from the Shimazu of Satsuma, potentially the most threatening of all tozama in Kyushu.[19]

Obviously, a Bakufu which could gamble with the foundations of its military security in this way no longer regarded the tozama as a threat. The inevitable corollary was that it would come to see the fudai daimyo as no longer any particular asset, and this attitude appears unmistakably in the pattern of Bakufu attainders, where family history failed to afford any special protection to those fudai daimyo who had earned official censure. Certainly none were involved in the disenfeoffments following the Battle of Sekigahara, but, from this point on, the Bakufu began to use attainders to make examples of daimyo—any daimyo—who either infringed its laws or obstructed its progress toward central governing power. From 1603 to his death in 1616, Ieyasu passed sentence of disenfeoffment on forty daimyo, of whom twenty-six were tozama and twelve fudai. These figures indicate that, in this area at least, the fudai received no special solicitude from their overlord. Ieyasu's evenhandedness was to be continued by his son and grandson; under Hidetada, both the number and proportion of fudai attainders increased in relation to the attainders of tozama—fourteen fudai as against twenty-one tozama—while under Iemitsu, the third shogun, there was a further increase in numbers, with sixteen fudai attainders in contrast to twenty-six tozama.[20]

In the reign of the fifth Tokugawa shogun, Tsunayoshi, fudai disenfeoffments actually came to outstrip those of tozama. Of a total of forty-six acts of attainder, more were directed against fudai

19. Kuroya Naofusa, *Nakatsu han shi*, pp. 145–54; Kodama Kōta and Kitajima Masamoto, eds., *Dai ni ki monogatari han shi*, 7: 424–37.
20. Fujino, *Bakuhan*, pp. 193, 201, 251–52.

daimyo than against tozama. After this time, attainders took place so infrequently that it is impossible to discern a pattern in them. Later, in the Bakufu's last large-scale attempt to make use of its prerogatives in this direction, Mizuno Tadakuni's ill-fated *agechi-rei* of 1843, fudai daimyo stood to loose far more than anybody else. Had Tadakuni remained in power long enough to enforce it, every daimyo holding land in the vicinity of Edo and Osaka would have lost it and received in return less productive land elsewhere. Of the twenty-four daimyo thus brusquely shoved aside, twenty would have been fudai and four tozama.[21] At the end of its career just as much as in the beginning, the Tokugawa Bakufu showed no great inclination to offer its traditional vassals any greater clemency than other daimyo.

This was so, too, with the sankin kōtai system. When first formally established in 1635, it was to apply only to tozama daimyo. Seven years later, in 1642, it came to be demanded of fudai daimyo also; this can only be a sign of an impartial approach to government in a period when the traditional distinctions no longer were valid. Whatever the motive, the effect was to impose the heavy financial burden of regular travel and maintenance of residences in Edo on the backs of fudai and tozama alike.

There are grounds for believing that the early Bakufu's policies were not so far dominated by mistrust and caution as has often been claimed. After all, the greatest beneficiaries of the Battle of Sekigahara were the tozama daimyo who had supported Ieyasu, since, of the total of six-and-a-half million koku distributed among daimyo, tozama received five million. Even after the battle of Osaka, some tozama daimyo continued to forge ahead. Arima Toyouji, for example, a Toyotomi vassal who had been rewarded with a fief of 70,000 koku at Fukuchiyama for his support at the Battle of Sekigahara, was moved to Kurume with a staggering increase of 210,000 koku in 1620. In 1632 Hosokawa Tadatoshi was raised from 320,000 koku to 540,000.[22]

21. Tsuji Tatsuya, *Kyōhō kaikaku no kenkyū*, pp. 46–47; Kitajima Masamoto, *Mizuno Tadakuni*, pp. 426–27.
22. Nakamura Kōya, *Tokugawa Ieyasu monjo no kenkyū*, 2 : 814–20; Kodama Kōta and Kitajima Masamoto, eds., *Monogatari han shi*, 5 : 303; Kuroya, pp. 35–36.

If the tozama were asked to pay the greater share of the building projects of the early Bakufu, this was no more than reasonable, since they had been given the lion's share of the fief increases and held the largest domains. Had it been the Bakufu's
intention to impoverish the tozama daimyo, as is so often con-
tended, it must be recognized that a great many opportunities
were missed. The building of the mausoleum at Nikkō during
the reign of Iemitsu, for example, which was the most expensive
single architectural undertaking the Bakufu entered upon, saw
no tozama daimyo called on for assistance. Instead, the Bakufu's
own treasury provided the greater part of the money required
for labor and materials, at prodigious cost.

It is impossible to estimate just which category of daimyo was
most affected by the early Bakufu's demands of money, materials,
and labor. What is certain, however, is that fudai daimyo were
not spared participation in these building projects. At Edo
Castle, work on the keep in 1607 was allocated to the Kantō
daimyo, who were all fudai, while the main pavilion was built
at the expense of four fudai daimyo in 1622. Extensions to the
castle in 1628 involved contributions from more than seventy
fudai. Work on the moats and walls in 1636 involved large
numbers of tozama, but also equally large numbers of fudai. If
Nagoya Castle was built by tozama daimyo in 1609, then Hikone
Castle was built between 1608 and 1615 almost entirely by fudai
contributors, among them Honda Tadakatsu and Okudaira
Nobumasa. It must not be forgotten, too, that during this building boom many fudai daimyo were in the process of establishing
new domains of their own. The tozama daimyo were almost all
in well-established domains, which already had their own castles;
the fudai, however, being sent to what had been fragments of
older and larger domains, often had to set about building castles
for themselves. When Fukuyama was carved out of the old domain of Fukushima Masanori, it had no castle of its own, and
Mizuno Katsushige, the first daimyo, had to build one. On his
entry in 1619, the Bakufu gave him 12,600 ryō in gold and 380
kan of silver, to help toward building a castle, but this was only
a fraction of what was needed. Fukuyama was surrounded by
rich tozama from whom the Bakufu could have commanded as-

sistance had it been concerned to cherish its fudai daimyo at all costs.[23]
If this is not enough to suggest that the Bakufu refused to allow great disparity between the way it treated fudai and the way it treated tozama, then it might be added that the Bakufu seemed to make no great distinctions between those tozama who were manifestly cordial and those who were not. Date Masamune, for example, was on good personal terms with both Ieyasu and Hidetada, yet the early building impositions drove him into debt. Tōdō Takatora was an even more astonishing case. He, too, had been a personal friend of Ieyasu, receiving his trust to a remarkable extent; his position in the Bakufu under Hidetada was such that he has been ranked with Ii Naotaka as one of the shogun's advisers. Certainly, when Hidetada called his fudai counselors together in 1619 to discuss the attainder of Fukushima Masanori, the tozama, Tōdō Takatora, was among them. Yet even so he was subjected to as many demands for building contributions as other less trusted tozama.[24]
Additional evidence that the early Bakufu was not primarily engaged in driving the tozama daimyo into penury can be found in the cautious spacing of its demands upon them. All daimyo who had helped fight in the Osaka campaigns of 1615, for example, were given a period of three years in which to catch their breath before being asked for help again—this, too, took no account of whether they were fudai or tozama. After Shimabara, in 1638, when many of the western daimyo had sent large numbers of troops to help put down the rebels, they were not asked for building contributions for some time. Some western daimyo who had special functions by virtue of their location, like the Kuroda and Nabeshima, each of whom was required to pay constant attention to the port of Nagasaki, were seldom or never asked for contributions.[25] It is doubtful if the Sō, the daimyo of Tsu-

23. *Hikone-shi shi*, 1 : 367–68; *TJ* 38 : 430; *Chiyoda-ku shi*, 1 : 482–85; *Fukuyama-shi shi*, 2 : 36.

24. Fukushima Kimiko, "Edo Bakufu shoki no seiji seido ni tsuite—Shōgun to sono sokkin," *Shiso* 8 : 91.

25. Yoshizumi Mieko, "Tetsudai bushin ni tsuite, *Gakushuin Daigaku Bungakubu kenkyū Nempō*," pp. 91, 116.

shima, who played such a large part in relations with Korea, were imposed upon, either.

In its role as moderator of interdomainal disputes, too, the Bakufu had a prime position from which to vent any dislike it may have had for tozama domains, particularly in those issues upon which tozama sought judgment against fudai daimyo or against the Bakufu's own daikan; after all, the Bakufu tribunal, the *Hyōjōsho*, which adjudicated disputes of this sort, was hardly an independent body. It was composed of the Senior Councilor on duty, the Superintendents of Temples and Shrines, the Superintendents of Finance, and the Edo City Magistrates, all of them Bakufu officials, and so presumably instruments of what they and their fellows defined as the best interests of the Bakufu. Hence, it was by no means anything like the independent judiciary which today is our own protection against the will of the central government. Yet, without going into an elaborate analysis of the decisions—if indeed there is any evidence to permit such analysis—it is possible to say that, in the course of general reading, one keeps finding examples of cases taken before the tribunal in which the verdict has gone to the tozama rather than to the fudai or the Bakufu daikan. When the tozama daimyo of Sendai and the fudai daimyo of Shōnai fell out, at the beginning of the nineteenth century, the latter apologized and dismissed his chief counselor rather than have the affair called to official attention, from which one may assume that not even impeccable fudai antecedents could compensate for a weak case. Nor, to extend the Bakufu's impartiality into the commercial field, of increasing importance in the nineteenth century, is there anything to suggest that any use was made of the Bakufu's authority to favor the commercial activities of fudai domains over those of tozama.[26]

As the Tokugawa period progressed, the fudai daimyo came to be involved more and more in the engineering projects developed by the Bakufu after its enthusiastic castle construction. One of these was the repair of castles, which, in effect, came to be limited to Edo Castle (although by no means to all parts of it needing repair). The work ranged from small-

26. Wakabayashi Kisaburō, *Maeda Tsunanori*, pp. 39–43, 194–96; *Tsuruoka-shi shi*, 1 : 372; Horie Yasuzō, *Kokusan shōrei to kokusan sembai*, pp. 65, 114.

scale tasks like cleaning the moats and drains and rebuilding gates damaged by minor fires (in 1732, Toranomon and Saiwai-bashi-mon were repaired by a fudai and a tozama respectively), to rather more ambitious repairs and rebuilding in the wake of larger fires. After the great fire of 1657, the initial repairs were allocated to Maeda, Hosokawa, Niwa, Toda, Sanada, Sōma, Naitō, Mizutani, Makino, and Okabe, of whom six were fudai and four tozama. The fire of 1838 which destroyed the Western Enclosure was followed by impositions upon thirteen daimyo, more than half of them fudai; a similar proportion of fudai daimyo met the cost of repairs after the next major fire in 1844. If in major repairs like these there was no tendency to batten on the tozama exclusively, it seems unlikely that the smaller incidental repairs would devolve more upon one sort of daimyo than another (*TJ* 41 : 600; 41 : 221, 242; 49 : 387, 520, 527–28).

A further form of obligation imposed on the daimyo was that of repairing the various shrines and temples associated with the Tokugawa family—Kan'eiji, now a grimy bomb-damaged remnant of what was once a vast and opulent metropolitan temple, and Tōeizan, at Ueno (both temples had strong associations with the Tokugawa and both had shogun buried within their grounds), and above all Nikkō. Although the Bakufu built the gaudy mausolea at Nikkō at its own expense, it did from time to time call upon other daimyo to help with the upkeep. Yet there is no particular sign here that one group of daimyo tended to be singled out to meet this obligation along fudai-tozama lines. What did happen was that demands usually were made on daimyo in the area. The Okudaira, while they were nearby in Utsunomiya, were called on for assistance in 1638, 1641, 1643, 1645, 1650, 1654, and 1659. This extraordinary shower of requests—from which their impeccable fudai status afforded them no shelter—was determined solely by their proximity to Nikkō. Various tozama were asked to contribute at one time or another —Kuroda and Arima in 1645, for example—but after 1651 such assignments tended to go to daimyo in the Tōhoku area, irrespective of whether they were fudai or tozama. It does not seem as though the weight of these obligations was particularly punitive towards tozama daimyo, or was even necessarily calculated in proportion to their enfeoffment. The tozama, Date of Sendai, with 625,000 koku, spent 12,300 ryō on Nikkō repairs in 1711, but the fudai, Sakai of Shōnai, with 140,000 koku—less than one-quarter of the Date holding—were called on to spend almost four times as much in 1739.[27]

Perhaps the most frequently employed form of extraordinary imposition upon the daimyo, once the castle construction had ceased, was that of civil engineering constructions, and of these the most important was work on rivers. Many of the Japanese rivers, and in particular those of the east coast, where in places a fairly broad coastal plain intervenes between the mountains and the sea, presented severe flood problems. Heavy rain, or the spring thaw, would often send huge masses of water hurtling down from the mountains upon shallow riverbeds and meandering courses unable to contain them. The result was usually flooding and devastation. In an attempt to counter this, the Tokugawa period saw a great amount of civil engineering on these watercourses, to build up their banks and deepen their beds. Throughout the seventeenth century, such work was usually assigned—when not done voluntarily—to the daimyo through whose domains the rivers ran, and who would receive the benefit of any improvements. Yet it became apparent that the daimyo of the two areas where these problems were most marked—the Kantō and Tōkai—were not sufficiently wealthy to afford the large-scale work necessary. For a time, the Bakufu joined in by contributing a supplementary allowance to domains engaged in such work, but it soon found the cost too high and after a time began to assign these projects to daimyo from other areas. It may appear in this instance that the fudai were being given favored treatment, for in the Kantō and Tōkai, where the daimyo were largely fudai, they were all spared considerable expense. Other daimyo were being brought in to pay for costly engineering projects from which the small Kantō and Tōkai daimyo would be the sole beneficiaries. Yet the way the Bakufu applied these impositions supports no such interpretation. Of the nine daimyo assigned to engineering work on the rivers of Kai, Mino, and Ise in 1766, six were fudai; only one of them, Ishikawa Fusazumi, the daimyo of Kameyama in Ise, held land in the area, and even then he was assigned to work in Kai, nowhere

27. Yoshizumi, "Tetsudai bushin," pp. 103–05.

near his own domain. One of the tozama daimyo involved, Tsugaru Nobuyasu, of Hirosaki (in the northwest corner of Honshu), had his domain devastated by an earthquake the day after the imposition was announced and for this reason was freed of his river obligations a few days later. One could ask for no clearer evidence of Bakufu solicitude for tozama daimyo. Had there been implacable hostility, the Tsugaru would most certainly have been forced to continue with their obligations. Instead, they were later given a Bakufu loan to help repair the earthquake damage. In this particular task of flood control, the daimyo with the largest domains contributed more, and so the contribution of the Honda of Nishibata in Mikawa (15,000 koku) cannot be compared with that of the Mōri of Chōshū (369,000 koku). However, the significant fact is not that the tozama paid more, for they could afford to do so, but rather that the fudai were ever called upon at all.[28]

A similar concern for equal treatment—or at least freedom from discrimination—can be seen in the Bakufu's other demands. In 1707, when Mt. Fuji erupted for the last time, it only provided cause for momentary excitement in Edo. Arai Hakuseki tells us that, after hearing a noise he took to be thunder, he went outside to find white ash falling over Edo like snow. Later that day, on his way to the castle, "the ground was covered with white ash, and the grass and trees had turned white." To the farmers of the three provinces which lay at the foot of the mountain, however, the ash, the tremors, the fires, and the lava combined to wreak a major disaster. Accordingly, the Bakufu called upon all daimyo to contribute two ryō for each hundred koku of their fief (OSK p. 199).

There is no evidence of partiality in the Bakufu's other impositions, either. Repairs to roads and bridges along the Tōkaidō in 1707, for example, were borne by three fudai. In the early 1840s an attempt to drain the Imbanuma, the great Kantō swamp which measured fourteen miles in length and four miles in breadth at its widest point, involved substantial contributions from five daimyo; four of them were fudai. As with all other attempts to drain the marsh, this too was ultimately abandoned, but not before it had cost those involved a great deal. It has

28. Ibid., pp. 96–103; TJ 47 : 211–12, 227.

been calculated that the fudai Sakai of Shōnai paid for the employment of 354,443 day laborers on this scheme.[29]

Other occasional expenditures demanded of daimyo seem to have been no less impartial. The fifth shogun, Tsunayoshi, who loved to go visiting, made a formal visit to the Maeda mansion (where Tokyo University now stands) together with five thousand of his companions, and stayed for five hours. By these marks of favor, he sent the Maeda immediately into debt. Such expensive honors were by no means monopolized by wealthy tozama daimyo, however. A similar jaunt, this time with 562 followers, to the fudai Tsuchiya mansion, was no less disastrous. The important visitors were fed on rice cakes, sweetfish (*ayu*), sea bream, salmon, and eels, entertained with performances of Nō, and given presents of swords, money, and salted sea bream. After two days they departed, leaving behind them a pile of broken crockery worth 288 ryō. The whole escapade cost the Tsuchiya 25,736 ryō, a sum they could ill afford.[30]

It is obvious from this account that the fudai daimyo were not spared the demands of the central government. Nor was there any great discrimination in the frequency with which such calls came. It is beyond the bounds of this work to attempt to tabulate the incidence of Bakufu demands for assistance from the 250-odd domains of Tokugawa Japan, but nevertheless it is possible to get some idea from a casual comparison of an ordinary tozama domain with an unexceptional fudai han. In each case, to avoid the complications of the building boom of the early seventeenth century, and the defence impositions of the Bakumatsu period, a much clearer picture is given if the years 1650–1850 are taken as the period to be examined.

Taking the Ikeda domain at Okayama as a convenient example of a tozama han—if anything possibly a little harder hit by Bakufu demands than many—the following picture emerges. In 1682 the domain entertained one of the twelve Korean embassies to visit Japan during the Tokugawa period. This was an honor that could hardly be avoided, since Okayama lay on their customary route to Edo; it was also rather more onerous

29. *TJ* 47 : 675; *Tsuruoka-shi shi,* 1 : 444–49.
30. Wakabayashi Kisaburō, *Maeda Tsunanori,* pp. 165–70; "(Tsuchiura han) Onari nikki."

than it might seem, since the number of emissaries and their attendants sometimes reached five hundred, and was never less than three hundred. Then, in 1699 came an order to survey the neighboring Fukuyama domain, from which the Mizuno had recently been removed. The following year Okayama was commanded to help with work on two Kantō rivers, the Kanamegawa and the Sakawa. In 1708, in the train of the eruption of Mt. Fuji, the domain presented the Bakufu with 6,304 ryō, and further visits by Korean embassies in 1711 and 1719 again enmeshed the Ikeda house in their entertainment. The year 1742 saw a contribution to work on the Tone River, near Edo, while 1748 and 1764 saw further receptions for Korean diplomats. In 1781 and 1787, Okayama again contributed to engineering work on Kantō rivers, and in 1789 it presented the Bakufu with 1,623 ryō. Work on Tokai rivers occupied the domain in 1792, 1799, 1809, 1829, and 1836, while in 1811 it entertained Korean ambassadors again. In 1845 Okayama gave the Bakufu 15,760 ryō. In summary, over a period of two hundred years, Okayama entertained Korean ambassadors on six occasions, presented the Bakufu with money on three—1708, 1789, and 1845—and contributed nine times to civil engineering projects.[31]

Against this can be placed the record of the fudai Okabe of Kishiwada, near Osaka, who held a domain of 53,000 koku. In 1655 they, too, entertained the Koreans, and two years later they were called upon to provide guards for two of the gates at Edo Castle. This was a dubious privilege reserved for smaller fudai and tozama daimyo; where the Ōtemon, the central palace gate, was concerned, such guard duty required the attendance of ten officers, thirty musketeers, ten bowmen, and fifty pikemen, amongst others, for periods of up to twelve months at a time. Then, after the great Edo fire of 1657, the Okabe contributed labor and materials towards rebuilding Edo Castle. The year 1669 saw more guard duty on the Edo gates, and in 1682 they entertained the Korean ambassadors shortly after the Ikeda at Okayama. Work on the nearby Yamato River in 1676 was followed by an order to help prevent soil erosion in the provinces of Settsu and Kawachi in 1684. This was to be repeated in 1691–92, after assistance in 1687 with the restoration of the Daitoku-in,

31. Imaizumi, 1 : 62–63; Ono Kiyoshi, ed., (Shiryō) Tokugawa Bakufu no seido, pp. 464–78; Taniguchi Sumio, Okayama han, pp. 307ff.

one of the temples at Kōyasan, the enormous monastery in Kii. Like the Ikeda, the Okabe also entertained the Korean embassies of 1711 and 1719, and, in 1714, between these duties, the daimyo Okabe Nagayasu was sent to Nikkō as the shogun's deputy. This last position was one of the few real prerogatives limited to the fudai daimyo; but it was a dubious honor, being simply the shogun's way of paying respect to the tombs of Ieyasu and Iemitsu without having to submit himself to the expense and trouble a formal journey to Nikkō entailed. For the deputies, although the expense and trouble were admittedly reduced, they were by no means negligible; the whole business usually occupied the best part of a month. In 1699 Nagayasu was ordered to help on an engineering project which changed the course of the Yamato River; his contribution cost him 16,930 ryō. In 1748 another Korean embassy was entertained, at the Nishihonganji in Osaka, and the Okabe entertained them again in 1768, on which occasion one of the Koreans was assassinated, to the marked discomfort of the domain authorities. Once more, in 1796, the daimyo went to Nikkō as the shogun's deputy—or more accurately, this time as assistant deputy. In 1775 they provided guards for the inner Sakurada gate and in 1787 were ordered to surrender 1,500 koku of rice to the Bakufu during the period of general food shortage which marked the end of the Tanuma regime.

Okabe Nagamoto, the tenth Okabe daimyo of Kishiwada, crammed a great deal of activity into his reign of twenty-nine years—notably guard duty at the Castle in Edo on ten occasions, and a policing action in which almost a thousand men were despatched to take charge of Sagara Castle for fifty days after it had been taken from the attained Tanuma. His duties included also the pacification of a peasant revolt in 1782 on land belonging to the Hitotsubashi branch of the Tokugawa family, which engaged 150 troops for ten days, and the policing of a Russian shipwreck in 1791, as well as participation in river work in three Tōkai provinces in 1782.

Nagamoto's successor, Okabe Nagachika, daimyo for thirty years, from 1803 to 1833, was also to provide Edo Palace guards on ten occasions, and he contributed toward engineering work on Tōkai rivers in 1813. Finally, in this chronicle of expenditure imposed on the Okabe of Kishiwada by the Bakufu between 1650 and 1850, under the twelfth daimyo, Okabe Nagayori, there was one journey made by Nagayori to Nikkō as a deputy in 1834. Nagayori also sent over three hundred soldiers to Osaka for four days in 1837 to give assistance in quelling the Ōshio Heihachirō revolt, and in 1834 contributed towards repairs on Edo Castle.[32]

The Okabe, then, entertained visiting Korean diplomats on a total of six occasions, comparing most tidily with the Ikeda of Okayama, who also were called upon six times. They were ordered to contribute to civil engineering projects on six occasions, to the Ikeda's nine, but to this should be added the two occasions on which the Okabe contributed to repairs on the castle at Edo, and also at Kōyasan. If it is objected that, of their six ventures into civil engineering, four were in nearby areas from which they may well have obtained some benefit, then one must also point to the twenty-three instances of guard duty at Edo, and the four instances of police work, where samurai were sent outside the domain for varying periods of time. Against this record of miscellaneous impositions, the Ikeda can show only the 1699 survey of Fukuyama. The one recorded instance of the Okabe being forced to give to the Bakufu—the amount of rice in 1787—compares very badly with the three occasions on which the Ikeda gave money. However, it is quite possible that the officials who compiled the chronicles of Kishiwada Han did not feel compelled to mention those occasions on which their daimyo joined all the other daimyo in making contributions at the Bakufu's command. The fact that the contributions after the eruption of Mt. Fuji in 1708 and after the agemai-rci a few years later were not mentioned, although they applied equally to all daimyo, would seem to indicate this. In any case, it is quite clear from the comparison of the incidence of Bakufu demands in the two domains that the tozama han does not emerge as the victim of harsh and inequitable demands. There is nothing here to suggest that fudai managed to evade the burdens laid upon the tozama.

So far, we have seen the Bakufu simply as an initiator of demands which, whatever the intention, were punitive in their

32. Ochiai Tamotsu, *Kishiwada han shi kō*, pp. 33–106.

impact on the daimyo, but it did have another aspect which warrants our attention. The shogun was not only the seat of temporal authority; he was the fount of benevolence to those who gave him their allegiance. For the most part, this took the aspect of formal gifts bestowed upon his daimyo—gifts of seasonal attire, for instance, or of characters written or pictures drawn by the shogun's own hand, or of cranes taken by the shogun's own hawks—as symbols of the appreciation of one for the services of the other. There was, however, a more tangible expression of the shogun's concern for the well-being of his vassals, and this came in the form of ready money. It was disbursed, sometimes as gifts, but more usually as loans to be repaid, at such times as the Bakufu judged the daimyo to be most in need, often to relieve a domain suffering from a famine, or ravaged by fires, floods, earthquakes, or typhoons. All of these were frequent visitors to the Japanese people; just how frequent can be judged by the record of the Nagaoka domain which, despite its location on the comparatively sheltered and prosperous west coast, saw no fewer than four major famines, forty-five floods, nineteen major fires, four typhoons and three violent earthquakes all in the space of two centuries. Another common occasion for such assistance was when a daimyo felt his castle keep was in need of repair, although oddly enough, that of Edo Castle had never been rebuilt. Repairs, too, were often required for the daimyo mansions in Edo, a city which witnessed eighty-nine large recorded fires during the lifespan of the Tokugawa Bakufu.[33]

To determine whether the Bakufu discriminated in apportioning such aid between the fudai daimyo and the others, let us take as an example the assistance given during the Kyōhō famine. In the summer of 1732, a plague of locusts swarmed over the young rice in large parts of western Japan. Some sixty-six daimyo saw the rice crops of their domains substantially damaged, forty-five of them losing over half of their crops. The result was a famine of massive proportions, affecting more than two-and-a-half million people. Perhaps as many as twelve thousand died. The Bakufu's reaction was prompt. Loans were to be given immediately to those domains most in need. The first

33. Imaizumi, 2 : 121; Ono Kiyoshi, *Tokugawa Bakufu*, pp. 130–40.

list of daimyo to be given loans by the Bakufu was made up almost entirely of tozama names, among them the most lustrous—Shimazu, Mōri, Ikeda, Yamanouchi, and Hosokawa—reflecting the fact that the area worst damaged was made up almost entirely of tozama han. Each daimyo was to be loaned a sum of money fixed in proportion to his assessed fief productivity and was to repay it over a five year period. In addition to this, the Bakufu spared no effort to get as much rice as possible to the afflicted areas, even sending out its own officials to the northern provinces to buy up rice for distribution where it was needed.[34]

Other disasters, if neither so pressing nor as widespread as this, evoked a response from the Bakufu which was equally free of consciousness of who was or was not a fudai daimyo. After the Edo fire of 1657, the Bakufu gave loans to all daimyo who had sustained damage to their mansions. As was the case with impositions, the loans were to vary only according to the kokudaka of the needy daimyo, giving yet another example of Bakufu impartiality. Still more limited crises were met with just as much concern for the interests of all. If a local famine in the province of Dewa, on the Japan Sea coast, brought a series of loans to three local fudai daimyo in 1756, then a famine in the domain of Hosokawa Shigekata of Kumamoto, a tomaza, was to elicit a loan of 20,000 ryō a few months later. The fudai Sakai of Himeji borrowed 15,000 ryō from the Bakufu to help with flood damage in 1749 with no more ease than Nabeshima Shigemochi, the tozama daimyo of Saga Han, could borrow 10,000 ryō in 1762 to help his domain over a bad season (*TJ* 41 : 214; 46 : 655, 657, 662; 47 : 103).

This evenhandedness was also evident when dealing with the problem of damage to one's castle or Edo mansion; the tozama Maeda of Kanazawa were given a loan of 50,000 ryō to help restore their castle and the surrounding city, damaged by fire in 1759; in similar circumstances in 1756, the fudai daimyo of Yodo Han, Inaba Masamori, was lent 10,000 ryō. There seems nothing to suggest that some tozama were more favorably treated than others, particularly not on the grounds of historical ties with

---

34. Tsuji Tatsuya, *Tokugawa Yoshimune kō den*, pp. 150–52; *TJ* 45 : 611, 622.

the Tokugawa. The Shimazu of Satsuma, last of the tozama to make peace with the Tokugawa, and leaders of the movement which ultimately overthrew them, seem to have suffered no discrimination. They received a loan of 20,000 ryō when their Edo mansion was destroyed in 1762, while the Tayasu branch of the Tokugawa family, whose mansion burned down at the same time, were given only 10,000. In 1785, a food shortage in the Ryūkyū Islands, part of the Shimazu domain, resulted in a loan of 10,000 koku of rice and 10,00 ryō. A visit to Edo by Ryūkyūans in 1843 provided the excuse for a Bakufu loan of 20,000 ryō to the Shimazu daimyo (*TJ* 46 : 654, 732; 47 : 75–76, 481; 49 : 466).

It must be conceded, I think, that neither by the gentleness of its impositions nor the warmth of its expressions of concerned interest did the Edo Bakufu demonstrate a willingness to treat the fudai daimyo as their history dictated. Nor can this have been a matter of accident, since the very Bakufu which followed this policy—or perhaps nonpolicy—was for the majority of the Tokugawa period thoroughly dominated by councilors who were themselves fudai daimyo. Originally, perhaps the Bakufu consciously followed a conciliatory policy toward those daimyo of whose good intentions it could not be sure; the intermarriage of fudai with tozama, which, permitted by the Bakufu, must surely have been a part of such a policy, soon worked to provide a group of fudai daimyo to whom the history of sixteenth century loyalties can have been of little practical relevance. In the everyday life of daimyo there was not the slightest reason to invoke the loyalties of 1600. Ōkubo Hikozaemon could, in his *Mikawa monogatari*, but then he was a minor hatamoto, not a daimyo, and could afford such antiquarian fancies. Alliances with tozama families were not an issue he or his children would ever have to resolve.

To the fudai daimyo, maintaining no special sense of identity, and certainly receiving no external confirmation of it, there was thus little to prevent them from making common cause with tozama daimyo when the course of events warranted. The only barrier which lay between them was the eligibility of the fudai daimyo for certain Bakufu official positions, and it is to a discussion of the significance of these that we must now turn.

4. Fudai Daimyo and Bakufu Office

Lord Akifusa . . . spoke to the rōjū and then . . . gave orders to the Tribunal. However, these men were thoroughly preoccupied with their own interests and those of their houses, and did not perturb themselves with national affairs.

Arai Hakuseki, 1716 (*OSK* p. 462)

In many aspects of life during the Edo period, the traditional distinctions between the various kinds of daimyo, although they may have been of interest to antiquarians, and the compilers of the annual bukan registers, were of little practical significance to the daimyo themselves. In one major area, however, the division between fudai daimyo and others was maintained largely unimpaired; this concerned their eligibility for official positions within the Tokugawa government. From its establishment to its collapse, the Bakufu recruited its senior administrators almost exclusively from among the fudai daimyo, thereby conferring on them the greatest and most durable proof of their special status. If anything could retard the corrosive effects of greater familiarity with other daimyo groups, and the growing confluence of their interests, it would surely be just such a privilege.[1]

To historians, this monopoly of Bakufu office has always seemed one of the most obvious features of the fudai daimyo. Few would disagree with Albert Craig in his claim that office provided the most gifted of the fudai with "a positive sense of bureaucratic identification with the Bakufu . . . (which) . . . overshadowed their identity as daimyo of autonomous areas." [2] Few would deny the reverse of this proposition, that exclusion from official positions within the Bakufu was a source of mortifi-

1. Although only a few senior administrators were ever to come from outside the fudai ranks, there is evidence to suggest that Bakufu office was by no means closed to other daimyo. Of the 195 men appointed Superintendent of Temples and Shrines during the Tokugawa period, seventeen, or more than eight percent, were tozama. Another seven tozama daimyo were to become Senior Councilors or the equivalent.

2. Albert M. Craig, *Choshu in the Meiji Restoration*, p. 17.

cation and chagrin to the tozama and ichimon and was in large part responsible for the erosion of support for the Bakufu among these groups in the 1860s.

This last and most formidable bastion of fudai privilege may also have been decisive in shaping their view of those areas in which their interests as daimyo lay opposed to the demands of central government. If it can indeed be assumed that the fudai valued their monopoly of Bakufu office, then it is quite a logical step to pass to an assumption that they were ready to jettison the more limited interest of their own domains in their enthusiastic pursuit and exercise of this privilege. The function of this chapter will be to challenge both assumptions.

There is no space here for a full description of the machinery by which the Edo Bakufu maintained itself.[3] The majority of positions within it were held by the lesser Tokugawa vassals, hatamoto and below, who had far less than the 10,000 koku representing the threshold of daimyo status in Tokugawa Japan, and most of them held no such rights to any specific tracts of land as did the daimyo. The lesser duties of the Bakufu were theirs—policing the Tokugawa lands, keeping their accounts, staffing their inadequate standing army—and within these limits, they may have had as much or more real power than their nominal superiors, the officeholding daimyo. Nevertheless, in those areas which concern us here, the manifestations of the Bakufu's central powers over the daimyo, the most potent and influential positions were the preserve of the fudai daimyo.

Of all the positions nominally restricted to the fudai, the least important was that of *sōjaban*, or Master of Shogunal Ceremony. The date at which the office was founded is uncertain, but it was not later than 1632, and it is not uncommon to find references to daimyo being appointed to this, or an analogous position, in the years following the Osaka battle of 1615. The Masters of Shogunal Ceremony were responsible for the protocol which surrounded all formal expressions of the relation between the Tokugawa shogun and his vassals (protocol for relations with the Imperial Court, if anything more complex and demanding, was left in the hands of a special group of families known as *kōke*). One

3. For fuller descriptions, see John W. Hall, *Tanuma Okitsugu,* and Conrad Totman, *Politics in the Tokugawa Bakufu.*

of the duties of the sōjaban was to carry gifts from shogun to vassal and from vassal to shogun in a ritual which gave form, but no longer substance, to the vanished personal ties between the two. They also supervised seating arrangements for formal occasions, arranged processions, and dealt with the various issues of precedence and form which arose in an age—and amongst a people—where such matters received unusual emphasis. The sōjaban can be observed in the pages of the *Tokugawa jikki* in their varied capacities: transmitting to the assembled daimyo the news of the death of the shogun, Iemitsu, enquiring after the health of ailing daimyo, or taking the customary gift of incense money to a daimyo whose mother has recently died. In 1652, on behalf of the eleven-year-old shogun, Ietsuna, who has not yet mastered his Chinese ideographs, we see the sōjaban prepare lists of presents he has received, using *kana*, the simplified syllabic script. The Buddhist service commemorating the twenty-seventh anniversary of the death of a concubine of the shogun, Tsuna-yoshi, himself dead for fifty years, is attended by a Master of Shogunal Ceremony as a Bakufu representative in 1764.[4]

In one sense the duties of this position were complex, for it was a time when much meaningless elaboration went into the public expression of the ties between the shogun and the daimyo. Okabe Nagakazu, who became a sōjaban in 1843, managed to fill several notebooks while learning his duties from his colleagues, and it was by no means exceptional for a daimyo in this position to appoint one of his vassals to prepare a list of duties for him as each ceremonial occasion arose.[5] Nor was it unusual for sōjaban to commit mistakes which could earn them brief periods of suspension.

Yet, for all the complexity, it was an office of no real political significance. Those who held it had duties but no powers. The position may have taxed their memories, their purses, and their powers of discretion, but little else of practical political value. Nevertheless, it served as a proving ground for those who wished official careers. In the constant contact with the shogun, Senior

4. Matsudaira Tarō, *Edo jidai seido no kenkyū*, pp. 133–34, 136; *TJ* 41 : 2; 45 : 597, 599; 47 : 155–56.

5. Ochiai Tamotsu, *Kishawada han shi kō*, p. 95; Matsudaira Tarō, (*Kōtei*) *Edo jidai seido no kenkyū*, p. 134.

Councilors, and daimyo which the position demanded, it was not unusual for sōjaban to attract such favorable attention as would bring promotion to higher Bakufu positions. After the middle of the seventeenth century, very few fudai daimyo moved into higher office within the Bakufu unless they had first served as Masters of Shogunal Ceremony, so it was obviously regarded as the first step toward higher political office. However, one cannot claim that all who held it had political ambitions. To men as conspicuously underemployed as were the daimyo of Tokugawa Japan, a position which carried no great responsibilities, yet gave promise of activity and excitement as well as the opportunity to rub shoulders with the major figures of the Tokugawa world, had its own rewards.

In numbers, the Masters of Shogunal Ceremony usually stood between ten and twenty strong and performed their duties in rotation, which apparently meant they were free to return to their domains whenever their sankin kōtai obligation permitted. The average age for appointment was somewhere in the mid-thirties, although younger appointments were not unusual. Both Kuze Shigeyuki and Aoyama Yoshimasa, for example, were appointed in their twentieth year.[6]

It was from among these men, for the most part, that fudai daimyo were appointed to the first of the important administrative positions open to them. This was Superintendent of Temples and Shrines, a post invariably held concurrently with that of Master of Shogunal Ceremony. One is tempted to assume that this promotion went to those who had distinguished themselves in the latter position, but the careers of people like Nishio Tadanao, who was appointed to both positions on the same day, show that this was by no means always the case (*TJ* 45 : 594).

Founded in 1635, the position of Superintendent of Temples and Shrines, was customarily held by four men at any given time. Their primary duties, as their title suggests, were concerned with the government and administration of those pieces of land which, under the control of religious foundations officially recognized by the Bakufu, lay outside the network of feudal obligations covering the rest of Japan. These four men were responsible for the tranquillity of the areas entrusted to their charge, and that

6. Matsudaira, p. 136; *KCS.*

included hearing lawsuits involving the religious foundations and their members. They were also given charge of maintaining order in those parts of the Bakufu's own domain which lay outside the Kantō provinces. In addition, they were among the officials who customarily conducted the affairs of the Bakufu tribunal; unless a Senior Councilor happened to be in attendance, the duty Superintendent of Shrines and Temples was the senior official present.[7]

From this dual post of Master of Shogunal Ceremony-Superintendent of Temples and Shrines, promotion came in one of two forms. The lesser, or least successful, of those destined for advancement would generally go to the position of Junior Councilor, or *wakadoshiyori*. It was to these men, usually four or five in number, that the administration of the Tokugawa kashindan was entrusted. From the time the office was formally established, with Iemitsu's "group of six" in 1633, there was a clear intent that they should be in charge of the "lesser matters" of administration, as distinct from the "greater matters" which fell to the *rōjū*, or Senior Councilors. Hence the Junior Councilors had jurisdiction over the members of the Tokugawa kashindan from the hatamoto downward, giving particular attention to their organization, welfare, behavior in official positions, private lawsuits, and so on. As was the case with the other major positions, the Junior Councilors each took turns as duty officer, a month at a time. At first this position served many fudai as another stepping-stone on the way to higher office, but it gradually became recognized as a position for the smallest of daimyo and, in the second half of the Tokugawa period, seldom led to any higher office.[8]

The more usual course for those destined for important office, after serving as Superintendent of Shrines and Temples, was that which led through either—or sometimes both—the positions of Keeper of Osaka Castle and Kyoto Deputy. Of the two offices, it is clear that the latter was the more prestigious, since, for many fudai pursuing official careers, promotion led from Osaka to Kyoto, but never the other way. The Keeper of Osaka Castle,

7. Matsudaira, pp. 466–71; Fujino Tamotsu, *Bakuhan taisei shi no kenkyū*, p. 245.
8. Matsudaira, pp. 376–83.

first appointed in 1619, when Osaka was proclaimed Bakufu property, had as his immediate jurisdiction the city of Osaka and its vicinity, but he was also empowered to settle disputes and to keep the peace in those parts of the Tokugawa private domain lying in the adjacent provinces of Settsu, Kawachi, Izumi, and Harima. He also had wide discretionary powers relating to the general security and stability of the west country, and, as his title infers, he was responsible for the safety and upkeep of Osaka Castle.[9]

If the Keeper of Osaka Castle used his position as a vantage point from which to survey western Japan, the Kyoto Deputy did so from a still higher level, for his status was only just below that of Senior Councilor, and indeed whenever he was in Edo he was ranked among them. In a sense, he was the Bakufu's ambassador to the Imperial Court, and this was his major function, but he was also responsible for the general government of the Imperial City, the security of the Imperial Palace, and the tranquillity of the neighboring city of Fushimi.[10]

The highest position in the Bakufu official hierarchy generally open to fudai daimyo was that of rōjū (Senior Councilor). Known by various informal titles for the first three decades of the seventeenth century, the position finally came to be dubbed "rōjū" in 1633, and had its duties given as firm a definition as one can hope for in the institutional history of the Tokugawa period.

As distinct from the Junior Councilors, who were in charge of "lesser matters," the Senior Councilors were given jurisdiction over "greater matters," which were basically the relations between the Bakufu and the daimyo, and between the Bakufu and the Imperial Court, as well as Bakufu finances, foreign affairs, distribution of fiefs, and the more ambitious building schemes. As was the case with the Junior Councilors, the rōjū, usually a group numbering between four and six, adhered to a duty roster under which each member of the council took responsibility for the general functioning of the government for one month at a time. Any grave decisions which lay beyond the routine competence of the Senior Councilor on duty required the signature of

9. Yagi Akihiro, "Ōsaka shūhen no shoryō haichi ni tsuite," *Nihon rekishi* 231 : 4.
10. Takigawa Seijirō, ed., *Nijō jinya no kenkyū*, pp. 57–60.

all. Regular council meetings obliged the Senior Councilors to remain in constant attendance at Edo Castle, as did the brisk ceremonial life, which kept off-duty councilors visiting shrines to the memory of various members of the Tokugawa family, visiting graves of former shogun, or arranging and attending Buddhist services in their memory. They also visited prominent daimyo bereft of close relatives and attended the *gembuku* ceremonies of their sons to witness the traditional rite in which the adolescent boys had their forelocks shaved in token of maturity.[11]

Finally, in the catalog of official positions within the Bakufu open to fudai daimyo, one should mention the post of *tairō*, or Great Councilor. During the 268 years of the Tokugawa Bakufu's existence, this post was filled on only thirteen occasions, for a combined total of seventy years. Since, of the thirteen tenants of the position, six came from the Ii family and three from the Himeji branch of the Sakai family, it can hardly be ranked among the most accessible of fudai offices. The duties of the position were even less clearly defined than was usual with Edo Bakufu offices, but they would seem to have included giving personal counsel to the shogun, and freedom to participate in council debates on matters of moment, without any obligation to perform the more trivial administrative tasks.

The institutional history of the Tokugawa Bakufu, such as is known of it, cautions against accepting any one of these definitions without substantial reservations. The workings of despotic governments are by their very nature secretive, impenetrable to contemporaries, and no less so to the historian. The Edo Bakufu, by profession, if not accomplishment, one of the more despotic governments, was no exception to this. Historians are aware of the workings of the Bakufu only in the vaguest and most general terms and can say with little precision exactly how these various offices meshed together in practice.[12] The evidence available, however, would suggest that, although the definition of powers remained fairly constant throughout the period, their content did not. At various times the Senior Councilors probably decided Bakufu policy in those areas formally assigned to them; at others

11. Matsudaira, pp. 366–76.
12. This sort of limitation is to be seen in Matsudaira, and also in Totman, *Tokugawa Bakufu.*

they seem to have acted simply as intermediaries between the shogun and his personal friends, who made the decisions, and the administrative assistants who saw that they were carried out. The office of Great Councilor, an even more personal position, seems to have fluctuated wildly in the extent to which incumbents exercised the powers open to them. Until Ii Naosuke burst upon the Bakufu in 1858 and proceeded to make his subordinates do as he wished, the most influential member of his family in Bakufu politics, despite five ancestors who had preceded him to the office of Great Councilor, had undoubtedly been Ii Naotaka, who had held no formal position at all. What impressed the Korean official, Nam Yong Ik, most about Naotaka when he saw him in 1655, apart from a "countenance full of dignity," and hairy forearms, was that he seemed the most formidable of the senior officials, a surprising judgment on a man who had no official position and who was being compared with men like Hoshina Masayuki and Sakai Tadakiyo.[13]

By contrast, Naotaka's son Naozumi, the first of the Ii to become Great Councilor, had little impact upon the Bakufu. Naotaka, in his last recorded testament, said of him that "it would be pointless for him to marry," and ordered him to adopt one of his nephews, lending fuel to the suspicion that in Naozumi appeared the first signs of the mysterious hereditary disease which was to incapacitate the Ii family for the next six generations. For whatever reason, however, his influence in office could not compare with that of his father out of office. Similarly, Ii Naohide, who became Great Councilor over one hundred years later, was to resign from the position claiming that he was "unable to bear the exhausting duties," when it would appear that, despite his exalted station, he was actually forced out by Matsudaira Sadanobu who, as a Senior Councilor of three months' standing, was his titular subordinate. Clearly, senior positions within the Bakufu were no guarantee in themselves of any great influence, although the potential was always there. It is true that Bakufu office did not always confer upon those holding it the authority to which they were entitled, but it is also true that it did at least place them in a position from which they could begin to compete for it.[14]

13. *Hikone-shi shi*, 1 : 451.
14. Ibid., pp. 455, 467.

It is doubtful, however, whether the authority conferred in theory upon the senior Bakufu officials ever really amounted to a monopoly of political influence. Certainly office gave monopoly of the right to administer the decisions taken by the Bakufu, but whether it also gave the right to make those decisions free from external pressures is another matter. There is nothing to suggest that daimyo otherwise ineligible for Bakufu office were deprived of the right to advise and remonstrate. Ikeda Mitsumasa was just as free to express his dissatisfaction with the Bakufu leadership in 1668 as the Ōbiroma daimyo were in their letter of 1841. Political pressure, too, could be applied by other daimyo, particularly by the sanke, who were called in to confer on various occasions. Matsudaira Sadanobu came to the position of chief Senior Councilor with their assistance in 1789, while their opposition was to play a large part in Mizuno Tadakuni's fall from office in 1843. The influence of Tokugawa Nariaki after 1853 is well known, but a glance at the records of Mito Han reveal him showering shogun, rōjū, and various lesser officials with increasingly ambitious demands and proposals from 1834 onward. His well-known "1838 Memorial" (*Bojutsu no fūji*), presented to the shogun in 1839, containing as it does both outspoken criticism and detailed suggestions for improvement, is hardly the work of a man diffident about his political standing.[15] Many of those who, like Nariaki, were to grumble in the Bakumatsu period of Bakufu unresponsiveness were really complaining that the Bakufu had considered, and then rejected, their advice, which is not quite the same thing.

Rewards of Office

Although Bakufu office may never have offered a total monopoly of political power and authority, it certainly gave to those occupying it positions of some prominence, and it may also have offered other incentives. In the previous chapter we saw that the fudai monopoly of Bakufu office was not necessarily followed by privileged treatment for all fudai, yet it was not impossible that office might have presented a legitimate opportunity to increase

15. For the *gosanke* in general, see *TJ* 41 : 21, 22, 123; Shibusawa Eiichi, *Rakuō kō den* p. 117; for gosanke political influence, see Kitajima Masamoto, ed., *Seiji shi*, 2, p. 291; for Tokugawa Nariaki, see *Mito han shiryō (bekki jō)*, especially pp. 77ff., (for *Bojutsu no fūji*), 114ff., 160ff.

one's material possessions, and so have constituted an enviable prerogative in this sense.

During the seventeenth century, official positions within the Tokugawa Bakufu did result in the enrichment of those holding them. Of the twenty-two Senior Councilors appointed between the formal inception of the post in 1633 and the turn of the century, only three were to register no increase at all in their formal enfeoffment during their official careers. The remainder all had their kokudaka raised by at least twenty percent and often much more. Hotta Masamori, for example, after a lifetime of service to the Tokugawa shogun in positions like page, guard commander, Junior and then Senior Councilor, saw his enfeoffment appreciate from 5,000 koku to 110,000, while Toda Tadamasa rose from 10,000 koku to 70,000 koku.

After this time, however, office was rewarded with fief increases to a far lesser extent. The next fifty years saw twenty-five fudai made Senior Councilor, but of these, twelve received no increases at all during their careers in office, while the increases given to the others were almost all insignificant. Only four of the thirteen to be given such increases received more than 15,000 koku. From 1750 until the fall of the Bakufu, of the eighty-odd Senior Councilors who held office during those years, perhaps only seven or eight would have received augmented enfeoffments, but with the exception of Tanuma Okitsugu (who increased his holdings from 600 koku to 57,000 during his career) such increases were small. Abe Masahiro, for example, during his very active and important career in Bakufu office, was rewarded with a mere 10,000 koku in 1853. His ancestor, Abe Masatsugu, holding a position analogous to that of Senior Councilor between the years 1623 and 1626, a much shorter period, and an infinitely less distinguished career, rose from 1,300 to 86,000 koku. There is no doubt that, compared with the early period, later officeholding came to hold out only a slight prospect of increased kokudaka which could be passed on to one's heirs (*KCS*).

High office, however, does seem to have given fudai daimyo some leverage if they were unhappy with the domain they held and wanted to be moved elsewhere. The great majority of fief movements after 1750 would seem to have been prompted by such circumstances, but even this leverage can only have been effective within certain restrictive limits. There can have been little to tempt the Hotta to remain in a Kantō fief like Sakura, where a third of its land lay hundreds of miles away on the Japan Sea coast, and where, as a vassal once wrote with gloomy emphasis, "there have never been many local commercial commodities," and there was every reason to tempt them away, given the opportunity. But they never moved, not even when Masayoshi was a Senior Councilor for a total of five years.[16]

It is true, also, that Bakufu office placed fudai daimyo in a position where they were constantly being given presents or being entertained. The Bakufu occasionally attempted to prohibit its officials from accepting gifts and bribes, but this never seems to have been particularly successful. When Mizuno Tadakane, daimyo of Karatsu in the late eighteenth century, was attempting to build an official career for himself, he received encouragement from one of his counselors, who wrote to him that not only would office be an ornament to the Mizuno house, but that also "as your lordship is promoted there will be gifts from others; if you accept these, in accordance with customary usage, I do not think things will be unduly difficult." Before any aspirant to office reached it, however, he usually had to offer bribes himself. Mizuno Tadakuni, for example, Tadakane's grandson, maintained a special fund from which to buy the benevolence of his superiors, and it is hardly coincidental that his demands on this score slackened immediately on winning promotion. That this is not an isolated case is demonstrated by the case of Ogasawara Tadakata; he spent so much in his pursuit of office that he was forced to reduce the stipends of his vassals in 1813, thus provoking their mass desertion the following year.[17]

Bribery of one sort or another was a fact of Bakufu official life. Tanuma Okitsugu won a reputation for accessibility to bribes which, although well known and well established, is nonetheless misleading in that one tends to regard him as the excep-

16. Kimura Motoi and Sugimoto Toshio, eds., *Fudai hansei no tenkai to Meiji ishin*, p. 205.

17. For prohibition of bribes, see *TJ* 46 : 731, 762, and also Kitajima Masamoto, *Mizuno Tadakuni*, pp. 285–86. See p. 103 in *Mizuno Tadakuni* for the Tadakane quotation and p. 144 for mention of Tadakuni's special fund. For Ogasawara, see Kodama Kōta and Kitajima Masamoto, eds., *Dai ni ki monogatari han shi*, 7 : 65–68.

tion rather than the rule. In the clearest case of Tanuma's venal-
ity for which there is evidence—the matter of Date Shigemura's
overeagerness to advance his court rank in 1767—a bribe was
also taken by Matsudaira Takemoto, who, as leading Senior
Councilor while Tanuma was still only Grand Chamberlain, was
far more culpable.[18]

Yet bribery in the sense in which we know it—giving something in return for some specified service—was by no means the
only form in which officials received presents. Far more pervasive was the custom of giving regular gifts to officials to keep
them at least neutral and receptive to bribes for more specific
projects. This occurred particularly at the New Year, always the
most active of Japanese gift-giving occasions, but there were
other opportunities as well. After receiving a gift of seasonal
clothing from the shogun in 1781, on the completion of work
done on some Kantō rivers, Tsuchiya Yasunao presented the
rōjū with gifts in his turn, amongst them a sword, bolts of
cloth, and boxes of seaweed and dried fish. Dinner invitations—
accompanied by gifts—were a common part of their official lives.
In 1681, for example, we see Ogasawara Tadayū, daimyo of
Kokura, entertaining the Senior Councilors at his Edo mansion
as a way of paying his compliments to the new shogun, Tsunayoshi, just as he had done a dozen years earlier when he inherited his father's domain. That such entertainment was not
uncommon can be seen from a set of instructions issued in 1747
asking daimyo to have their mansion gates free of loiterers on
those occasions when Junior or Senior Councilors come to visit.[19]

Gifts were as common to the more salient parts of official life
as they were to less public aspects, but they were usually more
flattering than substantial. As a Junior Councilor in 1712, Mizuno Tadayuki received a scroll of mountains and rivers by
Sesshū from among the belongings of the late shogun, Ienobu.
As Kyoto Deputy, between 1714 and 1717, he received twenty
gold pieces, five sets of seasonal clothes, a coat, a sword by Kuni-

18. Ōishi Shinzaburō, "Tanuma Okitsugu ni kansuru jūrai no shiryō no
shimpyōsei ni tsuite," *Nihon rekishi* 237 : 30.
19. For Tsuchiya, see "(Tsuchiura han) Kantō kawagawa gofushin gotetsudai ikken." For Ogasawara, see *Buzen sōsho*, 12 : 11, 29. The instructions of
1747 are contained in *TJ* 46 : 433.

toshi, and a chestnut horse from the shogun on commencing his duties. During his time in Kyoto he received various gifts of fish and tea from members of the Imperial family, a sword from the emperor, a few bolts of satin, and various copies of poetry collections, including the *Kokinshū* and the *Hyakunin isshu,* and poems inscribed by the emperor and empress. As a Senior Councilor from 1717 to 1730, he was given, amongst other tokens of esteem from the shogun, Yoshimune, swords, various small sums of money in lieu of the customary gifts of horses, bolts of cotton cloth, and seasonal habits. In 1729 Yoshimune, noted for his thrift, gave all his Senior Councilors paintings which he had done himself—not as bad as it could have been, for, as a draftsman, the eighth shogun towered above the others, many of whom were abnormally untalented. To Mizuno Tadayuki he gave a painting of tigers and bamboo, to Toda Tadazane one of a sage under a pine tree, to Matsudaira Norimura one of a dead tree with pigeons, and a painting of clouds and dragons to Sakai Tadaoto.[20]

When compared with the estates, palaces, and jewels with which European monarchs occasionally rewarded their ministers, even Sesshū scrolls make a painfully modest showing. The closest Mizuno Tadayuki came to what is usually thought of as Oriental splendor was in 1719, when the Korean ambassadors gave him two tiger skins, two leopard skins, various sorts of exotic cloth and paper, and, amongst other things, a catty of ginseng, for which Korea was famous throughout the Far East.[21] Aside from an increase of 10,000 koku, Tadayuki's formal gains from twenty-six years in Bakufu office—cloth, swords, and scrolls—are certainly not enough to convince one of their power to attract into the bureaucracy any fudai daimyo concerned with his material situation.

Another possible material benefit from office could have been sanctuary from Bakufu impositions, for it might be anticipated that those who manned the guns of central power would not train them on their own houses. In some instances this was true. Those Senior Councilors who issued the agemai-rei in 1722 were themselves exempt from its provisions, for example. There seems

20. "Hiyōroku."
21. Ibid.

scant evidence, however, for one scholar's assertion that as a general rule Bakufu officials were spared forced contributions to the Bakufu's building and engineering projects, and the evidence brought forward in this case does not bear the weight placed upon it.[22]

The Masters of Shogunal Ceremony were as vulnerable to Bakufu impositions as any other daimyo. The position did not save Akimoto Takafusa from being ordered to help clean the Edo Castle drains in 1733, nor Abe Masatomo from visiting Nikkō as the shogun's deputy in 1776, at no little expense. Inaba Masamori, a sōjaban in 1833, was not spared a contribution to the expense of rebuilding the Western Enclosure simply because of his office.[23]

What was true of those filling the humblest official positions open to fudai daimyo in the Bakufu applied equally to their superiors. Itakura Katsukiyo, a Junior Councilor in 1759, nevertheless had to work on Edo Palace, while in 1843 the Junior Councilor, Ōoka Tadakata, had the costly pleasure of entertaining the shogun, Ieyoshi, at his castle at Iwatsuki when the latter was on his way to visit the Nikkō shrines, and this was followed promptly by an order from an increasingly defense-conscious Bakufu to begin making cannon for the coastal defense of his domain.[24]

Although one can imagine that Senior Councilors might use their powers to make demands on their junior colleagues, it is a little harder to realize that they were unable to spare themselves. Hotta Masaaki had been a Senior Councilor for five years when he was ordered to contribute to repairs on the Nikkō mausolea in 1750, and he was selected again, in 1759, together with his colleague, Itakura Katsukiyo, for work on Edo Castle. Toda Ujinori, occupying the same post, suffered a similar imposition in 1795, while both Senior Councilors and Junior Councilors alike were compelled to contribute toward repairs after the fire of 1844.[25]

22. Yoshizumi Mieko, "Tetsudai bushin ni tsuite," *Gakushūin Daigaku Bungakubu kenkyū Nempō*, p. 115.

23. For Akimoto, see *TJ* 45 : 629; for Abe, see Kodama and Kitajima, *Dai ni ki monogatari han shi*, 6 : 263; for Inaba, see "Inaba kafu."

24. For Itakura, see *TJ* 46 : 742; for Ōoka, see *Saitama-ken shi*, 6 : 37.

25. For Hotta, see *TJ* 46 : 519 and for Itakura, see p. 742; for Toda, see *Ōgaki-shi shi*, 1 : 511; and for the repairs of 1844, see *TJ* 49 : 520.

By far the most singular example of the vulnerability of office-holders to Bakufu demands is that of the unfortunate Makino Tadamasa, who was daimyo of Nagaoka, in the Japan Sea province of Echizen. In 1838, while he was a Superintendent of Temples and Shrines, he contributed 3,000 ryō toward repairs on the Western Enclosure of Edo Castle. This was followed in 1840, while he was Kyoto Deputy, by the announcement of the three-sided fief transfer, to which I have referred before. Had it been carried out, Tadamasa would have been given for his domain another which, as one of his inspectors was quick to observe, had "no income other than its formal productivity." Then, in the middle of 1843, while he was still Kyoto Deputy, a scant five months before becoming Senior Councilor, it was announced that he was to transfer to the Bakufu some 604 koku of land at Niigata Hamamura, in exchange for a like amount of land in Mishima county, some thirty miles inland. At first glance an insignificant transfer of a trifling amount of land, this was in fact a great blow to the finances of Nagaoka, for what the Bakufu had appropriated was Niigata harbor, then, as now, the major port for northwestern Japan. It had brought the domain a regular 10,000 ryō in various fees and taxes every year and had been its greatest single source of income outside tax rice; now it was gone. Although Tadamasa became Senior Councilor shortly afterwards, and was to hold this position for the next fourteen years, Niigata harbor was never restored to him. To complete this chronicle of depredations, in 1844, now a Senior Councilor, Makino Tadamasa was forced to contribute 12,000 ryō to repairs on the main fortress of Edo Castle.[26]

Tadamasa's case, while providing ample proof that Bakufu office was of itself no guarantee of immunity from the enthusiastic intrusions of the power of the central government, is nevertheless an exceptional one. He was in office at a time when the Bakufu leadership was more than usually assertive of its authority, and it has been claimed—perhaps not altogether wisely—that he had incurred the dislike of Mizuno Tadakuni, his superior. Had this been the case, one might justifiably wonder how he came to be appointed Kyoto Deputy when Tadakuni was at the very peak of his powers. In any case, even if the unusual

26. For the inspection of Kawagoe, see *Nagaoka-shi shi*, p. 492, and for the rest see pp. 84, 121–22, 415–17, 433–34.

severity of this example is granted, there are still many other examples of Bakufu impositions on senior officials to be explained away.

Part of the explanation can be found in the Confucian rhetoric, so much a part of life in the Tokugawa period, which laid great emphasis on the personal tie of loyalty between the daimyo and the shogun. If loyalty was expected of all daimyo, then conspicuous loyalty was demanded of the shogun's ministers, since all political opposition to these advisers was likely to be couched in terms of their 'disloyalty.' This encouraged ostentatious acts of fealty; for example, Hoshina Masayuki, in 1651 was ordered by the Bakufu—at a time when he virtually was the Bakufu— to provide 1,000 men to work on a tomb for his brother, the dead Iemitsu (*TJ* 41 : 6). In such a climate any overt action by Bakufu officials to provide for their own material wants at the general expense risked being characterized as disloyalty.

Another part of the explanation lies in the system by which authority within the Bakufu tended to be wielded in rotation. In most of the major offices, each member took his turn on duty for a month at a time. It is certainly possible to exaggerate the importance of this, as almost every commentator of the "checks and balances" school has done; it did not give any durable protection against the emergence of one strong political figure, like a Sakai Tadakiyo or a Mizuno Tadakuni. Yet, as Ogyū Sorai complained, for most of the time the system of monthly rotation of duties served to produce a stifling degree of caution; "the result is," he noted, "that the officers are disinclined to act and are concerned only that there should be no cause for complaint against them during their period of tenure." [27] This, as much as the pressure to conform to the pattern of the ideal Confucian servant, prevented the use of one's official position for the satisfaction of individual material wants. Whether either prevented the pursuit of more general group needs is rather more open to question.

Part of the explanation, too, may lie in the actual power and status of Bakufu officials. That they should from time to time impose unpleasant duties upon themselves at the same time as they forced them upon other daimyo is puzzling only if one be-

27. J. R. McEwan, *The Political Writings of Ogyū Sorai*, p. 88.

gins with the assumption that, since the Tokugawa Bakufu—the organ representing the personal government of the Tokugawa shogun, the feudal overlord—was supreme in Japan, so those who headed its administration were equally supreme. Why should those who controlled the authority of the Bakufu turn it against themselves when they could not be touched from outside? The answer is that the Bakufu was by no means immune to outside pressures. What is inexplicable, when it is assumed that those outside the charmed circle of Bakufu office have no influence, becomes much more readily understandable once it is seen that at no time was the Bakufu totally in the hands of its fudai officers. It was from daimyo who held no office that one could expect protest to arise if Bakufu officials used powers entrusted to them for their own advantage.

That officials were unable to evade the impositions over which they themselves had control is clear enough. It is also true that they were unable to use their powers to wrest for themselves a larger share of Bakufu largess. The aid they dispensed, in the Bakufu's name, to daimyo laboring under particular hardships, capable of being extended to themselves when conditions warranted, quite plainly did not begin exclusively at home.

This is not to imply that officials felt any compunction about availing themselves of Bakufu loans in obvious cases of need. This was so common as to need no documenting. With no exceptions, however, the loans given by Bakufu officials to themselves and their colleagues in office in time of necessity seem to have been calculated by the same rules of thumb which decided the amounts other daimyo were given as loans. Flood damage to his domain at Himeji may have earned the Senior Councilor, Sakai Tadayasu, a loan of 15,000 ryō in 1749, but nearly twenty years later, in 1767, in a like predicament, the daimyo of Owari— no official—was given a loan of 30,000 ryō, a larger amount, for his was a larger domain (*TJ* 46 : 496; 47 : 264). Crop damage saw Matsudaira Yasuyoshi, the Senior Councilor, lent 5,000 ryō in 1767, but this was not exceptionally generous for a daimyo in this situation. A local famine in the province of Dewa brought a loan of 10,000 ryō to the Senior Councilor, Sakai Tadayori, and 3,000 ryō to the Junior Councilor, Sakai Tadayoshi, in 1756, but 3,000 ryō also went to Tozawa Masanobu, a local daimyo who had no connection with Bakufu office (*TJ* 46 : 655, 657). On occasions this refusal to turn their office to their own advantage could become self-denial. In 1717, for example, a fire in Edo destroyed the mansions of the daimyo of Mito and two Senior Councilors, Tsuchiya Masanao and Kuze Shigeyuki, but while the former was given the loan of 20,000 ryō, the two officials were merely given some sets of seasonal attire as an expression of the shogun's sympathy (*TJ* 45 : 54).

To those who held it, however, Bakufu office did more than merely block opportunities to advance one's own material position. Rather, like political office in the more carefully supervised modern societies, it actually involved those who sought it in a fair measure of material sacrifice. The climb to the highest official position was seldom made with any great speed, and never without the goodwill of at least some of one's superiors. Ogasawara Tadakata recognized this when he tried to buy his way into the affections of two Senior Councilors in 1813. Of course, had he been successful and managed to reach the topmost rung in the Bakufu, it is possible that with bribes and gifts from others he could have recouped the losses sustained in the climb to the top. There was always the risk, however, that one's official career would fall short of a position which was, after all, open only to five or six men at any one time. It was quite possible that a daimyo covetous of the highest official position would have his career terminated by death, incapacity, or dismissal before obtaining any return on his investment. Another possibility, just as serious, was that of being passed over for promotion. Mizuno Tadakuni can be seen agonizing about this in a frank report to his vassals in 1825; if the position he desires should go to another man at the next vacancy, he observes dispiritedly, "I shall have squandered my time needlessly, and our financial position must inevitably be critical." [28]

Even to those who were successful, the expenses of office usually succeeded in outstripping the income from bribes and presents. After all, Senior and Junior Councilors alike were required to live permanently in Edo, to be on hand for every discussion, and it was acknowledged by all that the expenses of life in one's domain paled beside the cost of living in Edo. They were also

28. Kitajima, *Mizuno Tadakuni*, p. 140ff.

required to be on hand for a multitude of ceremonial occasions; the calendar of events in Edo shows such occasions on fifty-three days of the year, from the height of the social season in the New Year, through the great festivals of the Tokugawa house, down to ceremonies marking the change of season.[29] This is quite exclusive of the myriad ephemeral ceremonies, like the birth, or the gembuku, of the shogun's children, and anniversaries of the deaths of former shogun or their relatives, as well as those occasions when the shogun went hawking, or watched swimming or horseback riding. Presence at these events alone, together with appropriate clothes for oneself and one's attendants, and the stray gifts which custom demanded be given to those with whom one had even the most fleeting contact, combined to make Bakufu office an expensive form of service for most fudai daimyo.

Certainly it is difficult, past the rich fief increases of the seventeenth century, to find any signs of fudai actually enriching themselves in office. All the evidence leads to the opposite conclusion. At Shōnai Han, where of twelve successive daimyo only one—Sakai Tadayori (Senior Councilor from 1749 to 1764)—held Bakufu office, the general downward progression of the han finances was not notably arrested by having a daimyo as a Bakufu official. If anything, the trend would seem to have been accelerated. In 1752 he confiscated the salaries of his vassals, in 1760 he took 45 hyō from each 100 koku of their income, and in 1760 and 1764 he borrowed extensively from the Homma. Nevertheless, despite this, and despite the fact that he also managed to increase his domain taxation rate during his term of office, he died leaving a debt of 200,000 ryō (which at contemporary market rates represented his total income for the next three years), and left his *vassals* in such a predicament that they were forced to ask for an advance on their stipends for the following year. In Sakura, too, the same result is to be observed. Hotta Masayoshi worked his way up through the various official posts within the Bakufu, beginning as Master of Shogunal Ceremony in 1827 and finally reaching Senior Councilor in 1841. This was the very period that his han debt rose from 835 ryō in 1822 to 24,637 ryō in 1833, after which his credit ran out. This situation cannot have lasted, however, for by 1860, two

29. Ono Kiyoshi, ed., (*Shiryō*) *Tokugawa Bakufu no seido,* pp. 281ff.

years after Masayoshi's long official career had ended, Sakura was in debt 140,000 ryō. Sakai Tadanobu, daimyo of Obama, and Senior Councilor from 1815 until his death in 1828, bequeathed his heir a sizeable debt of 300,000 ryō.[30]

The same phenomenon occurred in those few fudai families with very strong traditions of officeholding during the latter part of the Edo period. The Abe of Fukuyama, for instance, who had a daimyo in Bakufu office of some sort for a total of seventy-six of the last 123 years of the Tokugawa period, were no better off than most other fudai families. Their notable record of peasant rebellions—which occurred in 1717, 1753, 1770, 1786, and 1831— is symptomatic of financial malaise, as they were all occasioned by unwonted taxation. Abe Masakiyo's jaundiced appraisal of domain finances under his two predecessors, both of whom had been—as he was also—Senior Councilor, has been quoted in an earlier context. The Ogyū Matsudaira of Nishio, whose daimyo served as Bakufu officials for seventy-five years between 1764 and 1868, were in no better situation because of it, and their domain at Nishio reveals all the marks of financial crisis: borrowing outside the han, forcing loans from merchants and vassals within, and taking taxation from peasants in advance; that is, taxing on crops not yet planted, let alone harvested.[31]

If the likelihood of financial disadvantage alone was not sufficient to make fudai daimyo hesitate before they expressed a commitment to the Tokugawa family by participating in their government, there were other handicaps which could also be brought into the balance. For one thing, holding office in the Bakufu was never really unattended by some risk. By far the most spectacular punishments of fudai daimyo during the Tokugawa period were due to enmities incurred during an official career. This was as true for Ōkubo Tadachika in 1613, when he lost all of his 65,000 koku domain, as it was for Ii Naosuke, whose son in 1862 found his domain reduced from 350,000 to 250,000 koku by a Bakufu trying desperately to repudiate the memory and policies of his

30. For Sakai, see *Tsuruoka-shi shi*, 1 : 289, 341–42; for Hotta, see Kimura and Sugimoto, pp. 200, 208; and for the Obama Sakai, see *Fukui-ken shi*, vol. 2, pt. 2, p. 100.

31. For peasant rebellions, see *Fukuyama-shi shi*, 2 : 953–79; and for Nishio, see *Aichi-ken shi*, 2 : 371.

purposeful father. Others who attracted more temperate hostilities often won lesser chastisements, as for example having their
domains moved to less favorable locations. Yamagata was notorious as a domain to which the Bakufu often sent out-of-favor
politicians or, if they were beyond mortal reach, their sons. This
happened to Hotta Masanaka in 1685, to Matsudaira Norisuke
(Norimura's son) after his father's resignation in 1745, to Akimoto
Suketomo after his difference of opinion with Tanuma in 1767,
and to Mizuno Tadakiyo after his father Tadakuni had been
forced into retirement in 1845.

A further drawback to an official career within the Bakufu,
particularly chafing to a daimyo with energy and ability, was
that it precluded giving much attention to the conduct of domain
affairs. From Superintendents of Temples and Shrines upward,
fudai daimyo in office spent all their time in Edo, except for
occasional ceremonial journeys to the shrines of Ieyasu and
Iemitsu at Nikkō. Ōkubo Tadatomo, who was Senior Councilor
between the years 1677 and 1698 had his domain moved from
Sakura to Odawara in 1686, but although his new han lay just
fifty miles to the southwest of Edo—a two-day journey at most
—he was never free to pay it a visit until after his retirement in
1698, a good twelve years later. Hence, daimyo in office who
wished to keep abreast of affairs in their domains were forced to
do so by correspondence with their vassal administrators, who
were themselves often little known to the daimyo, and whose
loyalty to a lord seldom or never seen was bound to be bloodless
at best. Within fudai families strongly connected to Bakufu official positions, it is notable that those who made the most impact
on the affairs of their domain were invariably those who had no
office. Among the Ii of Hikone, for example, the daimyo who
spent most energy on han affairs were Naooki (daimyo from 1676
to 1701, and again, by default, from 1710 to 1714) and Naonaka
(daimyo from 1789 to 1812). The former spent only three years
in Bakufu office, as Great Councilor, a position which his family
almost monopolized, and the latter held no office at all. Abe
Masasuke, daimyo of Fukuyama for twenty-one years between
1748 and 1769, was in office for seventeen of them, and so left his
domain government to his vassals. His son and successor, Masatomo, daimyo from 1769 to 1803, seemed bent on following the

same course, entering office in 1774, and becoming Senior Councilor in 1787, but instead he resigned the following year and spent the rest of his life as an energetic reformer of the han government. Just as he was one of the most successful daimyo among the Abe, so Mizuno Tadateru, daimyo of Okazaki between 1730 and 1737, who held no Bakufu office, seems to have been the one daimyo in the Mizuno family to make a success of his han government.[32]

Competition for Office

A contemporary chronicle of the life of Makino Tadakiyo (1760–1831), noting that "he rose from Keeper of Osaka Castle to Kyoto Deputy, and finally Senior Councilor, as a result of which his expenses increased and his treasury was completely emptied," would seem to have the last word on the advantages of officeholding in Tokugawa Japan.[33] There need be little astonishment, then, that the fudai daimyo throughout the Edo period, on the whole evinced no great enthusiasm for careers within the Bakufu administration. It was no easy way to towering political eminence nor to material riches; success in competition for office brought with it a very real chance of increased expenditure, considerable hazard to their possessions if they made an error, and, for those who cared, it weakened their authority in their own domains. If, nonetheless, a monopoly of the highest positions in the Bakufu was something which the fudai prized, then it was certainly not reflected in the way in which they competed for it amongst themselves.

Historians have long been aware that in the lists of senior Bakufu officials certain family names keep recurring with remarkable persistence, while others appear seldom or never. Confronted with this, they have drawn up ingenious theories of the exclusiveness of Bakufu office which would seem to accord with the evidence. Kitajima Masamoto speaks for many in his claim

---

32. For Ōkubo, see Kodama Kōta and Kitajima Masamoto, eds., *Monogatari han shi*, 2 : 452; for Ii, see *Hikone-shi shi*, 1 : 456–61, 469–71; for Abe, see *Fukuyama-shi shi*, 2 : 535, 540–41; and for Mizuno, see Kitajima Masamoto, "Meikun no higeki," *Kokumin seikatsu-shi kenkyū*, ed. Itō Tasaburō, pp. 249–50.

33. Imaizumi Shōzō, *Nagaoka no rekishi*, 2: :119.

that, "putting it in the strongest terms, the fudai daimyo may be seen as, in a sense, bureaucrats. Naturally not all the 120–130 fudai daimyo obtained important Bakufu office; this was limited to those among them with special pedigrees. On the whole, many of the families had provided Senior Councilors in the early Edo period, and they had formed a clique by marrying among themselves." [34] To this assertion of the importance of traditional ties with Bakufu office, reinforced by intermarriage, Conrad Totman has added a further factor. "The head of only about forty vassal daimyo families," he argues, "could customarily seek the positions leading to Senior Councilor: they were families with fiefs (*han*) officially rated at 30,000 to 100,000 *koku* of rice or equivalent agricultural productivity. The few vassal daimyo with larger *han* (101,000–350,000 *koku*) usually held no functional bakufu offices, and the seventy-odd lesser vassal daimyo (with 10,000–29,000 *koku han*) held less important posts."; nor is he alone in insisting on kokudaka as a measure of eligibility.[35]

In each case, the argument is persuasive. Of the hundred or more fudai daimyo to serve as Senior Councilor from the beginning of the eighteenth century onward, perhaps as few as fifteen were from families which had not previously provided senior officials during the seventeenth century; perhaps a score would have maintained an income outside Totman's limits throughout their careers. Yet, nevertheless, both hypotheses are faulty. Not only did any such exclusive definition of eligibility fail to be enunciated in Tokugawa Japan, but also the exceptions to each are too numerous to be ignored. The entry into office of politicians like Tanuma Okitsugu, Toki Norinobu, and Honjō Munehatsu, and perhaps a dozen others after 1700 who had no family antecedents in office, is sufficient to cast doubt on the theory of exclusion by ancestry. Similarly, the official careers of various

34. Kodama and Kitajima, *Monogatari han shi*, 2 : 15; Kitajima expressed similar sentiments elsewhere, for example, in his *Bakuhan-sei no kumon*, p. 430.

35. Conrad Totman, "Political Succession in the Tokugawa Bakufu; Abe Masahiro's rise to power, 1843–1845," *Harvard Journal of Asiatic Studies* 26 : 105. W. G. Beasley, in his *Select Documents on Japanese Foreign Policy 1853–1868*, p. 327, can be seen as narrowing this further with his assertion that "in practice, in the late Tokugawa period, *Rōjū* were only chosen from those with fiefs of 50,000 *koku*."

members of the Sakai branches, and the Hotta family also, are sufficient to bring into question Totman's assertion that daimyo with more than 100,000 koku were barred from Bakufu office, for these families held well in excess of that figure.[36]

At first glance, there would appear to be more justice in establishing 30,000 koku as the minimum enfeoffment necessary to qualify for office, for nobody with less was ever to become a full Senior Councilor (although a handful reached an equivalent position as *rōjū kaku*). It is misleading, however, to consider this a barrier to recruitment from below the line. The Bakufu could always alter lesser enfeoffments by the simple expedient of augmenting them. This happened to Itakura Katsukiyo, for example. In 1749, as a Junior Councilor, he had his kokudaka increased from 15,000 to 20,000 and was raised to 30,000 koku in 1767, two years before he became Senior Councilor. The same process can be seen at work in the case of Tanuma Okitsugu. Kuroda Naokuni, given an increase of 5,000 koku while a Superintendent of Temples and Shrines, and another similar increase to a total of 30,000 koku when he was appointed Senior Councilor to the shogunal heir apparent in the Western Enclosure in 1732, was well on the way to carving out a similar role for himself, and, had he lived long enough to see his charge made shogun, he would undoubtedly have become Senior Councilor. That lesser fudai or upper hatamoto did not often move up to higher Bakufu office is true, but it was for want of neither precedent nor the necessary machinery (*KCS*).

The arguments for exclusive recruitment within the Bakufu all assume that the Bakufu could select at will, except insofar as it chose to impose limits on eligibility, from all the daimyo who lay within the appropriate categories, leading to the implicit assertion that only those who did attain high office could have done so, and that those who did not, could not have. In fact, a closer examination of the various lists of Bakufu officials seems to reveal not so much that those who did not could not, but that they would not. Selection may not have been so much in the con-

36. Totman, in his *Tokugawa Bakufu*, p. 163, notes that the Inaba, Hotta, and Obama Sakai were regular officcholders, despite their kokudaka, and imputes this to the service which members of these families gave under Iemitsu and Ietsuna.

trol of the Bakufu, as in the control of the individual daimyo; in other words, there was a fair degree of self-selection in the careers of those who reached high Bakufu office.

The most casual glance at the names of those who filled the position of Senior Councilor will reveal the frequent recurrence of a surprisingly small number of family names. Even if one were to grant the exclusion of all fudai except those with fiefs of 30,000 to 100,000 koku, it would have to be admitted that there was by no means equal representation for all eligible families. The list is dominated by Matsudaira, Abe, Sakai, Honda, and Mizuno, while other names receive little or no representation: the Okabe have none, the Ogasawara only two, the Suwa and Manabe only one, and so forth. Of course, the Matsudaira represent a combination of many families with the same name, as do the Abe and the Sakai, so in that sense it is only to be expected that they receive a greater exposure. However, a close look reveals that certain branches of these families were unusually well-represented in this highest of Bakufu offices. Historians have noted that five families—the Hotta, the two main Abe branches, the Ogyū and Ōkōchi branches of the Matsudaira, all descended from Iemitsu's key officials in the early seventeenth century— seem to have had a particularly strong affinity for high Bakufu office.[37]

The frequency with which these families provided Senior Councilors for the Bakufu is indeed striking, but it could easily be dismissed as fortuitous; after all, the position could be held by only four or five men at a time, and a certain amount of ability was demanded of those occupying it. The numbers involved were small enough to reflect accidents of health, capability, and longevity. But, if we turn to a more numerous sample, the lists of Masters of Shogunal Ceremony, lowest of the official posts open to fudai daimyo, we still find a marked imbalance; once again the same families dominate, while the others receive only token representation. The Okabe, Suwa, Yamaguchi, Miyake, and Takagi, for example, provided only two members each over two-and-a-half centuries, while the Inagaki and Yonezu managed only one each. Here the imbalance is much more significant.

The duties of a Master of Shogunal Ceremony, as we have

37. Totman, *Tokugawa Bakufu,* p. 169, is an example of this.

seen, were not intellectually taxing, and the position was often held by men who had just reached maturity, so the imbalance cannot be attributed to accidents or ability. The total representation of fudai family names—together with the occasional minor tozama daimyo, or upper hatamoto—is far too broad to permit the application of theories of exclusion by virtue of family background or kokudaka. The fact that it was the first step in an official career can eliminate all but the grossest accidents of longevity. In addition, it was a position which seems to have been quite elastic in the numbers it could accommodate—in 1800, for example, there were twenty-two in this position, but there were often fewer.[38] There is seldom evidence of any correlation between the number of appointments to it and the number of resignations; this, together with the occasional appointment of people who were not fudai, or sometimes not even daimyo, would seem to suggest that it was far from difficult to enter this position, and indeed that it was usually understaffed.

That the imbalance should persist in such an open position as that of Master of Shogunal Ceremony, the first step on the way to higher office in the Bakufu, can only be explained in terms of self-selection. Some families went into it constantly, and were plainly more eager for office than others. The self-selection can be seen at its highest in the record of the Inoue family, that branch of it which held Hamamatsu Han from time to time. From the time of the third daimyo, Masato, who entered Bakufu office as a Master of Shogunal Ceremony in 1669, each successive daimyo held an official position of some sort. Only two were destined to go no further than the lowest position, two did not rise beyond Superintendent of Temples and Shrines, and four became Senior Councilors.[39]

With other well-known official families, the pattern can be seen repeated in a rather diluted form, for not all were able to provide healthy daimyo in each generation or remain free from mistrust invited by the mistakes of fathers in office. The Hotta family followed this route quite well. The first two daimyo, Masamori and Masatoshi, each held important Bakufu office, but after the latter's assassination in 1684 the family fell under a

38. From *Ryūeibunin*, vol. 1.
39. "(Kazusa Tsurumai) Inoue kafu."

cloud which did not lift until 1728, when Hotta Masatora was appointed Keeper of Osaka Castle. From this time on, until the family fell into disfavor again after Masayoshi's controversial career as Senior Councilor in the 1850s, three of the six generations of daimyo held Bakufu office. At first glance, this may not be very impressive, but of those not to do so, one, Masaharu, died in his sixteenth year, far too young for any office to be anticipated, and another, also named Masayoshi, died in his twenty-fifth year, just when he might have been expected to enter the lists. This leaves us with only one Hotta daimyo, Masatoki, who was both old enough (fifty when he died) and eligible enough (he had become daimyo six years before) for office, but who made no attempt for it.[40]

The other famous official families—the Ogyū and Ōkōchi Matsudaira, the Fukuyama and Shirakawa Abe—all show signs of this sort of enthusiastic competition for office when circumstances permitted. Yet the majority of fudai houses show nothing like it at all. Much more usual is the lackluster performance of families like the Okabe and Ogasawara, who occasionally wandered out into the political arena, and then abandoned it.

To explain the success these few families obtained in their search for office, one need do little more than point to their persistence. They simply tried harder than the other families. With each generation in pursuit of office, the Inoue were certain to have more success than either branch of the Inagaki family, which between them could produce only one candidate for office.

Further evidence for the theory of self-selection can be found in the career patterns of some of the conspicuously successful officeholding families. If, granted a minimum of ability, members of certain families were predestined for promotion to the Bakufu's most powerful positions, many of them had records which belied this.

Of seven generations of daimyo in the Ogyū Matsudaira family between the Kyōhō period and the fall of the Bakufu in 1868, the first six all held official positions. All but the first, Norimura, began their careers as Masters of Shogunal Ceremony. Norimura, appointed Keeper of Osaka Castle in 1722, without any prior official position, and after a little more than six months, winning

40. "Hotta kafu."

promotion to Senior Councilor, had an infinitely more painless official career than any of his successors. The only one to approach the ease with which he gained promotion was his son, Norisuke, who became Master of Shogunal Ceremony in 1760, Superintendent of Temples and Shrines eight months later, and Keeper of Osaka Castle in 1764, a position he held until his death in 1769. This was much the sort of career one would anticipate from daimyo who had special access to political office—a token period as Master of Ceremonies, followed by a promotion to the joint office of Superintendent of Temples and Shrines, followed by promotion to Keeper of Osaka Castle, when his turn fell due, and a period of waiting for an opening to develop among the Senior Councilors—in his case a wait cut short by death, before his turn for further promotion had come.

The next three Ogyū Matsudaira daimyo, however, all had to wait some time for their promotions to Superintendent of Temples and Shrines. Norisada waited six years, Norihiro eight, and Noriyasu three. This is the first indication that at least some members of this prominent official fudai family were not eagerly welcomed into higher Bakufu office simply by virtue of their birth. Had Bakufu office been their birthright, one might have expected an earlier end to their apprenticeship period. None of the three was so young on his appointment to sōjaban that it made a period of apprenticeship here at all mandatory: the first was nearly thirty, the second was twenty-three, and the third was forty-six.

Perhaps even more surprising is the fact that their promotion was not as rapid as it could easily have been. In the case of the first, Norisada, between his appointment as sōjaban in 1781 and his promotion in 1787, he saw six of his colleagues, at least three of them from less prominent families, promoted before him, and one of these actually appointed over his head. The second, Norihiro, saw four from lesser families appointed before him, among them Ōkubo Tadazane, who was four years his junior, and whose ancestors had last provided a Bakufu official more than eighty years before. After this initial hurdle, further promotions tended to come more quickly, but this was universally so; Superintendent of Temples and Shrines was not a position in which daimyo lingered, for there were only four of them at a time, and they provided the pool from which promotions to Osaka and Kyoto came; once there, promotion tended to be automatic, as long as you could outlive at least one of the Senior Councilors.[41]

What was important, then, in showing how rapidly an officeholder was going to be promoted was how quickly he was given his first promotion, to *jishabugyō*. Yet it was just here that all five of the great officeholding families show themselves to be only average performers. As we have seen, of the five Ogyū Matsudaira who went along this route to promotion, only two moved on to Superintendent of Temples and Shrines in under a year. The others took three, six, and eight years, respectively, and two of them saw members of lesser families promoted ahead of them. In the case of the Hotta, of the three daimyo to make this progress from 1741 onward, one took seven years, while another took eight. The three Ōkōchi Matsudaira (of the senior branch) to hold important office from the mid-eighteenth century onward took four, seven, and six years, respectively, while Fukuyama Abe tended to take four years, etc. The showing is no more than average. Certainly there is nothing in their record of promotions to imply that the Bakufu was willing to give them special consideration because of their names; on the contrary, because no particular favor was shown them, the impulse must have come entirely from them.[42]

The imbalance visible among the names of Bakufu officeholders, then, was a real one, but it was largely self-imposed. Those who wanted Bakufu office, from whatever family, from whatever kokudaka, were free to try for it, with their capability the only restriction placed upon them. That many did not want Bakufu office is clear, and given the unrewarding nature of the positions, is also reasonable. What is more intriguing is why a small number of families, without any noticeable encouragement, should have applied themselves each generation with obsessive energy to the contest for office. No clear-cut answer to this is possible. However, in the case of the Iemitsu families, whose ties

41. "Ogyū Matsudaira kafu"; *Ryūeibunin*, vol. 1; Takayanagi Mitsuhisa and Takeuchi Rizō, eds., *Nihonshi jiten*, pp. 1042–55.

42. From "Hotta kafu; (Mikawa Toyohashi) Ōkōchi kafu"; *Fukuyama-shi shi*, 2 : passim.

with office are so clear-cut, it is quite possible that they regarded Bakufu office as in part an obligation laid upon them by their ancestors, and indeed derived some personal pleasure from it, as something which engaged their filial piety and antiquarian and even philanthropic leanings. The obligation was a personal one, and a private one, yet it was an obligation to an office, not to a man or a philosophy of government. It could neither dictate their behavior in office, nor the way in which they formulated their policies—it merely prompted them to official positions.

There is one further aspect of the fudai daimyo in their relationship to the Edo Bakufu and to office within it which commands our attention here, and that is the rapid decline in adherence to the concept of the "bureaucratic fief," the idea that office in the Bakufu carried with it possession of one of the smaller fudai domains within the Kantō and that removal or retirement from office automatically involved removal to a more distant domain. The failure of this principle carried profound implications for the course of relations between the central government and those daimyo who exercised power in its name.

The general stabilization of fief possession which took place during the Tokugawa period has been described in an earlier chapter. Here I should like to demonstrate that the Kantō "bureaucratic han" felt this movement almost as much as the more distant parts of Japan, using as an example Iwatsuki Han, a domain in the heart of the Kantō plain. In the history of its tenure can be seen the initial application of the principle of bureaucratic holdings, and also its subsequent lapse.

The first of the daimyo of Iwatsuki during the Edo period was Kōriki Tadafusa, who held no major position in the Bakufu but was moved out in 1619 to Hamamatsu and replaced by Aoyama Tadatoshi, who had just become a senior Bakufu adviser. In 1623, when Aoyama fell into disfavor, for some cause which is now obscure—his biography in the *Kansei chōshū shokafu,* the collection of genealogies compiled at the Bakufu's request in 1799, merely remarks cryptically that "there was a reason"—he lost both office and domain simultaneously.

Abe Masatsugu, the next occupant of Iwatsuki Han, became a Bakufu councilor in the same year (1623) and was promptly moved in to replace Aoyama. During his term of office (which lasted until his death in 1644), his domain increased substantially, and in 1638 he gave 46,000 koku, including the castle of Iwatsuki, to his eldest surviving son, Abe Shigetsugu. Shigetsugu had built up a substantial political career of his own, and was at that time one of Iemitsu's "group of six" (from which the office of Junior Councilor later developed); shortly after, he was to become one of the first of the formally appointed Senior Councilors.

So far, since 1619, the daimyo of Iwatsuki had all been leading Bakufu officials, but on Abe's death in 1651, the bureaucratic principle was allowed to lapse for twenty years; this was a feature of the tenure of many other Kantō domains during these years also, and its significance will be discussed in the following chapter. For the moment, let it suffice to say that, after two Abe daimyo without Bakufu office, the bureaucratic principle was reasserted in 1680, when Abe Masakuni was moved away to Miyazu on the Japan Sea coast, not far from Kyoto, and was replaced as daimyo of Iwatsuki by Itakura Shigetane, a Superintendent of Temples and Shrines, who was to be made Senior Councilor within a few more months. Like his predecessor, Aoyama Tadatoshi, Itakura too came shortly under a cloud ("there was a reason" in this case too), was deprived of position and domain, and was placed under house arrest after the new shogun, Tsunayoshi, took office in 1680.

Early the following year, Toda Tadamasa, a newly appointed Senior Councilor, was moved into Iwatsuki from Shimodate Han. Within five years, he was moved on to Sakura Han, another of the well-known "bureaucratic han," and Iwatsuki had a new daimyo, this time Matsudaira Tadachika, who at the time was a wakadoshiyori, or Junior Councilor, and one of Tsunayoshi's personal advisers as well. In 1697, he was moved into Kansai, but his replacement in Iwatsuki was Ogasawara Nagashige, who had just become Senior Councilor.

At a decent interval after his death in 1710, Ogasawara Nagashige's son, Nagahiro, who held no Bakufu office, and was destined to hold none, was moved away to Kakegawa, near the modern city of Shizuoka, and replaced by Nagai Naohiro, who had been a Junior Councilor since 1704.

To summarize then, in the first hundred years of the Tokugawa Bakufu, this central Kantō han saw eight changes of daimyo family, with the han going to an incumbent Bakufu official on each occasion. Of its first twelve daimyo, all but three held major positions in the Bakufu. This was plainly a "feudal bureaucratic han," and with a history like this, there was little to encourage daimyo to think it would stay long in the hands of their descendants unless they too secured office in the Bakufu.

Yet the relaxation of the Bakufu's powers over the daimyo is visible here, too. Nagai Naohiro's death in 1711 saw Iwatsuki pass into the hands of his second son, and then his third son (neither of whom held any office), who held it until 1756. In that year, Ōoka Tadamitsu, a favorite of the ninth shogun, Ieshige, and one of the last self-made fudai daimyo, was moved in. After his death in 1760, Iwatsuki remained in the hands of his descendants, only one of whom had anything like important Bakufu office, until the Bakufu collapsed.[43]

The same was true of other han which had been occupied by Bakufu administrators under Hidetada and Iemitsu. Kawagoe Han, which had been the domain of five prominent Bakufu officials in the seventeenth century, among them Sakai Tadakatsu and Matsudaira Nobutsuna, saw no more officials from 1714 onward; rather it saw fifty years of occupation by faineant Akimoto, followed by a century of occupation by an ichimon Matsudaira branch. Tsuchiura Han, which under Iemitsu had provided a home for Kutsuki Tanetsuna, a Junior Councilor, did the same later for Tsuchiya Kazunao, first as Junior, then as Senior Councilor, and for his son Masanao who was also a Senior Councilor. Yet it also did the same for their descendants for the next two hundred years. Some of these were to hold minor ceremonial positions in the Bakufu, but only one attained a post of any seniority.[44]

This is a pattern which has been ignored by Japanese historians. One of them has noted that "into Kantō fudai han like Sakura and Odawara there was a constant coming and going of daimyo who had obtained important Bakufu offices like rōjū," but does not think it necessary to add that this was not a lasting phenomenon. Indeed, the very domains chosen as examples are

43. From *Saitama-ken shi*, vols. 5, 6.
44. For Kawagoe, see Kishi Dembei, *Kawagoe hansei to bunkyō*, pp. 11–13; for Tsuchiura, see "Tsuchiya kafu."

evidence of the slowing pace of fudai daimyo transfers. In Sakura Han, the Hotta regained possession in 1746 and held it until the Bakumatsu, although some of them occupied no Bakufu office at all. In Odawara, the Ōkubo returned in 1686 and stayed there until the Meiji restoration and its aftermath, yet from 1713 onward they produced only one daimyo who held Bakufu office of any sort.[45]

In the combination of circumstances which saw official careers within the Bakufu rewarded less and less, and tenure and location of fiefs determined by birth and succession rather than by possession of, and performance in, Bakufu office, one can see the seeds of the Bakufu's failure to transform itself into anything approaching a centralized monarchy, and hence the seeds of its ultimate fall.

The decline in the rewards available to those participating successfully in the Bakufu's official life not only prompted less competition for office, and therefore probably won the Bakufu only a small share of each new crop of talented daimyo, but, far more significantly, it provided no incentive to those who did seek office to give all their enthusiasm to the aggrandizement of a government from which they could anticipate few rewards. This was something which European commentators on the problem of counsel had had very securely in mind. Machiavelli saw quite clearly the necessity of rewarding one's advisers, observing that "the Prince . . . ought to take a care to his servant, honouring him, enriching, and obliging him to him to the end that . . . those many charges cause him to fear changes that may fall, knowing he is not able to stand without his master." [46] In failing to continue to do this, the Bakufu provided no incentive to its officials to look to it exclusively for their rewards, and so one has no right to expect the "positive sense of bureaucratic identification with the Bakufu" attributed to them by Craig.

A further impediment to strengthening Bakufu power may be seen in the competing incentive each office-holding daimyo had to look to his greatest good through the management of his own domain. Machiavelli was aware of the danger of this, too, advis-

45. The quotation is from Kodama and Kitajima, *Monogatari han shi*, 2 : 14; for Hotta, see "Hotta kafu," and for Ōkubo, see "Ōkubo kafu."

46. Niccolo Machiavelli, *The Prince*, chap. 22.

ing that those who gave counsel should not be allowed to develop independent sources of power or interest of their own.[47] Had the Tokugawa been as aware and kept recruiting their officials from modest backgrounds, rewarded them generously, given them domains in the Kantō, close to the center of Tokugawa influence, and made clear to them that continued tenure of those domains depended upon their participation in Bakufu administrative duties, it is quite likely that the result would have been a move toward centralization and accumulation of powers by the Bakufu.

Instead, after the first fifty years of its existence, the Bakufu turned largely to established daimyo for its ministers, and "new men" of the sort against whom Ōkubo Hikozaemon had railed in 1622 appeared only rarely during the next two centuries. Yanagisawa Yoshiyasu, Manabe Akifusa, Ōoka Tadamitsu, and Tanuma Okitsugu were all exceptional in their rise from obscurity. It may be argued that the later Bakufu still recruited its officials from the families of those who had been "new men" under Iemitsu, but this is not the same thing at all. The quality of service and personal loyalty to be expected from a man like Abe Tadaaki, who began his career as a page, with an income of 6,000 koku, must have differed vastly from the attitude of his remote descendant Masatō (Senior Councilor from 1864 to 1865), born and bred the daimyo of a domain of 100,000 koku. To Tadaaki, official position in the Bakufu offered the only way to wealth available, and the stronger the Bakufu the more his strength, as its servant, was likely to be. To Masatō, the Bakufu was no longer a source of wealth, and the stronger it became, the more precarious would be his hold on the only wealth he knew, the fief of 100,000 koku passed down to him by his twelve predecessors.[48]

The Bakufu also ceased demanding that its senior officials have their domains within the Kantō. Of the twenty-two Senior Councilors appointed between 1633 and 1700, only one had his han located outside the Kantō for the duration of his career, and only nine of the twenty-four appointed between 1700 and 1750 did not have Kantō fiefs. Of those appointed between 1750 and 1800, the majority (eleven out of seventeen) had domains which were

47. Ibid.
48. "(Tanakura) Abe kafu."

not in the Kantō, as did the majority (sixteen out of twenty-six) of those appointed up to 1853. All but two of the Senior Councilors appointed thereafter had their han outside the traditional location for Bakufu bureaucrats.[49] This too must have caused a change in the quality of service, for these men, with han remote from the center of Tokugawa influence, were far more likely to have commercial and strategic interests of their own. The general slackening of fief transfers, already described, affected officeholding daimyo no less than anybody else. This, too, can only have restricted their enthusiasm for their role as servants of the Bakufu by intensifying their concern both for the prosperity of their domains and their continued tenure of them. Of the rōjū in 1850, for example, one, Makino Tadamasa, had a fief held by his forebears since 1618; two, Abe Masahiro and Matsudaira Tadayū, were from han settled by their ancestors nearly 150 years earlier. The two remaining Senior Councilors, Toda Tadaatsu and Matsudaira Norimasa, had ties with their fiefs going back to 1774 and 1764, respectively.[50] The devotion these men gave to the central government, while no doubt sincere, must have lacked the single-minded intensity of their forefathers in the early years of the Bakufu. By the mid-nineteenth century, Bakufu office was, for them, simply a fact of life, no longer *the* fact of life. Untoward manifestations of Bakufu power—like the attempt to move three daimyo a decade earlier —can have seemed hardly less menacing to them than to the tozama daimyo who signed the petition opposing it.

Arai Hakuseki, in a comment on the senior Bakufu officials of the early eighteenth century, accused them of caring only for themselves and their family interests (*OSK* p. 462). Perhaps it would be incautious to accept too readily the judgment of one who, as a "new man" and a political rival, had so many personal reasons for despising them. Nevertheless, it must be admitted that the Bakufu took no steps to ensure that their reaction should be otherwise. The fudai daimyo in office may have been too con-

49. Calculated from Mitamura Engyō, *Buke jiten,* pp. 395–401; the figures do not include either second appointments, or those appointed only to the post of *rōjū kaku.*

50. Calculated from Takayanagi Mitsuhisa and Takeuchi Rizō, eds., *Nihonshi jiten,* pp. 1056–85, and Fujino Tamotsu, *Bakuhan taisei shi no kenkyū,* pp. 718ff.

spicuously placed to pursue his own selfish interests, but there was nothing to prevent him from fostering the best interests of his class. In any case, even as an official, he was surrounded by his own vassals who, whether in formal or informal capacities, continued to offer him advice. Given the fact that their dependence on the domain was even more explicit than his, one can imagine what lines that advice would follow. It comes as no surprise to learn that Nishimura Shigeki, as a prominent vassal of a fudai domain, was opposed to the sankin kōtai system, despite its contribution to Tokugawa political stability. Any vassal had reason to resent such a constant drain on domain resources. It accords rather less with the common theory of fudai daimyo in office to realize that, although aware of these views, the rōjū, Hotta Masayoshi, retained Nishimura's services as a vassal and used him as a confidential adviser on all questions of Bakufu policy.[51]

The continued employment of fudai daimyo as administrators and the failure to build up a staff of permanent senior bureaucrats from among the direct vassals of the Tokugawa house simply ensured that the Bakufu would be staffed by men whose attitude toward centralized power was at best ambivalent. If those fudai officials ever felt their identity as daimyo of autonomous domains overshadowed, they gave little sign of it. As a Kyoto Deputy, one might have expected Sakai Tadamochi to insist that his domain policies take the national interest into account. Instead, while he was in office, in 1755, his han at Obama stopped the export of grain which might otherwise have gone to help relieve the Tōhoku famine. In 1819, showing a similar unconcern for the national interest, the Obama domain banned grain exports again; the daimyo, Sakai Tadanobu, who was a Bakufu Senior Councilor, presumably did not see this as conflicting with the interests of the state. No doubt this can be said also of Mizuno Tadakuni, who held the same office, for his domain followed suit in 1840. Comparable bans took place at Fukuyama from time to time, despite the frequency with which the Abe were to attain high positions within the Bakufu.[52]

51. Kojima Shigeo, "Bakuhan-sei hōkai-ki ni okeru kaimei-ha kanryō no keisei," Nihonshi ronkyū pp. 453–54.

52. For Obama, see Fukui-ken shi, vol. 2, pt. 2, p. 99; for Mizuno, see Kitajima, Mizuno Tadakuni, p. 174; for Abe, see Fukuyama-shi shi, 2 : 690.

Their obligations as daimyo forced them into positions like this during their tenure of Bakufu office. Similarly these obligations placed them under constant pressure to neglect when they could, and resist when they could not neglect, those Bakufu powers which threatened the prerogatives which as daimyo they prized. If by so doing they ranged themselves with the tozama and ichimon daimyo against the Tokugawa house, there was little to inhibit them.

5. Fudai Daimyo and Bakufu Policy: 1600–1853

> When government is impeded and ministers are estranged
> from the ruler, certain people can acquire power, like the
> eunuchs [in China] . . . by acting as intermediaries . . .
> and accepting bribes. . . . Since ancient times such peo-
> ple have been likened to "foxes in the city wall and rats
> in the altar."
>
> Tokugawa Nariaki, 1838 [1]

It is a truism that the personal administration of hereditary
monarchs is no guarantee of sound government. The workings of
genetics are mysterious and often flagrantly wayward to the eye
of the observer, but it seems certain that no bloodline can hold
unto itself forever those elements that produce gifted rulers.
Certainly, the Tokugawa knew of no way to do so. Although
Ieyasu's son and grandson had the mettle to maintain, even to
intensify, the powers of the position they had inherited, this was
by no means true of all their successors. The hazards of birth and
death, of sickness and health, of temperament and proclivity,
which had for the moment favored the Tokugawa, were soon to
produce shogun for whom personal government was impossible.

The alternative to chaos, under such circumstances, was to de-
vise a system of government which, in the case of a competent
shogun, could provide counsel when necessary and protection
from administrative minutiae, and in the case of an incompetent,
could make decisions in his name. In giving shape and permanence to the office of Senior Councilor, in defining its duties, and
providing for regular rotation of responsibility, Iemitsu may well
have been providing such an alternative in the 1630s. If the intention was to provide continuity for the government, and protection for the shogun, then it was successful. Despite the occasional emergence of shogun who were infants, eccentrics, or in-
valids, the institution itself was to survive until the Bakufu fell
in 1868.

Observing this, historians have customarily sung the praises

1. *Mito han shiryō (bekki jō)*, p. 85.

of the "system of checks and balances" by which prescient early shogun provided for the perpetuation of their line and their office. Yet the perpetuation was only mechanical. The title was preserved, together with the claim of the Tokugawa house to it, but the system was unable to maintain the substance of authority. It was too much to expect of those who had held unusual powers under an incompetent shogun that they would surrender them meekly to his more competent successor. No Tokugawa shogun was to inherit the full measure of power to which his position in the Bakufu entitled him. Those who wanted it had to fight for it.

It was a battle which could not be waged unaided. Any shogun wishing to restore the autocratic prerogatives of the Iemitsu period, and so free himself from the deferential restraints of his fudai daimyo counselors, had to do precisely what Iemitsu had done, which was to make use of personal favorites. This entailed installing them in formal positions within the official hierarchy, rewarding them generously to preserve their loyalty, calling on them for counsel, and using them to the exclusion of fudai daimyo in the performance of administrative tasks. From men of this kind, such a shogun could anticipate advice and assistance which, if not wholly unselfish, was free of commitment to the status quo.

The matter of counsel has always presented something of a problem to autocratic monarchs. Men like Machiavelli and Bacon, who could seriously consider no other form of government, saw the chief difficulties confronting the monarch as, first of all, providing himself with able counselors, and then assuring their loyalty to him. As a solution to the first, both would have rejected, without hesitation, the theory perpetuated by the fudai daimyo, that counsel was a prerogative of a certain group of traditionally loyal vassals. Aware of the unlikelihood of the loyalty or the ability of the grandfather being transmitted intact to the grandson, both men would have urged the monarch to take his counsel where he could find it. To make sure of the continuing loyalty of advisers, Machiavelli recommended plentiful rewards, while Bacon, with less pessimism, thought the monarch should select as his counselors only those personally well known to him.

The Tokugawa, half a world away, knew nothing of the Florentine official or the English lawyer, yet those shogun who wished to assert their absolute prerogative were led to comparable conclusions. As Bacon suggested, they made use of men well known to them—often from childhood—and as Machiavelli suggested, they rewarded them handsomely. The counselors of their choice were usually to find themselves counted among the fudai daimyo by the end of their careers, and sometimes they were destined to establish long and glittering fudai lines, but in almost every case they were not daimyo by birth. With no inherited assumptions about what a Bakufu should or should not do, with their loyalty directed only to themselves and to the master who rewarded them, with no stable domains or long-established vassal bands competing for their allegiance, dependent for their fortune upon their wits, they were the ideal weapons of despotism.

No doubt it was for this reason that they were so hated. Under despotic governments anywhere, the matter of counsel was usually as much a subject of concern to the ruled as to the ruler. To the outsider, the processes of despotism, secretive and arbitrary, have always seemed particularly vulnerable to dubious influences; the ruler as the impersonal head of the state, acting for the good of all, and the ruler as mortal fallible man, swayed by personal and private likes and dislikes, seem too close for comfort. The one is considered good government, the other bad, and only the monarch straddles the line between them. It is therefore important that he be not susceptible to unworthy influences; hence the importance assigned to those who help him reach his decisions. Are they to be men of independence, thinking only of the good of the state, ready to counsel the king fearlessly, or are they to be sycophants, people who advance themselves by telling the ruler only what he wants to hear, and by using their personal influence with him to determine policy? As the reputation of the courtier in Europe and the eunuch in China suggest, few people have been more universally execrated than the personal servants and companions of the monarch. Whig historians have long taught us to dislike the king's friends, and the great villains of modern history, stretching in a long line from Machiavelli to Rasputin, are generally those close to the king's person.

The landed aristocracy has always provided the strongest critics of such men. To the mass of the people, it is a matter of indifference whether the tyrant is one man or many; those most threatened by autocratic power are those who stand to lose most by its use. Any monarch increasing his powers will do so at somebody's expense, and it is usually the landed nobility—sometimes the Church—that suffers. Therefore, its members were the most uncompromising opponents of those surrounding the monarch, and their most vehement critics. Shakespeare's Bolingbroke spoke for them all in his denunciation of Richard II's cronies as insects, "the caterpillars of the commonwealth"; so too, from another civilization, did Hsieh Kun, the Ch'in Dynasty statesman who likened the personal favorites of the ruler to vermin, the appearance of which foreshadows the ruin of the state, "foxes in the city wall and rats in the altar." [2] The king's friends were no more welcome in Tokugawa Japan. As the agents of autocracy, which is by definition not subject to external restraint, they personified all the menace which unbounded and capricious autocratic powers held for the Japanese daimyo. The daimyo, both fudai and tozama, regarded men like Yanagisawa Yoshiyasu and Tanuma Okitsugu, who were the personal confidants of shogun, with quite as much suspicion as ever an English Parliament lavished on the Duke of Buckingham.

This is why so few of the shogun's personal advisers have come down to us with favorable reputations. The shogun himself was beyond open reproach, but those resentful of his policy could at least attack his "evil counselors" with all the weapons at their disposal, including slanders. Hence, of all the "new men" to whom different shogun turned for advice, Arai Hakuseki alone has maintained a good reputation, simply because his own literary and scholarly skills transcended the opinions of the daimyo who were his contemporaries. They loathed him. Others, with no such weapons at their disposal, found attributed to them all manner of financial and sexual irregularities by their contemporaries and have been consistently vilified by later generations of Japanese Whigs. Yanagisawa Yoshiyasu, the Genroku political figure, survives in the history books as the man who, like the Duke of Buckingham, pandered to his master's grosser vices—

2. From the life of Hsieh Kun, in the Ch'in History, quoted in Kanno Michiaki, *Jigen*, supra *jōko*.

lending Tsunayoshi his wife, fathering his son, and sharing his bed. Similarly, Mizuno Tadaakira's influence over the eleventh shogun, Ienari, was rumored to have originated from a homosexual amour. Manabe Akifusa, although to his ally Arai Hakuseki a man of so noble a character as to rival the princes of antiquity, was charged with a similar relationship with Ienobu, the sixth shogun. He was also reputed to have enjoyed a less than platonic friendship with Ienobu's concubines. Naturally, such men were also accused of accepting bribes; Tanuma Okitsugu was accused of doing so on such an heroic scale as to make his name synonymous with corruption. To some were attributed worse crimes. Manabe Akifusa was rumored to have heedlessly brought on the fatal illness of Ietsugu, the seventh shogun, by keeping the ailing child outside in the cold while carousing with his mother. Tanuma, going one step further, was actually said to have murdered his protector, the tenth shogun, Ieharu.[3]

The general consistency underlying these judgments of "new men" in the Bakufu is impressive. It need not, however, be accepted as evidence that they actually did whatever has been imputed to them. Not one of the sources is above suspicion, whether in terms of the motives of its author, or his proximity, physical or chronological, to the events he describes. The *Sannō gaiki* for example, source of most of the uncharitable stories about Yanagisawa and Manabe, is no longer accepted uncritically by modern historians, one of whom has warned of a high proportion of gossip amongst the information it provides (*OSK* p. 568). In the case of Tanuma, too, most of the evidence comes from suspect sources.

What this unflagging vilification of a certain type of Tokugawa political figure does suggest, however, is the fear and hostility they engendered among men who felt most threatened by their activity within the Bakufu. This has often been interpreted as simply the natural resentment of fudai daimyo who saw these men as intruders, usurpers of their favored position by the shogun; but in fact, it was by no means confined to fudai. With a

3. For Yanagisawa, see Kodama Kōta, *Genroku jidai*, p. 292; for Mizuno Tadaakira, see Kitajima Masamoto, *Mizuno Tadakuni*, pp. 211–12; for Manabe Akifusa, see Arai Hakuseki's appraisal in *OSK* p. 576, and pp. 569, 580–81 for slanders about him; for Tanuma, see the judgments referred to in John W. Hall, *Tanuma Okitsugu*, pp. 54–56, 139.

unanimity transcending fudai-tozama lines, the daimyo of Toku-gawa Japan feared and resented the autocracy of the shogun, and those who abetted it. Fearing and resenting this power, whether in office or not, by word and by deed, they fought it as best they could.

They had reason for their fear and resentment. Their privileges as autonomous daimyo were threatened as at no other time by a shogun intent upon restoring his prerogatives. Had the shogun been one who submitted meekly to the advice of his traditional counselors, they would have had little to fear. In this respect, Bakufu policy underwent marked fluctuations according to the complexion of its government; when dominated by Senior Councilors, its demeanor toward daimyo was more permissive, but, when either the shogun or his personal representatives were in control, Bakufu policy changed. Instead of solicitude for their welfare and respect for their rights, there were assaults of various kinds upon the daimyo, their domains, and their tenure of them.

To imply that this seesaw between the daimyo, represented by the fudai, on the one hand, and the shogun and his friends, on the other, dominated the policy and the politics of the Bakufu for 250 years would be an unpardonable exaggeration. It is more likely that for much of that time nobody was particularly conscious of it. Far more important and constant were the day-to-day administrative problems common to each generation—what to do about fires, what to do about famines, what to do about dishonest tax collectors, what to do about peasant unrest, samurai poverty, and so on. Nevertheless, the centripetal-centrifugal tension, even if seldom consciously realized, and never brought out for open discussion, underlay many issues on which some policy was demanded of the Bakufu. Each time the Bakufu disenfeoffed or transferred a daimyo—or conversely, failed to disenfeoff or transfer him—for a particular reason, it was in effect making a choice for central power or for daimyo autonomy. This was also the case whenever it prohibited or gave permission to some form of domain economic activity, and it also lay behind the Bakufu's willingness, or unwillingness, to place impositions upon the daimyo.

At the beginning of this work, I described a general weakening of the Bakufu's central position in Tokugawa Japan, laying the responsibility for this upon the fudai daimyo. In this chapter, I shall attempt to demonstrate this, comparing the various turns taken by Bakufu policy, as it was relevant to this issue, with the background of those who determined that policy. For, although the overall movement of the Bakufu's powers over the daimyo was downward, a movement of decline, there were occasions during the 250 years when the downward course was accelerated, and occasions when it was arrested, or even slightly reversed. No precise correlation of the nature of Bakufu policy with the identity of those who made it is possible—we are after all dealing with human beings, whose responses do not always permit tidy equations—but it is surely no accident that, in general, those periods in which the Bakufu's powers were pressed most strongly, and those periods in which they were most neglected, varied according to the status of those responsible for Bakufu policy. When policy was determined by the fudai daimyo who filled the positions of Great Councilor and Senior Councilor, that policy generally reflected a reluctance to assert Bakufu powers at the expense of daimyo prerogatives. When it was in the hands of the shogun, or his personal friends and advisers, the tenor of Bakufu policy was almost invariably that of a reassertion of the Bakufu's position of dominance over the daimyo.

Ieyasu, Hidetada, Iemitsu

By the time Ōkubo Hikozaemon wrote his *Mikawa monogatari* in 1622, the presence of "new men" in the counsels of the Tokugawa had become a matter for comment, particularly to men like Hikozaemon, who felt that generations of loyal service deserved more recognition. Addressing himself to his children, he wrote that men not from the province of Mikawa, and therefore strangers among the Tokugawa vassals, "are being employed without hesitation near to the shogun's person; people who are not fudai are being declared fudai and are brought into the shogun's service. Those like you who have been fudai for nine generations are treated as newcomers." [4]

It is quite plain that Hikozaemon recognized this as largely a post-1615 phenomenon, for he calls upon the dead Ieyasu to look down on the way the fudai—seven years later—were being ne-

4. *Mikawa monogatari,* p. 427.

glected,[5] and in this his memory and his observations did not play him false. There was a substantial difference in the employment of new men in the Bakufu after 1615.

Ieyasu had not hesitated to use new men in his service. Honda Masanobu, his son Masazumi, Itakura Katsushige, Naruse Masanari, the Buddhist priest Konchiin Sūden and the Confucian scholar Hayashi Razan all gave him counsel and assistance during the years after Sekigahara, first when he was shogun at Edo, and then in his active retirement at Sumpu after 1605. All were men of lowly origin, whose talents Ieyasu found valuable. He used them, and he rewarded them, but there was never any doubt that they were his men. Many of them were to become daimyo, but always as a favor, never as a right, and some of these, sent off as eternal advisers to Ieyasu's younger sons at Owari, Kii, and Mito, were destined never really to obtain more than second-class daimyo status.[6]

However, the use of such men did not imply a break with the fudai daimyo. Ieyasu used "new men" in the same sort of humble positions that he—and his forebears—had always used them: to run errands, keep accounts, and give him advice in those fields where his prominent military fudai were unskilled. If nothing else, the uncertain military situation precluded their employment in any way, or to any end, likely to give offense to the fudai daimyo. Some historians have claimed to observe signs of tension between Ieyasu and his fudai during the years which lay between Sekigahara and Osaka, a tension brought on, it is said, by resentment of Ieyasu's patronage of outsiders, but there is little beyond conjecture to support such a view. Those fifteen years, rather, were an Indian summer of mutual dependence, when, in the knowledge that more fighting was to come, Ieyasu relied on his fudai just as much as they on him. Substantially rewarded after Sekigahara, they stood in expectation of more rewards, their immediate attentions were fixed upon their new duties as daimyo, and Ieyasu's need of their support kept them in his military counsels.

After Osaka, and Ieyasu's death, however, the situation began

5. Ibid., pp. 426–27.
6. Fukushima Kimiko, "Edo Bakufu shoki no seiji seido ni tsuite—Shōgun to sono sokkin," *Shisō* 8 : 78–85.

to change. Hidetada may have had prominent fudai daimyo like Sakai Tadayo at his elbow, but he also was surrounded by men of origins far more obscure. The circumstances of Doi Toshikatsu's birth, for example, were mysterious. There were rumors that he was Ieyasu's bastard, while the official genealogy, the *Kansei chōshū shokafu,* which was not beyond fabricating ancestries, merely noted of him that his family records had been lost. Together with others among Hidetada's personal advisers, like Nagai Naomasa and Inoue Masanari, Doi Toshikatsu had been a companion to Hidetada when both lord and vassal were young (*KCS*).

This tendency to seek the company and counsel of old friends of low rank was carried still further by the third shogun, Iemitsu, from the 1630s onward, when it was accompanied by a slight, but perceptible movement toward deliberate exclusion of prominent fudai from positions of formal influence. The business of government, under Iemitsu, came to be more and more the function of a small group of men whose personal relations with him were lifelong, but whose claims to daimyo rank and fudai status were far from robust.

The best known among them was Matsudaira Nobutsuna, whose origins in Mikawa Province and family ties with the Tokugawa were substantial enough; but nevertheless the branch of the family into which he was subsequently adopted had only modest enfeoffments. His adopted father made his own way as one of Ieyasu's personal advisers and managed to have Nobutsuna assigned to Iemitsu at an early age, presumably to place him in a favorable position from which he could follow the same path. Abe Tadaaki was also from a leading fudai family, but from a minor branch of it, and without his Bakufu office would have remained a hatamoto. His cousin, Abe Shigetsugu, was admittedly the son of a daimyo—Abe Masatsugu—but a younger son, and was originally adopted into a hatamoto family. He remained there until, already an adult, the death of his elder brother brought about his return to his father's inheritance (*KCS*).

Hotta Masamori, too, could not have claimed to be either a fudai or a daimyo in his own right. His father had had an extremely varied career, including a rōnin period, until a purely fortuitous link with the Inaba family, and through them with Iemitsu's nurse, Kasuga no Tsubone, was to bring him into Ieyasu's service, and his son, Masamori, into service with Iemitsu, where it was said of him that "the shogun trusted nobody more" (*KCS; TJ* 41 : 22).

There were others, but it was these four men—Matsudaira Nobutsuna, Abe Shigetsugu, Abe Tadaaki, and Hotta Masamori —through whom Iemitsu carried out his personal government. He knew them very well. Nobutsuna had been assigned to Iemitsu on the latter's birth, Abe Tadaaki when Iemitsu was six, and Masamori when he was sixteen. His ties with Abe Shigetsugu, who did not join him until much later, can have been hardly less firm, since Shigetsugu committed suicide on Iemitsu's death in 1651. Between 1633 and 1638 all these men had become Senior Councilors, an office just newly established, and they were to dominate Bakufu administration until Iemitsu's death. Their personal relationship with the shogun, the insecurity and novelty of their daimyo rank, their lack of secure ties with their domains and vassals, all combined to make them ideal servants for an autocratic shogun.

With the advice and cooperation of men like these, and with the powers of decision held firmly in their own hands, it is not surprising that Bakufu policy was at its strongest under the first three Tokugawa Shogun, albeit rather less under Ieyasu and rather more under Iemitsu. In the fifty years during which they reigned, the Edo Bakufu introduced and exercised its most stringent forms of control over the daimyo.

It was under the first three shogun that daimyo were disenfeoffed and transferred on a scale never to be repeated, and for reasons which were never again to be applied with so much rigor. Misgovernment, disobedience, failure to provide an heir— all could, and often did, lead to outright attainders or to substantial fief reductions. It was in the first version of the *Buke shohatto,* in 1615, that the Bakufu affirmed its right to control the extent to which daimyo fortified their domains, and to control marriages between daimyo families. The third version, in 1635, demanded that all daimyo follow the principles of Bakufu law within their domains, and it also organized the haphazard hostage system into the sankin kōtai (*TK* 1 : 63 ff). In 1603, and

again in 1643, the Bakufu affirmed its position as mother and
father of the people, in accordance with Confucian precepts, by
giving sanction to the right of peasant protest, either in the form
of desertion or of direct appeal to the Bakufu.[7] Behind all these
claims, providing them with their cutting edge, was the Bakufu's
system of inspection, used to make daimyo more responsive to the
wishes of the central government. Finally, under the first three
shogun, the Edo Bakufu battered the daimyo with a series of
impositions, forcing them to build Edo Castle, the Nijō Palace,
and various provincial castles, and forcing them, too, to drain
large parts of the city of Edo and dredge its canals.

Ietsuna

Arai Hakuseki, looking back in 1716 over nearly a century to
the politics of the Iemitsu period, was conscious that a great
change had taken place in the Bakufu at Iemitsu's death and
Ietsuna's succession. He interpreted it as a victory for the forces
of conservatism, with the fudai daimyo driving Iemitsu's new
men away from government, an observation no doubt sharpened
by the knowledge that, as he wrote, a similar process was en-
folding him.

"In the time of the third *Shōgun*," Hakuseki observed,

> His Excellency Hotta Masamori, who was at first made a
> member of the council, was taken away from this position
> within a short time, and made the shogun's Chamberlain.
> All commands to the Senior Councilors, and all messages
> from them [to the shogun] were transmitted through him.
> In the time of the fourth shogun, who succeeded while still
> a child, government was entrusted to the Senior Councilors,
> and thenceforth there was nobody like His Excellency Masa-
> mori (*OSK*, pp. 574–75).[8]

Iemitsu's early death, at the age of forty-seven, placed the
shogunal prerogatives in jeopardy. After three shogun who were
able and adult, well fitted to govern the nation themselves, capa-

---

7. *Tsuruoka-shi shi*, 1 : 403.

8. Hakuseki was mistaken in stating that Hotta Masamori was removed
from the council and made Chamberlain. Rather, he remained a Senior
Councilor until his death in 1651, but this detail need not detract from the
flow of Hakuseki's argument.

ble of selecting their own ministers, came the boy Ietsuna, just ten years old when he took over the reins of government. His health was notoriously frail, as can be seen by the frequency with which the *Tokugawa jikki* records his receiving moxa cautery. His digestion was not good, and he was greatly susceptible to colds—all in all, even in his maturity, not one of the most robust of rulers (*TJ* 41 : 30, 52, 61, 79, 87).

Without the skill, the experience, and later possibly even the wit to choose his own confidants, Ietsuna allowed the system of personal government established by the first three shogun to lapse. Two of Iemitsu's companions had followed him into death, and of those who remained the longest lived was Abe Tadaaki, who died in 1666. These men, as they departed, were not replaced by further "new men" of the shogun's own choice, but, rather, by men who were already fudai daimyo in their own right and all from well-established families. For the very first time in the Tokugawa period, the fudai daimyo are to be seen filling the role in Bakufu administration which they were thereafter to claim as their right. There was nobody to prevent them. Ietsuna cared so little for the administrative routine that he was commonly, if disrespectfully, known as '*sayō-sei*' *sama*, the "so be it" shogun, a title earned by his unwillingness to express any opinion of his own. His most frequent comment to suggestions made by the fudai daimyo who gave him counsel was "so be it." [9] The shogun's uncle and guardian, Hoshina Masayuki, no doubt assured the physical security of the young shogun during a period of some danger, but there is no reason to believe that the interests of the uncle, himself a daimyo, were precisely those of his dead brother or his nephew.

When the Korean, Nam Yong Ik, whose idiosyncratic description of Ii Naotaka has been referred to elsewhere, saw the leaders of the Bakufu in 1655, the most influential among them appeared to him to be (apart from Ii Naotaka) Hoshina Masayuki, Sakai Tadakiyo, and Sakai Tadakatsu.[10] It is an interesting list for various reasons. In the first place, only one of them had not been born the son of a leading fudai daimyo, and this was Hoshina Masayuki, who, instead, was born the son of a shogun. This is

9. Shinji Yoshimoto, "Tokugawa Tsunayoshi," in *Buke no sekai*, ed. Okada Akio, p. 18.

10. *Hikone-shi shi*, 1 : 451.

already a perceptible departure from the men of the Iemitsu period, compounded by the fact that they all had enfeoffments well above the average. Secondly, only one of them was a Senior Councilor. This was Sakai Tadakiyo. Naotaka held no office, Masayuki was the shogun's guardian, and Sakai Tadakatsu was a Great Councilor. This, one may suspect, implies no denigration of the office of Senior Councilor. Since Tadakiyo was the only newcomer to it, after Iemitsu's death, the absence of any others rather reflects the diminished importance of the remnants of Iemitsu's political machine. Abe Tadaaki and Matsudaira Nobutsuna, were, at that time, the only other Senior Councilors.

Sakai Tadakatsu died the following year, Ii Naotaka in 1659, and Hoshina Masayuki in 1672, but even before the latter's death, Sakai Tadakiyo, named Great Councilor in 1666, had taken over the direction of the Bakufu and its policy. As the other figures faded from the Bakufu, they were replaced by Senior Councilors who were all recruited from among the established fudai daimyo, all the sons of daimyo. These men, between them, formulated and administered Bakufu policy until Ietsuna's death in 1680.

The contrast between the Bakufu leaders of the Iemitsu period and those of the Ietsuna period could hardly be more marked; the difference in the policies they espoused is equally sharp. Under the government of fudai daimyo, the Bakufu began to retreat from the use of several important prerogatives, some of which it was never to regain. If others were exercised again under later and stronger shogun, they were nevertheless blunted and were no longer weapons of attack, but of defense.

From the very beginning of Ietsuna's reign, there was little doubt that Iemitsu's policies were to be reversed. At the end of 1651, within eight months of Iemitsu's death, a major change in the Bakufu's attitude to deathbed adoptions was announced. Taking as justification the fact that the many attainders of the first half century of Bakufu rule had created samurai unemployment on a disturbing scale, the daimyo who determined Ietsuna's policy for him decided to relax the prohibition on deathbed adoptions. To restrict the number of fief confiscations, dying barons were now to be permitted hasty adoption of an heir, to keep name, fief, and vassal band intact. They had unerringly fixed on the one factor to which the great majority of attainders were due. Under Iemitsu, alone, twenty-five of the forty-three daimyo who lost their fiefs did so for this reason; during the years 1600–51, fifty-eight daimyo had been disenfeoffed for lack of an acceptable heir. Gamō Tadasato, one of the largest daimyo of northern Japan, lost his 600,000 koku fief on his death in 1627.[11] Nevertheless, of several possible counters to the problem of the rōnin, the unemployed samurai, the daimyo guiding Ietsuna selected that which gave the daimyo greater security from the Bakufu, for it inevitably detracted from the already tenuous pretense that a fief was given by the shogun to the daimyo at the former's discretion. They had thrown away one of the Bakufu's major trump cards, a power which, had it been maintained in use throughout the Edo period, would have provided the Tokugawa with a swelling store of private domain, as daimyo bloodlines dried up one after the other, and so helped them along the road to monarchy. As the shogun's servants, they had done less than their duty, but as daimyo, alive to the possibility that they or their children might one day wish to adopt to preserve the line and protect their vassals, they did merely as discretion demanded.

It is not necessary to look further for the reason behind the sudden slump in fief confiscations under Ietsuna. While Iemitsu had confiscated all or part of the domains of forty-three daimyo between 1632 and 1651, an average of over two for each year of his personal government, under his son, the average fell to less than one, or to be precise, 0.86.[12] However, in other matters relating to daimyo attainders, the Bakufu was also more lenient. In 1654, for example, after some three thousand of his peasants had run away to a neighboring tract of Bakufu land, Torii Tadaharu, the obsessively concupiscent daimyo of Takatō, in Shinano, was accused of misgovernment by a Bakufu official. Under earlier shogun this would have earned him disenfeoffment, but now his tenure of his domain was undisturbed. Retribution of a sort came to him ten years later, with his assassination at the hands of his own physician, but Ietsuna's Bakufu failed to punish him at all.[13]

11. For the Iemitsu figures, see Fujino Tamotsu, *Bakuhan taisei shi no kenkyū*, pp. 251–52; for the 1600–51 figures, see Kurita Motoji, *Edo jidai shi, jō*, pp. 283ff.

12. Tsuji Tatsuya, *Kyōhō kaikaku no kenkyū*, p. 46.

13. *TJ* 41 ; 117; for Torii Tadaharu's death, see *Hankampu*.

The celebrated Date *sōdō* was to provide a still more flagrant example. When both sides of this extremely violent domain dispute were called to Sakai Tadakiyo's mansion for an enquiry before the Great Councilor and three Senior Councilors, one of the parties to the vendetta cut another down; yet, the affair did not result in the confiscation of any part of the enormous Date domain.[14] The principals and their families were punished severely enough, but the domain itself, and the Date family's possession of it, was untouched, reflecting the daimyo-dominated Bakufu's concern with han order and stability of tenure. The same concern can be seen in the settlement of a dispute within the Honda family's domain at Kōriyama handed down by the Senior Councilors in 1671. The original domain of 150,000 koku was simply divided amongst the rival claimants in an attempt to keep everybody happy.[15]

The sluggishness which had overtaken the Bakufu's confiscation policy revealed itself also in a reluctance to transfer daimyo from one fief to another. Between 1632 and 1651, in the years of Iemitsu's personal government, daimyo were moved on no fewer than 117 occasions, an average of perhaps six per year. Under Ietsuna, where the years between his accession in 1651 and his death in 1680 produced only forty-seven examples of daimyo movement, the annual average sagged to less than two. This slackening of what had once been a torrent of transfers had its impact on the "bureaucratic fief" principle, which, as described in the previous chapter, suddenly lapsed during these years.[16]

Similarly, the three decades of Ietsuna's incumbency reveal a notable absence of any large-scale building or repair projects. Sasaki Junnosuke, in his studies of Suwa Han, has found that it suffered few or no Bakufu impositions during these years, and a glance at the records of a domain like Kokura reveals a like hiatus, with only routine matters like guard duty at Edo and visits to Nikkō to disturb the even tenor. Instead of contributing any money to the Bakufu, the daimyo received a loan of fifty kan of silver in 1660 to help with repairs to Kokura Castle. The curious decision not to rebuild the keep of Edo Castle after the great

14. Kitajima Masamoto, ed., *Oie-sōdō*, pp. 168–69.
15. Ibid., p. 203.
16. Calculated from Fujino, *Bakuhan*, pp. 718ff.

fire of 1657, by which the Bakufu was divested of one of its most unequivocal symbols of ascendancy, was taken by Hoshina Masayuki, daimyo of Aizu, acting in Ietsuna's name. Here, too, the same pattern emerges; the Ietsuna years provided daimyo with a long respite between the feverish castle-building of the first fifty years, and the civil engineering demands later to be introduced by Tsunayoshi.[17]

In other areas of Bakufu power, there also appeared slight but unmistakeable signs of relaxation. It was in the 1660s that daimyo were permitted to issue their own currency, and domains like Kaga and Sendai came to reassert control over goods passing across their borders. By 1667 Bakufu inspectors were instructed not to bother obtaining maps of the domains and castles allotted to their scrutiny. Until the 1660s the sankin kōtai system, irrespective of its formal wording, had required not only the daimyo but their chief vassals as well to send their children to Edo as hostages to ensure a still greater control of han government, but this was another casualty of the Ietsuna period.[18]

This is all part of an undeniable softening in the Bakufu's approach to the daimyo and their rights to their domains. Such detachment, appearing in a Bakufu dominated by fudai daimyo, was no coincidence; the proof is to be found in the abrupt policy reversal which followed the entry of a fresh group of "new men" into positions of influence under the next shogun.

Tsunayoshi

In the person of Tsunayoshi, the fifth shogun, the Tokugawa struck back. Ietsuna's death in 1680, in his fortieth year—since he left no issue—gave the title of shogun to his younger brother Tsunayoshi, Iemitsu's fourth son, who was then thirty-four years of age. The difference between the two brothers could hardly

17. For Suwa, see Sasaki Junnosuke, "Bakuhan kankei ni okeru fudai daimyō no chii," *Nihonshi kenkyū* 58 : 16; for Kokura, see *Buzen sōsho*, vols. 12, 13, passim; for information on the Edo Castle keep, see Murai Masuo, *Edo-jō*, p. 102.

18. For currency, see Chihōshi Kenkyū Kyōgi-kai, eds., *Chihōshi kenkyū hikkei*, pp. 163ff.; for Kaga and Sendai, see Ōkubo *et al*, eds., *Nihon no ayumi*, 3 : 153–54, as well as Sasaki Junnosuke, *Daimyō to hyakushō*, pp. 118ff; for Bakufu inspectors, see *OKS* p. 674, and for *sankin kōtai*, see Hanseishi Kenkyūkai, eds., *Hansei seiritsu*, pp. 805–06.

have been more conspicuous. Where Ietsuna had been frail, retiring, and content to leave government to whomsoever chose to conduct it, Tsunayoshi came to the office of shogun a fully grown healthy man, with a mind of his own, and a decided interest in the principles and practice of good government. In an age when all politicians declared their interest in Sung Confucianism as a matter of convention, Tsunayoshi stood out, surpassing his contemporaries in his patronage of scholars and his unflagging enthusiasm for lectures on the Confucian classics.

Nor was his enthusiasm confined to Neo-Confucianism. The fifth shogun was also a Buddhist of exceptional piety, and left behind him an extraordinary record of devotion. Obsessed by Buddhism's prohibitions against the taking of life, he forbade the killing or maltreatment of domestic animals like horses and dogs, and declared it a criminal offense to eat the flesh of birds and beasts, extending his protection to deer, boars, and even the humble *unagi,* the freshwater eel, and the *dojō,* or loach. A particular affection for dogs prompted him to special efforts on their behalf, earning him the title of "Dog Shogun"; to kill a dog was a capital crime, to wound one could result in banishment, and anybody who failed to treat dogs with respect, or who abandoned pups, risked a term of imprisonment. In 1695, homes for strays were established at Nakano and Ōkubo, on the outskirts of Edo, with daimyo assistance. By the time Tsunayoshi died, a daily 300 koku of rice was necessary to feed the 50,000 dogs being housed there.

No Tokugawa shogun generated more hostility than Tsunayoshi. Even the *Tokugawa jikki,* more or less obliged by the circumstances of its compilation to emphasize the positive aspects of those whose reigns it described, was terse with him. Of a policy which contained far more than its share of eccentricities, the *Jikki* observed that "no ordinary ruler would have committed excesses like this." Hearing of Tsunayoshi's death, the Kyoto courtier Konoe Motohiro was to note in his diary that "not one of the thirty years of this shogun's rule produced anything auspicious. The unhappiness of the people increased day by day, until of late they looked forward only to the end of his reign." [19]

19. For Tsunayoshi and his dogs, see the quotation from *Tōdaiki* contained in Kobata Atsushi, *Kinsei shakai,* pp. 185–86; for food and lodging

Undoubtedly, much of the opprobrium was deserved. He was an odd man—irascible, censorious, fanatical, probably mad. It is likely that animals were of greater concern to him than were the mass of his subjects; the rigor with which these laws were enforced in Edo is suggested in Arai Hakuseki's recollection that "tens of thousands of people were accused of these crimes, too many to count" (*OSK*, p. 225). Nevertheless, Tsunayoshi was accused of considerably more than mere lack of humanity. He has come down to us with the additional image of a notorious homosexual, so frantic in his pursuit of handsome companions that he was prepared to entice them with positions of prestige, power, and profit in his administration, and in so doing was content to ignore the rights of the fudai daimyo who were his traditional advisers.

It is on this point that the popular picture of the fifth shogun deserves attention. The malevolence of his critics was not directed at his sexual deviance, for the same taste had been accepted without adverse comment in his father, Iemitsu. What rankled was that, by whatever process they were selected, Tsunayoshi's favorites were outsiders. Their entry into the Bakufu dislodged the fudai daimyo from positions of authority, and their advice to the shogun was not always to daimyo taste. It is not difficult to trace, behind the usual descriptions of Tsunayoshi and his government, the enmity of daimyo whose privileges, sanctified as never before by three decades of immunity, now seemed likely to be overturned. Tsunayoshi's policies may in part have been inspired by doctrinaire piety, but not entirely so. In certain areas his motives were a good deal more pragmatic. They were designed to restore the personal prerogative of the shogun in the face of those who had been content, under Ietsuna, to participate or to acquiesce in its dismantling.[20]

In 1680 Tsunayoshi succeeded to a Bakufu largely in the control of the Great Councilor, Sakai Tadakiyo, and a group of

---

for the dogs, see Kodama, *Genroku jidai*, p. 301, and Shinji "Tokugawa Tsunayoshi," p. 32. The quotation from the *Jikki* is used in Tsuji, *Kyōhō*, p. 39, while that from Konoe is to be found in Kobata, *Kinsei shakai*, p. 191.

20. For the homosexual motive in Tsunayoshi's choice of companions, see Kodama, *Genroku jidai*, p. 293, where the *Sannō gaiki* is used, and also Donald Shively, "Tokugawa Tsunayoshi, the Genroku Shogun," in *Personality in Japanese History*, ed. Albert Craig and Donald Shively, pp. 97ff.

Senior Councilors, none of whom he had chosen. Had they remained, Tsunayoshi could have done little to assert his own authority, so he countered in the only way possible. Within twelve months, the key figures had gone. Sakai Tadakiyo was forced into retirement, to the amazement and unease of all, and two of the inherited Senior Councilors were abruptly turned out. On a third, Hotta Masatoshi, the shogun lavished so much attention and so many favors (bringing his enfeoffment from 40,000 to 130,000 koku within the brief space of four years) that Masatoshi, despite his fudai daimyo background, seemed more akin to the new men of the 1630s than to Sakai Tadakiyo, whom he replaced as Great Councilor.[21]

Apart from Masatoshi, however, the new shogun largely ignored the Senior Councilors, and after Masatoshi's assassination in 1684, did so completely. In obedience to the precedent of the previous reign, he created them, but he no longer used them. He attempted to limit their authority by insisting that reports from Bakufu magistrates come straight to him, and not go to the Councilors at all, and by forbidding daimyo to lobby with the Councilors.[22] Instead, his confidants and advisers were those linked to him by personal, not institutional, bonds. The first, appointed in 1681 to the position of Grand Chamberlain, with status equivalent to that of Senior Councilor, was Makino Narisada.

Narisada, born in 1636, just ten years before the man he was destined to serve, was the son of a hatamoto. His father had become a member of Tsunayoshi's household in 1648, when the future shogun was just an infant, with three elder brothers standing between him and the succession. Narisada, too, was to enter Tsunayoshi's service sometime during the 1650s, and by 1670, when his master was made daimyo of Tatebayashi, Narisada became his chief adviser. Here he would have remained, with his stipend of 3,000 koku, had Tsunayoshi's brothers lived. Since they did not, he was the new shogun's first choice as personal adviser in 1680, continuing in this capacity until retirement in 1695. Engelbert Kaempfer, who met him in Edo in 1691, de-

21. For unease about Sakai, see Tsuji, *Kyōhō*, p. 44, and, for Hotta Masatoshi's likeness to "new men" see p. 58.

22. For attempts to reduce the authority of the Senior Councilors, see ibid., pp. 102–03; for daimyo, see *TJ* 42 : 379.

scribed him as "formerly Chief Tutor to the now reigning Monarch, before he came to the Crown," and "now his chief favourite, and the only person whom he absolutely confides in." Apart from noting the Grand Chamberlain's interest in Dutch cheese, and remarking with approval on his "manly and german-like countenance" (being himself a native of Westphalia), it is significant that Kaempfer also chose to comment on that one aspect which unmistakeably identified Narisada as a weapon of personal government. By repute, observed the European, the Japanese politician was "no ways given to ambition." Makino Narisada was his master's man, as shown both by his personal proximity to the shogun and the magnitude of his rewards, for he rose in status from a hatamoto of 2,000 koku to a daimyo of 80,000 koku.[23]

If both Bacon and Machiavelli would have recognized Makino Narisada as an agent of autocracy, they would have been no less approving of the man, twenty years his junior, who was to inherit his prominent position in the shogun's counsel. Yanagisawa Yoshiyasu was also the son of a hatamoto assigned to Tsunayoshi at a time before it seemed possible that he should ever become shogun; in this Yoshiyasu resembled Narisada, but, where the latter's father had a respectable enfeoffment of 5,000 koku, Yanagisawa Yoshiyasu's father held only 160 koku and a supplementary allowance of 370 hyō. At the age of sixteen, Yoshiyasu had been assigned to Tsunayoshi as a page—a connection which in itself recalled Iemitsu and his personal advisers, most of whom had launched their careers from a similar position—and, together with his master, gradually increased in influence and prosperity. From an initial enfeoffment of 500 koku, he came to hold a domain of 151,000 koku, the most meteoric progress in Tokugawa history; the former page was to become, next to Tsunayoshi, the most powerful man in Japan. Arai Hakuseki, who knew him at the zenith of his powers, said of Yoshiyasu that "affairs of state were conducted as he wished, and all the Senior Councilors did was to relay what he told them." [24]

23. The details of Makino's career are to be found in *Hankampu;* Kaempfer's opinions are in his *History of Japan,* 3 : 84.

24. For Yoshiyasu's background, see Kitajima Masamoto, "Makano Narisada to Yanagisawa Yoshiyasu," in *Edo Bakufu—sono jitsuryoku monotachi.* ed. Kitajima Masamoto, 2 : 1–32, and for his career, see *Saitama-ken shi,* 5 : 495–96. Details on Arai Hakuseki are to be found in *OSK* pp. 574–75.

Tsunayoshi's purge of the senior officials inherited from his elder brother, together with his unwillingness to look beyond personal companions for advice, has provided the foundation for a theory of studied neglect of the fudai daimyo. His employment of five tozama daimyo as Bakufu officials, (attributed to lust by the Sannō gaiki, with characteristic generosity) would seem to substantiate this. Some historians have gone further, noting the frequency with which Tsunayoshi punished his fudai daimyo. Of the forty-six daimyo attainted by the Bakufu during Tsunayoshi's rule, no fewer than twenty-nine were fudai, representing a surprising reversal of the proportions of previous reigns, which has led Tsuji Tatsuya, for example, to accuse Tsunayoshi of a deliberate malice and hostility toward the fudai.[25]

There is, however, little other evidence of conscious malice. Despite the appointment of five tozama to lesser positions, the office of Senior Councilor continued to be filled by fudai daimyo, and Tsunayoshi made no consistent attempt to reduce the scope of their formal duties. Nor did he ignore them. Akimoto Takatomo, for example, Senior Councilor between 1699 and 1707, who had inherited 18,000 koku from his adopted father, was awarded a fief increase to bring his domain to 50,000 koku, while Abe Masatake, Senior Councilor between 1681 and 1704, enlarged his 80,000 koku fief to 100,000 while in office. Some fudai, whether officials or not, provided Tsunayoshi with his companions, and rivaled him in the intensity of their devotion to No dancing.[26]

The number of fudai attainders under Tsunayoshi is indeed both remarkable and undeniable, but it is difficult to see any implacable hostility in this. If the intention behind them was to purge the Bakufu, and Japan, of the "overmighty subject," one might have expected the fifth shogun to set his aim rather

25. The tozama daimyo were: Yamanouchi Toyoakira and Katō Akihide as Junior Councillors, Matsuura Takashi as Superintendent of Temples and Shrines, and Nambu Naomasa and Kanemori Yoritoki, both as Grand Chamberlain. For this, as well as for the judgment of the Sannō gaiki, see Kodama, Genroku jidai, p. 293. Tsuji's opinion is to be found in Kyōhō, pp. 39ff., and the attainder figures are on p. 47 of the same work.

26. For Akimoto, see Saitama-ken shi, 5 : 496–97, and for Abe, see "(Tanakura) Abe kafu." For an example of a fudai No enthusiast, see Imaizumi Shōzō, Nagaoka no rekishi, 1 : 74.

higher up the fudai ladder. The greater majority of those whose domains were confiscated were only small daimyo. True, Sakai Tadakiyo, one of the greatest of the fudai, was forced out of office, but this can more easily be attributed to his position and policy than to his status. Had it been otherwise, Tsunayoshi's hostility would have been transferred intact to Sakai Tadakata, who as Tadakiyo's son and successor shared in that status. Instead, relations between them were uniformly cordial, and included an official promotion for Tadakata to the post of Superintendent of Temples and Shrines before bad health cut short his career.[27]

Nevertheless, although it is not easy to sustain the argument that Tsunayoshi was actively waging a campaign against the fudai in particular, it is quite plain that he was far more strict in his handling of all daimyo than his predecessor had been. Eccentric though his policy was in many other respects, he is to be seen here as a man attempting, with the assistance of personal friends, to reestablish the prerogatives of his position.

As was his custom with whatever he undertook, Tokugawa Tsunayoshi set about restoring the shogunal authority with vigor and wholehearted commitment. No sooner had he removed from office all who might have hindered him than he began to make use of his powers with a severity not seen since Iemitsu's death in 1651. Where his elder brother Ietsuna had confiscated domains at a rate of 0.86 per year with an annual average of 26,000 koku, Tsunayoshi doubled the rate to 1.6 and 57,000 koku per year. The difference between the two reigns in this context reflects not opportunity, but attitude. Tsunayoshi was simply more severe. In the famous Echigo sōdō, the domainal succession dispute which embroiled one of the largest domains, Tsunayoshi gave notice of his new attitude. Although the succession had been formally decided by the Bakufu at the end of the previous reign, the new shogun declared his displeasure at the way the matter had been handled and called all parties before him for his personal adjudication. His decision, handed down the following day, was as ruthless as the previous settlement had been lenient and must have proved deeply disquieting to the other daimyo who had been present at the hearing. The enormous

27. *Gumma-ken shi,* 2 : 47–49.

Echigo domain was to be confiscated, as were the fiefs of two cadet branches which had failed in previous attempts at internal concilation. Two of the principals in the vendetta were ordered to disembowel themselves, and many others were exiled.[28]

The Kōriyama sōdō, which erupted afresh the following year, gave the daimyo fresh cause for anxiety. This particular dispute had been thought settled under Ietsuna, by a conciliatory decision which, simply by dividing the Honda domain at Kōriyama between the two contending parties, preserved the baronial prerogative, and so pleased everybody. However, it was a decision which failed to please the new shogun who, in 1682, reviewed the case, and, reasserting Tokugawa supremacy over the daimyo, confiscated the 60,000 koku fief of one of the disputants. There was little comfort to be had from this decision, and little more from Tsunayoshi's treatment of Ogasawara Nagatane, who saw his fief at Nakatsu reduced for his scandalous pursuit of women, a trait which in the case of his predecessor had merely incurred official disapproval.[29]

Hand in hand with this expansion in confiscations came a freer use of the Bakufu's power to order fief transfers. In answer to the rate of transfers under Ietsuna, rather less than two per year, Tsunayoshi diligently built up a record of 123 instances of fief movement, an average of more than four a year, which, although short of Iemitsu's best, set a pace which was never to be repeated.[30] The movement here is also reflected in a reassertion to the "bureaucratic han" principle. It was revived in Iwatsuki Han, for example, and many others, and can be seen at work in the career of somebody like Inaba Masamichi, a Master of Shogunal Ceremony and Superintendent of Temples and Shrines, who, until his resignation in 1685 held a Kantō domain at Odawara. After resigning he was transferred to Takada, in Echigo. Later in Tsunayoshi's reign, when Masamichi reentered Bakufu office as a Senior Councilor, he was moved back from the Japan Sea coast into another Kantō domain, this time at Sakura.[31]

28. The confiscations are referred to in Tsuji, Kyōhō, p. 46, while the Echigo dispute is covered in Kitajima Masamoto, ed., Seiji shi, 2, pp. 163–64, and Kodama, Genroku jidai, pp. 279–81.

29. For Kōriyama, see Kitajima, Oie-sōdō, p. 213, and for the Ogasawara, see Kuroya Naofusa, Nakatsu han shi, p. 40.

30. Calculated from Fujino, Bakuhan, pp. 718ff.

31. "Inaba kafu."

Tsunayoshi, while busily taking land from daimyo and moving them around, also attempted to augment the Bakufu's own landholdings with a spirit which had not been seen since Iemitsu's time and was never to appear again. After his death, the Bakufu not only failed to expand its territorial possessions, but even allowed them to decrease, making Tsunayoshi's reign the last occasion on which the Bakufu made more than a desultory claim to this prerogative.[32] In 1692, for example, when the Kanemori were moved to a new domain in Dewa, the Bakufu appropriated their former landholdings in the mountains at Takayama, placing them under the control of a daikan, an official who was appointed by, and responsible to, the Bakufu alone.[33] Similarly, when the Mizuno lost their domain at Fukuyama in 1698, the land was confiscated by the Bakufu, placed under a daikan, and a survey of it ordered from the Ikeda of Okayama. When this revealed that the Mizuno had built up the productivity of the domain from its stated 100,000 koku to an actual amount of 150,052 koku, the Bakufu gave 100,000 koku of it to the next daimyo, Matsudaira Tadamasa, and pocketed 50,052 koku of the most productive land in the old Mizuno domain.[34] Much the same thing happened at Kuwana in 1703.[35] Arai Hakuseki was to note as one of the characteristic policies of Tsunayoshi's government that "whenever daimyo or hatamoto had their fiefs transferred, the fertile fields and places blessed with mountains, forests, rivers and marshes were all made Bakufu domain; the remainder was given away as private domain" (OSK p. 329). In doing this, the Bakufu was doing no more than exercising the right—tacitly acknowledged by all daimyo—to ownership of all land, and in particular to those areas not specifically given in fief. However, it was a right which, used infrequently enough before Tsunayoshi, was not used at all after his death.[36]

Appropriately, in this renewed use of centralized powers under Tsunayoshi, Bakufu impositions upon daimyo also increased. From this time, for example, Suwa Han was subject to increasing demands for various forms of guard duty. The custom of sending

32. Kitajima Masamoto, Edo Bakufu no kenryoku kōzō, pp. 327–31.

33. Wakabayashi Kisaburō, Maeda Tsunanori, p. 171.

34. Fukuyama-shi shi, 2 : 394.

35. Kuwana-shi shi, 1 : 366.

36. Ōishi Shinzaburō, "Genroku, Kyōhō-ki no keizai dankai," in Nihon keizai-shi taikei, ed. Furushima Toshio, pp. 49–51.

daimyo to Nikkō as Bakufu deputies was begun in 1682, and in 1703–04, with a project involving the Yamato river, the practice of levying contributions for civil engineering projects, defunct since the late sixteenth century, was revived. There was also a new severity in the matter of Bakufu loans to daimyo. In 1681, not long after assuming office, Tsunayoshi began to demand the repayment of old debts, some of which had been outstanding since daimyo had borrowed money to repair damage suffered in the great fire of 1657. Some, indeed, dated back to the time of the Osaka campaigns, over sixty years earlier. Add to this such matters as the confiscation of the highly productive Besshi copper mine in 1704, and Tsunayoshi's conspicuous fondness for paying ceremonial visits to daimyo mansions, regardless of the cost to the host, and the impression of renewed Bakufu authority is overwhelming.[37]

There is a similar impression of vigorous interference in internal domain affairs. The hansatsu, which various fiefs had begun to issue, with Bakufu permission, in the 1660s, were finally banned in 1707, to the inconvenience of the thirty-four domains using them at that time. In 1699, when Mizuno Tadamitsu, daimyo of Okazaki, requested permission to have his nephew Tadateru declared his heir, one of Tsunayoshi's Grand Chamberlains suggested that he choose his brother Tadayuki instead, which he dutifully did. In 1685, when one of Mizuno Tadaharu's vassals borrowed money from a tradesman and then refused to repay it, Tadaharu was held responsible and dismissed from his joint appointment as Master of Shogunal Ceremony and Superintendent of Temples and Shrines, while the vassal was put to death. The erratic Honda Masatoshi, who had lost his domain for his part in the Kōriyama sōdō, and was exiled in the charge of the daimyo of Shōnai, found time there hanging heavily on his hands, and so amused himself by beating his two attendants, using a ladder on one occasion. They complained to the daimyo, Sakai Tadazane, who notified the Bakufu but received little

37. For Suwa, see Sasaki, "Bakuhan kankei," p. 22, and for Nikkō, see *Ōgaki-shi shi*, 1 : 408. For details on engineering, see Yoshizumi Mieko, "Edo Bakufu no kansatsu seido," *Nihon rekishi* 244 : 96, and for loan repayment, see Kodama, *Genroku jidai*, p. 378, and *TJ* 42 : 431. Information on the Besshi copper mine is contained in Kobata Atsushi, *Nihon kōzan no rekishi* 244 : 135.

thanks for it. Where a reprimand would have sufficed, Tadazane and his leading vassals were punished for their negligence in allowing such behavior in a man entrusted to their care. Tadazane was placed under house arrest for four months, and, for eight months, was obliged to let the shaven portions of his head go untrimmed as a token of remorse.[38]

In all these aspects, the policy of the Tsunayoshi years represents a distinct departure from that of the previous reign. By making forceful use of powers of attainder and of fief transfer, and by making fresh demands of the daimyo, Tsunayoshi's Bakufu, administered by his special companions, seemed both able and willing to overshadow the daimyo and, in so doing, restore itself to the position of hegemony laid down by its founders.

That Tsunayoshi himself was regarded with fear—if not respect—by his daimyo is beyond dispute. Date Tsunamura of Sendai is reputed to have said that, "when I had audiences with Ietsuna long ago, I always looked at his face. But in the case of the present shogun . . . I lower my head involuntarily." There is no doubt that the fifth shogun strived deliberately for this effect. Tsunayoshi may have been mad in many respects, but as an absolute ruler he could tell a hawk from a handsaw.[39]

Ienobu, Ietsugu

The death of Tsunayoshi at the beginning of 1709 was to alter the Bakufu in some respects. In 1683, Tsunayoshi's young son had died, and as the fifth shogun was never to beget another, he finally adopted as heir Tokugawa Ienobu, daimyo of Kōfu, and son of his long-dead brother Tsunashige. It promised to be a successful choice. The man who succeeded Tsunayoshi was very different from his eccentric uncle, being altogether more prudent, conciliatory and well balanced, and he proceded to give immediate proof of this.

Within ten days of his accession, even before Tsunayoshi had

38. For hansatsu, see Ono Masao, "Kambun, Empō-ki no ryūtsū kikō," in *Nihon keizai-shi taikei*, ed. Furushima Toshio, 3 : 376; for Mizuno Tadamitsu and Mizuno Tadaharu, see "Hiyōroku." Information on Sakai Tadazane is from *Tsuruoka-shi shi*, 1 : 315–16.

39. The quotation, from the *Sannō gaiki*, is translated by D. H. Shively, "Tokugawa Tsunayoshi, the Genroku Shogun," in *Personality in Japanese History*, ed. Albert M. Craig and Donald H. Shively, p. 94.

been interred at the family temple at Ueno, the new shogun
commanded a dramatic policy change. The laws which Tsunayoshi had introduced for the protection of his beloved animals,
and which he had intended to endure for a hundred years after
his death, were abruptly rescinded (*OSK* pp. 224–25). Five days
earlier, also, Ienobu had called the Senior Councilors before him
and informed them that, unlike the reign of his predecessor,
when all things had been decided by Yanagisawa Yoshiyasu, it
was his wish to hear their advice (*TJ* 44 : 5).

If indeed they believed him, the Senior Councilors were to be
disappointed. Ienobu was altogether more moderate and reasonable than Tsunayoshi had been, but he proved no more ready
to surrender his authority and no less jealous of his prerogatives. He too, like the fifth shogun, had come to the succession
as a mature man (forty-six years old), and, like the fifth shogun,
came experienced in directing the affairs of his own domain,
and had personal confidants and advisers of his own. Despite his
formal greeting to the Senior Councilors, and despite the prompt
retirement of Yanagisawa Yoshiyasu, Ienobu continued to seek
advice from those people of low rank who were well known to
him and, in this, as in the policies they suggested to him, he
resembled his predecessor far more than he differed from him.
Equally, like his predecessor, he and his confidants were slan-
dered for their pains.

As Tsunayoshi before him, Ienobu continued to appoint established fudai daimyo as his Senior Councilors during the three remaining years of his life, but he made little use of them. Instead, he relied on the advice and cooperation of two men, each
of whom had been associated with him in the years before he
became shogun. The first of these was Manabe Akifusa, whose
career had begun as an apprentice to a No dancer of the Kita
school; from here he had entered Ienobu's service, and, the two
men being much of an age, Akifusa became his trusted companion. Theirs was an association of nearly thirty years when
Tsunayoshi's death made Ienobu shogun, and it is not surprising
that it should have continued unchanged. Nor is it to be
wondered at that, as Ienobu's status rose, so did Akifusa's enfeoffment; from 3,000 koku at the outset of his career, he came
to hold 50,000 koku as daimyo of Takasaki, a progression which,

while more modest than that of Yanagisawa Yoshiyasu, is very much of the same sort.[40] Certainly it is not to be taken as evidence of dishonesty, for, like Makino Narisada, whom Kaempfer had considered "no ways given to ambition," Manabe Akifusa was judged "a selfless man," by the Confucian scholar Muro Kyūsō. Konoe Motohiro was to describe him as "a faithful servant of whom past and present cannot show the like" (*OSK* pp. 579–80).

The second of Ienobu's personal advisers was Arai Hakuseki, one of the greatest scholars of the Tokugawa period, who had entered Ienobu's service in 1693, after twenty years of sporadic employment under various daimyo. A man of more modest background could scarcely be imagined, for he had always earned his living as a scholar and writer under various daimyo patrons, and not even at the height of his influence in the Bakufu did his enfeoffment rise above 1,000 koku. Here also was an adviser whose origins were humble and who had been known to Ienobu for fifteen years before his accession. So trusted was he that Ienobu said of him: "What Buddhism calls 'two minds as one' (*ittai bunshin*) is the way it is between him and me. His mistakes are mine, and mine his" (*OSK* p. 309). Yet, despite this trust, and the consequent influence he wielded in Bakufu government and administration, he was even more self-effacing than Manabe Akifusa, holding at no time any formal official position. He spent his entire career as a *yoriai*, a hatamoto without office.[41]

At the end of his political career, after his return to private life, Arai Hakuseki wrote an autobiography, the *Oritaku shiba no ki*, in which he described the events of his years in power. From his description one is left in no doubt of the tension between the two "new men" and the Senior Councilors. "The men who were Senior Councilors," wrote Hakuseki in withering denunciation,

> were what are commonly known as "daimyo's sons," and they had neither studied the ways of antiquity, nor knew

40. Akifusa's career is described by Miyazaki Michio in "Arai Hakuseki to Manabe Akifusa," in *Edo Bakufu—sono jitsuryoku monotachi*, ed. Kitajima Masamoto, vol. 2.

41. For Hakuseki's career, see Miyazaki Michio, "Arai Hakuseki to Manabe Akifusa," in *Edo Bakufu—sono jitsuryoku monotachi*, ed. Kitajima Masamoto, and Tsuji, *Kyōhō*, pp. 81–82.

anything of the present. Usually they just transmitted the shogun's commands. They did not even know what the state of
government finances was, much less could they comprehend
the substance of complex political matters. When they came
before the shogun, so fearful were they of his power that
they were incoherent. Consequently the shogun would first
tell the Grand Chamberlain his own opinion, and then have
him transmit it to the Senior Councilors in a way they could
understand. The Senior Councilors similarly corresponded
with the Shogun through the Grand Chamberlain (*OSK*
p. 575).

Hakuseki had little reason to love the Senior Councilors, and
one must not accept the judgments in his autobiography too
readily, but this is nevertheless an interesting description of the
way government was conducted by Manabe Akifusa—the Grand
Chamberlain referred to in the text—and the shogun. Two
points are open to dispute: for one, Hakuseki was unduly modest
about his own role, which consisted of giving practical advice,
drawing up legislation, and then crushing opposition by citing
appropriate Chinese and Japanese precedents; for the other, the
Senior Councilors, although not Hakuseki's intellectual equals,
probably deserve more credit for their ability than the aggrieved
scholar was prepared to allow them. The rest of the portrayal,
however, seems substantially correct, and bears an uncanny resemblance to the words of Tokugawa Nariaki with which this
chapter begins. Despite the century and more between the two
descriptions, the situation in each is very much alike; the only
difference is in the sympathy of the author. Arai Hakuseki, as the
new man par excellence, sees the Senior Councilors as fools who
are very properly bypassed by men of ability, while Nariaki, as a
daimyo who is threatened by such activity, condemns this in
principle as a sign of the state in decay. The scholar has nothing
to lose, but the daimyo stands in considerable risk.

The situation was to change slightly with Ienobu's death in
1712, while still in his fiftieth year. His successor, his son Ietsugu,
was then only three years old and had only four more years to
live. Hakuseki, realizing that "after the death of [the former

shogun] . . . who had known me so well, my advice would no longer be accepted," considered resigning, but finally stayed on. He need scarcely have troubled himself, for it was one of the peculiarities of personal shogunal government that the personal advisers, the "new men," could not stand alone. They needed the shogun's active support to sustain their influence and could hardly hope for anything of this sort from Ietsugu.

No sooner had Ienobu died, in fact, than his political machine was in grave trouble. Akifusa and Hakuseki found themselves opposed by the Senior Councilors at almost every turn, even on the most trivial issues. Should the young shogun wear mourning for his father? Arai Hakuseki said yes, while his arch enemy, Hayashi Nobuatsu, official Confucian adviser to the Bakufu, said no, on the grounds that Chinese ceremonial restricted this to people above the age of seven, and the Senior Councilors agreed with him. This sort of division of opinion had frequently arisen under the previous shogun, who invariably settled the matter by overruling the Senior Councilors in Hakuseki's favor, but with Ienobu dead, it became far more difficult. To break this particular impasse, the new men had to draw on the support of Ienobu's mother and his widow (OSK pp. 413–17).

On the greater issues, like recoinage, and the reorganization of foreign trade at Nagasaki, the Senior Councilors were even more obstructive. Disliking the lack of antecedents of the Grand Chamberlain, whom they regarded as a usurper, and mistrusting the doctrinaire Confucianism of the scholar one of them had once called "a fiend," they made good use of their position to bring Bakufu affairs to a stalemate. Then, in 1716, when Ietsugu died, the Senior Councilors had their victory.[42]

Given that the policy adopted by the Bakufu in these years was more moderate than that of the Tsunayoshi period, and given also that the combined reigns of Ienobu and Ietsugu lasted for only seven brief years, only three of which saw capable direction from the shogun, there was little achieved for the Tokugawa in the struggle against the daimyo. However, enough was done to suggest that had these two reigns been longer more would have been won.

42. Tsuji, Kyōhō, pp. 78, 82, 91ff.

Certainly, as the rational Confucian scholar and the moderate shogun expunged the more bizarre policies of Tsunayoshi's reign, the number of fief confiscations fell markedly, yet, with an average of 0.7 confiscations, involving 25,000 koku per year, the Bakufu attitude was still conspicuously more severe than it was to be in the future, and the same was so of fief transfers. Impositions on daimyo, too, decreased, and they were ordered to refrain from the exchange of elaborate gifts, for Hakuseki was perturbed at the financial load they had to carry. The context in which this concern is voiced, however, makes it quite clear that his solicitude was not for the daimyo, whom he did not mention, but for the peasants, onto whose shoulders all such burdens inevitably found their way. He was not opposed to all impositions, and, significantly enough, had announced his intention of rebuilding the keep of Edo Castle, left untouched since the fire of 1657, before his fall from prominence prevented his carrying it out.[43]

It is also clear that Hakuseki's concern with the welfare of the peasantry was quite capable of being extended to the actual detriment of the daimyo's rights. In 1711, after some four thousand peasants from a daimyo domain had petitioned the Bakufu to dissolve their daimyo's control over them, and to substitute for it that of a neighboring Bakufu official, the Confucian scholar opposed the suggestion that they be punished. With some justice, he asked how it could be that "peasants who wish to belong to the Bakufu domain can be rebels against their superiors?" Such an attitude was obviously one which the daimyo, dependent for most of their income on a stable and docile peasantry, would find unpalatable. Even less to their taste would have been Hakuseki's assertion that all peasants should have the right to complain against bad conditions (*OSK* pp. 325–30).

There were other aspects of Bakufu policy during these seven short years which were symptomatic of a more rigorous attitude towards the daimyo. The Bakufu may not have increased its own landholdings, but it did reassert control over what it had by abolishing the system of *azukaridokoro*, under which in the past

43. For confiscation, see ibid., p. 46, and for fief transfers, see Fujino, *Bakuhan*, pp. 204–05; impositions are dealt with in *OSK* pp. 337–38, and Edo Castle is dealt with in Murai, p. 102.

many daimyo had been given almost total control over areas of Bakufu land adjacent to their domains. In 1709, too, on Ienobu's accession, an immediate repayment was ordered of one-third of all outstanding loans contracted before 1680. The elaborate instructions to barrier guards, cited in the first chapter, are a product of this period, as are a series of instructions to junkenshi, the Bakufu inspectors. These instructions were far more detailed and severe than any previously announced. The first of the new reign, for example, called the attention of the inspectors to a general lack of good government and crumbling of standards throughout the land, and reminded them of their duty to see this reformed. The inspection system had long since lost any meaning, and an attempt, under Ienobu and his two confidants, to breathe new life into it is a useful signpost to the policy of an era of Tokugawa autocracy which, while too short to be productive, had much promise.[44]

Yoshimune

Like Tsunayoshi and Ienobu before him, Tokugawa Yoshimune, the eighth shogun, came to his succession already mature. He was thirty-two in 1716, the year he took office, and had already been a daimyo in his own right for more than ten years. As a daimyo, like the fifth and sixth shogun, he had his own personal advisers in his domain, but he differed in that he did not take them with him into high Bakufu office. Nor did he seem prepared to follow the policy of centralization which had distinguished the Bakufu ever since 1680. In very many respects, despite a background which might have made him receptive to the enhancement of his own authority, Yoshimune adopted a low posture in his relations with the daimyo.

It is not difficult to see why he should have felt a certain constraint, for one element in his background set him apart from Tsunayoshi and Ienobu and placed upon him limitations to which they had not been subjected. Their claims to the succession were undisputed. Tsunayoshi had come to his position with-

44. For *azukaridokoro*, see Kitajima, *Kenryoku*, p. 331; for loan repayment, see Tsuji Tatsuya, *Tokugawa Yoshimune kō den*, p. 6; for guards and inspectors, see Ōkubo et al., *Nihon no ayumi*, 3 : 173, and *OKS* p. 679.

out difficulty, as the only surviving son of Iemitsu, the third shogun,[45] while Ienobu was formally designated Tsunayoshi's heir well before the latter's death. When the boy Ietsugu died, however, without brothers, cousins or uncles to succeed him, Iemitsu's bloodline vanished, leaving the Bakufu without a head, but with the responsibility of deciding the succession. Manabe Akifusa and Arai Hakuseki, having no influence of their own, were ill-equipped for survival in the power vacuum which followed and found themselves shouldered aside by the Senior Councilors, who selected the new shogun.

Their choice fell upon Ieyasu's great-great-grandson, Yoshimune, daimyo of Kii, but the identity of the man selected is perhaps less important than the circumstances of his selection. Regardless of his own feelings on the subject of Bakufu authority, or of his own convictions on the place of the fudai daimyo in government, it was highly likely that, once in office, he would defer to the Senior Councilors. As their nominee, attaining his position only with their imprimatur, he could do little else. So one might expect, and so it proved with Yoshimune, who, despite his reputation as the Bakufu reformer par excellence, introduced little to strengthen the Bakufu's hand against the daimyo and did much to limit the shogun's personal powers.

It is against these circumstances that one must see the haste with which the new shogun moved to disavow the people and policies of the preceeding reigns. Where the fudai daimyo had been ignored, Yoshimune was eager to assure them of his particular affection. Where the Senior Councilors had been estranged from the shogun, Yoshimune called on them to confer with him directly, and where Tsunayoshi had bluntly excluded them from access to reports from Bakufu magistrates, Yoshimune ordered the magistrates to report directly to the Senior Councilors, unless otherwise directed. Manabe Akifusa was dismissed, and Arai Hakuseki, having no office from which to be removed, simply surrendered his chambers and departed. No personal friends of

45. There is a theory that Sakai Tadakiyo had attempted to prevent this by inviting a member of the Imperial family to become shogun, but this has never been substantiated. Tsuji, in *Kyōhō*, pp. 43–44, considers it unlikely, suggesting that it was a rumor developed by people unable otherwise to explain the sudden dismissal of one so powerful.

the new shogun were to replace them. Instead he used only established fudai daimyo as his advisers.[46]

Yoshimune's eagerness to deny all sympathy with what had gone before extended even to the memory of his predecessors. Arai Hakuseki professed to see a dark symbolism in the decision to bury Ietsugu on the seventh day of the fifth month, which happened to be the hundred-and-first anniversary of the fall of Osaka Castle. "When there are so many months and days in a year," he wrote, "why hold the funeral on this particular day?" (*OSK* p. 562). Although he did not say so, he obviously felt that the Bakufu had been taken over by enemies of the Tokugawa house, who took this opportunity to make an oblique declaration of allegiance to the long-dead rebels at Osaka. Without going quite so far, it is possible to see traces of a certain contempt. Was it frugality, for example, which lay behind Yoshimune's complaint that Ietsugu's coffin was too elaborate, and should be replaced by something more economical? Hardly, since it involved the waste of a coffin already made and the special construction of a new one.[47]

In this, as in other matters, like the austerity of the ceremonies commemorating Tsunayoshi's death and the seventh anniversary of Ietsugu's death, when the sutras were chanted only 1,000 times instead of the customary 10,000, there is rather more involved than mere personal animosity. Each such economy, while it saved very little, served to reduce the position of the shogun, and, by comparison, render the daimyo less inferior and subservient than they had previously been.[48]

Such was certainly the tenor of the eighth shogun's policy toward the daimyo. There were very few fief confiscations, for example—only twelve instances in almost thirty years, producing an annual average of 0.4 confiscations, and 10,000 koku. This was by far the lowest rate of Bakufu activity in this area that the Tokugawa period had yet produced. With so few

46. See chap. 3 for the subject of special treatment for the fudai. The direct conference with Senior Councilors is handled in Tsuji, *Kyōhō*, pp. 98ff., while the matter of magistrates' reports is covered in Ōishi Shinzaburō, "Kyōhō kaikaku," in *Iwanami kōza Nihon rekishi*, 11 : 276. For Manabe and Arai, see Tsuji, *Kyōhō*, p. 98.

47. Tsuji, *Yoshimune kō den*, p. 93.

48. Ibid.

attainders, direct appropriation of land by the Bakufu was unlikely; more, in 1720 Yoshimune turned his back on the policy
on Bakufu lands enunciated in 1713, just seven years earlier.
Where Hakuseki and Akifusa had restored the Bakufu's direct
control, through its daikan, of all parts of Bakufu land, no matter
how remote, under Yoshimune individual daimyo were again
given permission to take over the control of those areas of Bakufu
land which lay adjacent to their own domains.[49]

In fief transfers, too, his reign saw a new low, an average of a
little more than one such transfer for each of the years during
which he was shogun, a rate rather less than the previous low
point under Ietsuna. As a natural corollary the "bureaucratic
han" principle was abandoned, and, for the first time in the history of the Tokugawa Bakufu, those appointed to high official
positions from fiefs outside the Kantō were permitted to retain
them during their terms of office. Of the twelve daimyo appointed
to the office of Senior Councilor by Yoshimune, seven came from,
and retained possession of, domains outside the Kantō, setting a
mischievous precedent.

Yoshimune's reign was also notable for the mildness of the
burdens it laid upon the daimyo. Occasional impositions did continue, but not as a regular feature of Bakufu policy; rather, they
were exceptional, and none of them was particularly spectacular.
Indeed it is possible during this period to find examples of the
Bakufu itself bearing the cost of work—as it did for work on the
Ōi River in 1722—which would previously have been allocated
to daimyo. With the agemai-rei of 1722, described earlier, Yoshimune's Bakufu made its most ambitious demand of the daimyo,
but in order to carry it out gave as much in compensation as it
took away.[50]

The period also saw other strange reversals. Instead of confiscations, or impositions, we find the Bakufu actually borrowing a
large sum of money from the daimyo of Kaga. Where the former
shogun had taken great pains to build up Edo Castle as a
symbol of their power, we see Yoshimune giving his assent to the

<hr/>

49. See Tsuji, *Kyōhō*, p. 46 for confiscation, and Kitajima, *Kenryoku*, p. 331,
for Yoshimune's land policy.

50. Work on the Ōi River is referred to in Tsuji Tatsuya, *Tokugawa
Yoshimune*, p. 69.

destruction of a fence which had topped the outer walls, for the
reason that keeping it in good repair was too expensive. Pine trees
were planted in its place. Instead of forcing daimyo to contribute to Bakufu engineering projects, as Tsunayoshi had done,
the eighth shogun offered financial assistance to smaller domains
with projects of their own.[51] If Arai Hakuseki had favored the
reduction of the amount daimyo spent on formal gifts, Yoshimune did so to an infinitely greater degree (*OSK* p. 339).

Other signs of retreat were equally significant. The Tokugawa
Bakufu, so long as it maintained pretensions to supreme authority
in Japan, could not afford to neglect the numerical strength of
its support. Tsunayoshi, in permitting the expansion of the
Tokugawa vassal band—the hatamoto and gokenin—gave proof
of his awareness of this. Yoshimune, on the other hand, began to
retrench; some newcomers were dismissed, the employment of
others was limited to their lifetime alone, deliberately excluding
their children, while still others received no right of adoption, so
that if they died without issue their stipend would be confiscated.
The right of peasants to complain to the Bakufu against their
daimyo was yet another casualty of these years. In 1603, and again
in 1643, the Bakufu had guaranteed this right, and Hakuseki re-
affirmed it in 1711, but in 1721 Yoshimune was to ban all forceful
presentations of petitions, and in so doing cut peasants off from
all legal recourse against a daimyo who maltreated them. This
was a direct reinforcement of the daimyo's right to determine the
fate of his own peasantry, and the Bakufu was the weaker for it.
Then, in 1730, came permission to reissue the hansatsu which
Tsunayoshi had prohibited in 1707; it was a popular move among
the daimyo, at least twenty-seven of whom proceeded immediately
to take up where they had left off, followed in the years to come
by many others, all of whom were prepared to thus limit the
effectiveness of the national currency.[52]

51. The Kaga loan is mentioned in Ōishi, "Kyōhō kaikaku," pp. 307–08,
and the matter of the pine trees on the moat appears in Kitajima Masamoto,
"Mizuno Tadayuki," in *Edo Bakufu—sono jitsuryoku monotachi*, ed. Kitajima Masamoto, 2 : 81. For help to smaller daimyo, see Yoshizumi Mieko,
"Tetsudai bushin ni tsuite," *Gakushūin Daigaku Bungakubu kenkyū nempō*,
14 : 99–100, and *Keiroku hen*, 2 : 267–68.

52. The reduction in Tokugawa vassal numbers is mentioned in Tsuji,
Tokugawa Yoshimune, p. 19; Tsuji, *Kyōhō*, p. 100; and Tsuda Hideo, "Toku-

Tokugawa Yoshimune is best known to history as the architect of the Kyōhō Reforms, the man who tried gallantly to stem the flood of commercialization in Tokugawa Japan with his call for a return to the sterner virtues of a simpler age. He is renowned as a ruler who, while urging frugality on others, lived frugally himself, who sought men of talent for his administration, who asked the advice of the common citizens in conducting the affairs of state. He remains in the history books as a model of the Confucian virtues, in sharp contrast to those who preceeded him as shogun—Tsunayoshi the frivolous and spendthrift homosexual and Ienobu, the dupe of the ambitious No dancer and the dogmatic intellectual. Some of the praise is deserved, for he did reduce government expenditure, even if it meant abandoning the illusion of supremacy, and he did increase income, although at the cost of increased taxes. Many of his reforms indeed were of a sort with which daimyo could find themselves in agreement; nobody was likely to quarrel with a restoration of the manners and deportment of the good old days. Currency reforms and control over the price of rice, to avoid extreme fluctuations, were matters of benefit to all daimyo. So too was the attempt, successful for a time, to put the economic affairs of the Bakufu on a more stable footing. In the context of this argument, however, the most important aspect of the reforms is that they took place at the expense of nobody, except perhaps the peasants. Certainly the daimyo did not suffer from Bakufu pretensions to authority under Yoshimune. He provided capable, efficient, and above all predictable government within decently circumscribed limits. For this he received the praise of his peers, and amply repaid the Senior Councilors for their choice.

Ieshige, Ieharu

In 1745, the eighth shogun retired to spend the remaining six years of his life coaching his son and successor in the art of government. It was a thankless task, by all indications. Ieshige, the new shogun, although holding office from his thirty-fourth year

gawa Yoshimune to Tanuma Okitsugu," in *Nihon jimbutsu-shi taikei*, ed. Hayashi Motoi, 4 : 75. The ban on petitions is mentioned in *Tsuruoka-shi shi*, 1 : 404, and the hansatsu calculations are from Chihōshi Kenkyū Kyōgi-kai, eds., *Chihōshi kenkyū hikkei*, pp. 163ff.

until his retirement at the age of forty-nine, was never to be an ornament to it. That he was no outstanding ruler is to be gauged from the space allotted to him in the *Tokugawa jikki*. With each shogun, the *Jikki* would first give a chronological description of the events of his reign and then launch into its obligatory hymn of praise, dredging up anecdotes—whether true or not—illustrative of his wisdom, piety, courage, and wit. The *Jikki* managed to fill 204 pages with such stories about Yoshimune; for Ieshige, the ninth shogun, it could find only enough for three pages, pointing out apologetically that "as he grew older, his health gradually became more frail" (*TJ* 46 : 769). He is generally believed to have been sickly, feebleminded, and afflicted with a stammer so severe as to render him incoherent—a picture of decrepitude which the sly suggestion, found in the *Zoku sannō gaiki,* that he had "many affairs with his maidservants," serves to make only more abject.[53]

His son Ieharu, who became shogun at the age of twenty-four, when his father retired in 1760, fares a little better at the hands of historians (since almost all ignore him) and even receives twenty-eight pages of individual attention from the *Tokugawa jikki,* but he, like his father, could find no place in a list of active and influential shogun. Though sick in neither body nor mind, he nonetheless failed to leave a distinctive mark on the government of which he was the head.

Paradoxically, it was from these two most unpromising rulers, the shambling degenerate and the pallid nonentity, that support came for a new onslaught on daimyo prerogatives. The forty years (1746–86) which made up their reigns saw some reassertion of the authority of the Tokugawa Bakufu, not on the part of the ninth and tenth shogun themselves, but from two men who relied implicitly on their support. Ōoka Tadamitsu and Tanuma Okitsugu were to dominate the politics of the Bakufu in this period, the former as Grand Chamberlain, until his fatal illness in 1760, and the latter first as Grand Chamberlain and then as Senior Councilor. Like all other willing servants of Bakufu

---

53. The usual impression of Ieshige can be found in Kitajima, *Seiji shi, 2,* p. 242. The comment from *Zoku sannō gaiki* is to be found in Saiki Kazuma, "Tokugawa shōgun seibō narabini saishō kō," in *Rekishi to jimbutsu,* ed. Nihon Rekishi Gakkai, p. 437.

autocracy, both rose from low rank and established a close personal relationship with the shogun they served. They too were as unpopular with contemporaries as any other newcomers to government.

According to hoary legend—never verified, and suspect as all such simplistic explanations should be—Ōoka Tadamitsu owed his eminence to two skills. He was a deft mimic and could amuse tumbledown Ieshige with his imitations, and he was also the only member of the shogun's entourage who could ever understand what Ieshige, behind his stutters, was trying to say. This may or may not be true. Certainly Ieshige's sudden retirement in 1760, less than a month after Tadamitsu's death, suggests a very strong tie between them. There is enough in his background and career, however, to make an explanation of this tie in terms of such arcane skills unnecessary. Like all other "new men," Ōoka Tadamitsu was the protégé, confidant, and old personal friend of the shogun he served. He had emerged from a modest background, for his father was a minor Tokugawa vassal, with an annual income of 300 koku. In 1724, when he was only fifteen, Tadamitsu was assigned as a page to Ieshige, then thirteen. By the time Ieshige had succeeded to his father's office, therefore, Tadamitsu was a friend of more than twenty years, and Ieshige lost little time in showing how much he valued that friendship. As soon as Yoshimune was safely out of the way, the ninth shogun began to give Ōoka Tadamitsu the rewards associated with "new men," making him a daimyo in 1751, Grand Chamberlain in 1756, and ultimately awarding him a fief of 20,000 koku at Iwatsuki.[54]

Tanuma Okitsugu was to follow a similar path a few years later, but, living longer, his path led further. His father, too, was a Tokugawa vassal of low rank, with 600 koku, who had originally come from the Kii domain with Yoshimune in 1716. Tanuma, like Ōoka, was assigned to Ieshige as a pageboy, and won his confidence to such an extent that in 1751 he was made Grand Chamberlain, and in 1758 became a daimyo in his turn. On his retirement, Ieshige commended Tanuma to his son,

54. *Saitama-ken shi*, 6 : 34; Shinji Yoshimoto, *Edo jidai no buke no seikatsu*, pp. 111–14.

Ieharu, then twenty-three years old, and the new shogun retained his services, showering him with favors until Tanuma, by the end of his career in 1786, was daimyo of Sagara, with an enfeoffment of 57,000 koku.[55]

With the direction of Bakufu policy in the hands of such men, each of them free of traditional ties to certain tracts of land and certain groups of men, one can see the pendulum swinging once more in the direction of greater Tokugawa authority over the daimyo. True, in government, there was no overt hostility toward the fudai daimyo; the office of Senior Councilor continued to be filled whenever a vacancy appeared, and filled, moreover, from among fudai daimyo ranks. Both Ōoka and Tanuma were to find particular allies among them. But nevertheless, historians have noted a perceptible waning of the influence of fudai daimyo upon Bakufu policy during these years and, not entirely coincidentally, a hardening of attitude toward the daimyo in general.[56]

One indication of this is to be found in Bakufu attainder policies. Where the rate of fief transfers remained constant and low throughout the eighteenth century, no matter who guided Bakufu policy, these years of revived shogunal authority did begin with a small but significant upturn in daimyo punishments. Yoshimune had chosen not to use his powers in this sphere and, as a result, had confiscated domains only when there was no reasonable alternative. Under Ieshige, by contrast, there were four instances of attainder between 1750 and 1760, all of them for reasons which Yoshimune would have ignored.[57] The case of Kanemori Yorikane, daimyo of Gujō (38,000 koku), is particularly interesting, for it developed out of a complaint about him that his peasants had made to the Bakufu. This, in itself, Yoshimune would not have allowed, but Ieshige's Bakufu did, and after confiscating Kanemori's domain, the Bakufu proceeded to discover why an attempt had been made to conceal the incident. In their investigation, the censors found evidence implicating a Junior Councilor, whose domain was confiscated as punishment,

55. For Tanuma, see Hall, *Tanuma Okitsugu*, pp. 34ff., and also Doi Akitaka, "Tanuma Okitsugu, Okitomo fushi," in *Edo Bakufu—sono jitsuryoku monotachi*, ed. Kitajima Masamoto, 2 : 93ff.

56. Kitajima, *Seiji shi*, 2, p. 172.

57. Ibid., p. 244.

and a Senior Councilor, Honda Masayoshi, who was in consequence stripped of his office (*TJ* 46 : 716, 719, 724).

Apart from these instances, the reigns of the ninth and tenth
shogun show little in the way of direct attacks on the daimyo.
Neither period produced any particularly severe impositions
upon the daimyo, although it is perhaps significant that Ieharu's
formal progress to Nikkō in 1776 was the first example of its
kind for nearly fifty years. It represented the revival of a custom
which cannot have been welcomed by the daimyo, who were
forced to go too. The Okudaira of Nakatsu spent 14,792 ryō on
their part of the ceremony, and other daimyo can hardly have
spent less.[58]

It was in its commercial policy that the Bakufu in these years
was to continue its struggle against daimyo independence. In a
world of growing commercialization, in which domain participation was mounting steadily, the Bakufu was falling behind. By the
latter part of the eighteenth century, the Tokugawa economic
position was no longer what it had once been, and, with this
in doubt, Tokugawa hegemony became still less certain. Slowly
and uncertainly the daimyo were beginning to adjust to an economy in which rice, the traditional source of all wealth, was losing
in importance to cash crops of various sorts, like cotton, dyes,
and tobacco, and in which a new commercial life was emerging
independently in the countryside. The Bakufu was rather slower
to confront these new realities, but in this period, particularly
under the direction of Tanuma Okitsugu, we can see the demar-
cation of a new arena on which the Bakufu-daimyo struggle was
to take place. For the first time, the Bakufu began to use its
political weight to challenge daimyo commercial enterprises.

The unfolding of this policy took various forms. One was the
renewed attempt—unsuccessful—to prohibit the use of hansatsu;
had it been effective, daimyo would have encountered much
more difficulty controlling the production of their domains. In
1755, notes based on gold and copper were declared illegal, and
a further, all-inclusive ban was announced in 1759.[59] In various
ways, too, the Bakufu insisted on greater knowledge of domain
productivity. In 1763, for instance, daimyo were instructed to

58. Kuroya, p. 335.
59. Ochiai, p. 397, and *TJ* 46 : 740.

provide Bakufu financial magistrates with information about the location and production of copper mines in their domains, fearing an attempt to wrest this source of wealth away from them. In 1766, this was followed by new action to regulate the sale of copper (*TJ* 47 : 113, 224).

Equally threatening was the new interest being shown in the marketing of goods of all sorts. There were several attempts to reinforce the dominant position of Osaka in national commerce, against an increasing tendency for interregional trade to develop more freely (and more rationally) as producers began to send their goods, not to Osaka, but to wherever they could command the best price. One such attempt took the form of an order limiting the sale of oil to the city of Osaka in 1766 (*TJ* 47 : 214). Still more menacing, however, was the Bakufu's own entry into the world of commerce. This took two distinct forms, one of them conventional, since it involved the Bakufu competing as a form of daimyo domain with other domains. In the 1760s, for example, when the Bakufu came to have control of 90,000 koku of the best safflower-producing land in Japan, in the Yamagata area, it proceeded to assert the right to buy up the production of the whole area—much as Hikone had done with its Takamiya cloth—regardless of where the safflower was actually being produced.[60] In 1767, too, a similar attack was made on the cotton production of the Kantō (*TJ* 47 : 244). Later, in 1785, a Bakufu official was sent to Aizu to learn their wax-making process, a development which that domain, famous for its wax monopoly and jealous as all domains were of special technical secrets, cannot have welcomed (*TJ* 47 : 785).

It was the unconventional form of competition, however, that was the major danger, because here the Bakufu was competing not simply as a larger and more powerful domain, which was bad enough, but as the national government, with powers reaching to all corners of the country, and with the right to compel the daimyo to cease all competition of their own. Under Tanuma's guidance, the Bakufu began to offer patents of monopoly to merchant groups in Edo and Osaka, in return for which it was to be paid an initial fee and a percentage of the volume of

60. Kimura Motoi and Sugimoto Toshio, ed., *Fudai hansei no tenkai to Meiji ishin*, pp. 139, 167.

business. The Bakufu could be expected to use its political might to enforce the monopoly rights it granted, whether these conflicted with preexisting rights established by daimyo or not. Under Tanuma, such patents were granted for the purchase and distribution of copper, silver, brass, sulphur, alum, camphor, cinnabar, ginseng, cotton, both crude and processed oil, and *tawaramono*.[61] In effect, such measures put the Bakufu, and the Bakufu's favored merchants, into direct competition with the daimyo and their merchants. The advantage Edo had may be seen, for example, in the terms of the order of 1780 which set up the Iron Guild, where any iron produced anywhere in Japan was to be sent directly to Osaka, reported to the magistrate, and then turned over to the merchants of the Iron Guild. Having bought the iron at the low official price, these merchants could then sell it on the open market, and the profit—which would otherwise have gone to the daimyo or their agents—would be theirs, save for the fee they returned to the Bakufu (*TJ* 47 : 636–37). That such competition was resisted can be seen from a later order which—noting that some iron was being sold independently, long before it ever reached Osaka—reminded producers and sellers of their obligation to turn all iron over to the Iron Guild (*TJ* 47 : 757). That it was also effective, and therefore resented, is evident from the haste with which Tanuma's enemies moved to nullify the Bakufu's monopoly efforts after his overthrow (see the following section).

There was one other area in which Tanuma's government showed a new and dangerous enthusiasm for asserting its supremacy over the daimyo, and this was in the very sensitive area of food resources. The calamitous seasons of 1782 and 1783 were to bring unprecedented crop failures, and this, together with the disastrous eruption of Mt. Asama, combined to give northeastern Japan one of its worst recorded famines, the effects of which were to last for five years and more. Domains like Sōma and Sendai lost from eighty to ninety percent of their crop, and, in three years, over one million people died.[62] In the face of such an emergency, the Bakufu took up a position appropriate to a na-

61. *Tawaramono*, or baled goods, included dried sea slugs, dried abalone, shark's fin, dried cuttlefish, and various kinds of seaweed and kelp.
62. Kitajima, *Seiji shi,* 2, pp. 267–68.

tional government, and ordered the domains to sell all of their rice stores, warning that any infringement would be severely punished (*TJ* 47 : 741, 748). Nevertheless, however natural a stance for a national government, and however laudable in humanitarian terms, this cannot have failed to touch a nerve with daimyo accustomed to disposing only of as much rice as they had to and conserving what remained for just such an emergency of their own.

Of all Tokugawa political figures, Tanuma Okitsugu has come down to us as the most unsavory; despite some notable attempts to salvage his reputation, he is still regarded as the archetypal venal politician. "Nothing refreshes me more after a hard day's work on affairs of state," he is reputed to have said, "than coming home to a house full of gifts." His residence, it is claimed, was so besieged by those eager to buy his favor that their swords, stacked in the antechamber, resembled "a drawing of the waves of the sea." There is no reason to believe that such stories were true. As Ōishi Shinzaburō has shown, the three major sources of such colorful slanders are suspect for various reasons: the *Zoku sannō gaiki* is notoriously untrustworthy; the recollections of Uezaki Masayori were written to be presented to Matsudaira Sadanobu, Tanuma's enemy and successor, in the hope—subsequently justified—of official preferment; and the *Kasshi yawa* was written by a daimyo, Matsuura Seizan, whose impartiality is questionable, since he was brother-in-law to two of Sadanobu's chief lieutenants. What little conclusive evidence exists to convict Tanuma of corruption also implicates other senior Bakufu officials; they were not execrated, but Tanuma was.[63]

It is necessary to look at Tanuma's policies, not his ethics, to see why his prominent contemporaries should have been eager to force him out of office and then blacken his reputation. It is no accident that his downfall was brought on by a concerted opposition of daimyo and that Matsuura Seizan, his most damaging critic, was also a daimyo. Tanuma Okitsugu offered the Bakufu, beset by financial difficulties, an escape which cut squarely across a region reserved by the daimyo of Tokugawa

63. For the statement attributed to Tanuma, see Takahashi Shin'ichi, "Tanuma Okitsugu," in *Buke no sekai*, ed. Okada Akio, p. 157; for Ōishi's criticism of the sources, see his "Tanuma Okitsugu" article.

Japan as their own. The daimyo, as unenthusiastic at the prospect of a strong Bakufu as they were resentful of such strengthening taking place at their expense, found this unacceptable. As soon as the tenth shogun, Tanuma's protector, fell desperately ill in 1786, they banded together to force the new man out and replace him with someone more acceptable. The blackening of his reputation which followed dismissal was a natural part of the political process, for the only way sudden changes in administration and policy could be justified was in the language of Neo-Confucian moralism. With Tanuma the blackening was successful, for he had no articulate Arai Hakuseki to vouch for him to posterity.

Ienari and Matsudaira Sadanobu

Ieharu had only two sons, and since both predeceased him, he adopted in 1781 a distant cousin, a boy from the Hitotsubashi house, who, like himself, was a direct descendant of Yoshimune. It was this boy, Ienari, now fourteen years old, who was to become the eleventh Tokugawa shogun at Ieharu's death. Once again conditions favored a retreat from shogunal absolutism. Tanuma, unable to survive without the active support of the shogun, was gone already, and his nominees in official positions were finding their tenure every day more precarious. Into this power vacuum stepped the daimyo, just as they had done over a hundred years earlier when the young Ietsuna had become shogun, to tell their young ruler, with all deference and politeness, just what had to be done to restore the country to health.

Together, the daimyo of the sanke and the sankyō—one of whom was the new shogun's real father—decided on who should lead the Bakufu. Not unnaturally, the man they chose was one of their own, a younger son of the Tayasu house, who had been adopted by a lesser kamon daimyo and who already had notable success in four years of governing his domain at Shirakawa. This was Matsudaira Sadanobu, famous for the moralistic legislation known as the Kansei Reforms.

In the few years in which he had governed his own domain, Sadanobu had made himself a reputation as a skilled administrator in a time of unparalleled disaster in northeastern Japan.[64]

---

64. Shibusawa Eiichi, *Rakuō kō den*, pp. 27, 115–16.

Surrounded by famine on all sides, he sent agents outside his do-main to buy up rice wherever they could. Like all Confucian reformers, he launched a severe economy drive, paring adminis-trative and personal expenses to the bone, but then, stepping out-side the conservative Confucian mold, he had begun an aggres-sive search for new sources of income. Like many other daimyo, Sadanobu turned to cottage industries and cash crops; to en-courage a lacquer industry, he planted sumac and invited lacquer masters from other domains to migrate to Shirakawa. He was prepared to do no less to give his domain a paper industry, nor did he hesitate to invite from Kyoto, Edo, and Osaka people qualified to give instruction in various other marketable skills, like pottery-making, sake-brewing, weaving, and dyeing. At his suggestion, experiments were made in planting bamboo, sweet potatoes, tobacco, rushes, and various medicinal herbs, including wolfsbane (*torikabuto*) and ginseng, and in raising carp, catfish, and *shijimi*.[65] By such measures, it was said, the Shirakawa do-main was spared the ravages of the Temmei famine, and not one inhabitant died of starvation.

Such was the man, who in 1787, in his twenty-ninth year, was nominated to the office of Senior Councilor, a post to which he was shortly to add that of *hōsayaku*, personal adviser to the young shogun. As a daimyo, he had shown himself energetic and capable, instituting policies that placed the prosperity of the domain and the security of its sources of income above all other considerations. Around him was a group of followers, daimyo of all kinds, who had in common the experience of governing their domains during a time of exceptional hardship.[66]

As might be suspected from his background, and from the in-terests and convictions of those around him and those who fol-lowed him into office, Matsudaira Sadanobu was an opponent of big government. "The people belong to Heaven," he once wrote, "but since Heaven cannot govern them, it has provided the em-peror to do so; since the emperor cannot govern them on his own, he has established the daimyo to do so." This was a de-scription of the government of Japan with which most Japanese daimyo would have agreed, but which, significantly, omitted all

65. Ibid., pp. 49ff., 338, 72.
66. For a list of Sadanobu's daimyo supporters, see Imaizumi, 1 : 91.

reference to the Bakufu and the part it played in organizing the daimyo on the emperor's behalf. When, later, he came to draw up a list of instructions for Ienari, he emphasized that the shogun had merely been entrusted with the government of the provinces by the emperor and that therefore they were by no means to be regarded as his own property. Should he come to consider them as such, Sadanobu warned, there would be great suffering. In his own policies, drawn up in the shogun's name, Sadanobu made it clear that all he demanded of the Bakufu was that it keep its own financial affairs in order without infringing upon the rights of the daimyo, and that it provide a stable economic framework within which the daimyo could govern their domains.[67]

Nevertheless, though he could denigrate the Bakufu's national role, recent experience had shown that the power of the shogun was too open to misuse to allow him any freedom in his choice of personal companions. In a series of instructions written in 1788, Matsudaira Sadanobu showed just how seriously he regarded this matter. To the Senior Councilors, he warned: "You should take care in your selection of attendants and tutors for the young shogun." To Ienari himself, he urged discrimination in the choice of companions, drawing his attention to the important distinction between ministers of state, who, out of servile flattery, will tell a ruler only what he wants to hear, and those who, from loyalty and selflessness, are prepared to differ with the ruler and even reprove him for the general good. Just in case Ienari could not tell the difference, the office of personal political counselor was abolished, and he was informed that he would be advised exclusively by the Senior Councilors, who were all daimyo.[68]

No matter how much such advice was dressed in the language of Neo-Confucian statecraft, it is clear that Sadanobu's chief demand of the shogun was that he take counsel of his daimyo rather than seek it elsewhere. It was clearly a recommendation of a sort which people everywhere have been concerned to force upon autocratic rulers, in the hope of rendering government less capricious and their own position more secure, but no absolute ruler has ever cared for such advice. Ienari, after reaching ma-

67. Shibusawa, pp. 27, 115–16.
68. Ibid., pp. 113–14, 117–19.

turity, paid as little heed to these precepts as he did to Sadanobu's moralistic warnings against women and song.

In 1793, Sadanobu resigned from office, comparing himself to a valuable sword, which is used when needed and then restored carefully to its case, lest constant use dull its edge.[69] He had held power in the Bakufu for six years, assisted by a group of devoted followers.

It was not a long time, certainly not long enough to effect his stated aim of the restoration of Japanese manners and customs to the state of uncorrupted innocence prevailing under Ieyasu. But it proved sufficient to carry out the major part of his brief, which was the elimination of all traces of Tanuma Okitsugu and his policies. This was the area in which Matsudaira Sadanobu worked most rapidly and most effectively. There was no more logical starting point for a repudiation of Tanuma's government than an attack on his collaborators. As soon as Tanuma had been driven from his post, his opponents launched a purge on a scale never before known in Bakufu politics. In the bureau of finance, thirty senior officials were dismissed within a few months, while the bureau of public works lost twenty. Not even the highest Bakufu officials were immune, and although retribution came to them rather more slowly, it was no less sure. Within a year of Sadanobu's promotion to Senior Councilor, three of his colleagues in this post had been removed, and the Great Councilor, his formal superior, was forced to retire. It has been calculated that, in the eight years between Sadanobu's appointment to the Tamarinoma in 1785 and his resignation in 1793, some ninety-two Bakufu officials were punished, in varying degrees of severity, for dereliction or for too close an identification with Tanuma and his policies.[70]

Long before this process of renovation was done, and the positions of those purged filled with officials more acceptable, Matsudaira Sadanobu had turned to launch a violent onslaught on those of Tanuma's policies he considered objectionable. One by one the patents of monopoly which Tanuma had granted were rescinded, and the guilds dissolved—first the iron and brass guilds, in 1787, the ginseng guild later that year, then monopoly

69. Ibid., p. 321.
70. Ibid., pp. 121ff.; Kitajima, Seiji shi, 2, p. 294; Tsuda Hideo, "Kansei kaikaku," in Iwanami kōza Nihon rekishi, 12 : 241.

rights to Kantō oil seeds the following year, and to Kantō cotton in 1790, and so on.[71] In so doing, Sadanobu was once more restricting the sources of Bakufu income, deriving it instead from a more traditional source and one that interfered with nobody else—the land tax. Even here, significantly, his approach was not to acquire more land for the Bakufu, or even to increase the rate of taxation on what it had, as Yoshimune had done, but simply to make tax collection more efficient and honest. He obviously had no intention of revitalizing Bakufu finances as Tanuma had done, but was content, as Yoshimune had been, simply to economize on ceremonials, building projects, and administrative costs as much as possible.[72]

To some extent, too, the Bakufu, under Matsudaira Sadanobu, showed an increasing unconcern with the maintenance of its traditional control over far-flung markets like Osaka, and this was balanced by a growing interest in the economic life of the Kantō as the basis for Bakufu economic life and the economic well-being of the city of Edo, which was its home.[73] It is possible to see this as isolationism, with the Bakufu deliberately turning away from the burdens of daimyo control and national order, and cultivating its garden in the narrowest sense. To some extent this involved marching over the rights of Kantō daimyo, but there can be little doubt that the majority were best pleased by this. Examples of this assertion of control for the sake of Edo and the Kantō are the denial of the right of the daimyo of five Kantō provinces to levy taxes on sardines caught on the shores of their domains. The purpose was to encourage more production, so that more fishmeal fertilizer could be sent down to the areas around Osaka, whence came the Edo oil supply.[74] In assuring itself of a steady supply of oil, at lower rates, the Bakufu gave permission to oil producers of the Osaka area to send their goods straight to Edo and bypass Osaka, using instead ports such as Nada, Nishinomiya, and Hyōgo.[75]

In some respects, the Kansei Reforms did see claims to

71. *TJ* 48 : 45, 51, 74, 136; see also Kitajima, *Seiji shi*, 2, p. 307, and Tsuda, "Kansei kaikaku," pp. 254–55.

72. Shibusawa, pp. 133ff., 160ff.

73. Kitajima, *Seiji shi*, 2, p. 314.

74. Tsuda, "Kansei kaikaku," p. 260.

75. Ibid., pp. 258–59.

authority over daimyo in other areas, as, for instance, when an attempt was made to survey the internal commerce of each domain to determine why prices were rising. But, even here, despite the pretended scope of the enquiry, it has been claimed that the Bakufu was really only interested in the Kantō.[76] Also, of course, in trying to keep prices stable, the Bakufu was working to provide an atmosphere of general stability which all daimyo regarded as desirable.

It is tempting to see in these various measures Sadanobu's distaste for the commercial process, and no more. This is, after all, in keeping with his image as projected in the work of Whig historians, Japanese and foreign. Nevertheless, it was not so simple. One of the interesting things about Sadanobu's dislike of commerce was that it applied only to Bakufu commercial activities. He was markedly less hostile to commerce within the daimyo domains. When daimyo of Shirakawa, as we have seen, he lavished considerable attention on commercial development, and was to resume this later, after his early retirement from politics. As the leading Senior Councilor, too, he jettisoned Bakufu monopolies but was prepared to encourage those developed by daimyo, even to the extent of underwriting them with Bakufu funds. It was in keeping with the precedent established in these years that the Kii domain was later to be lent an annual 10,000 ryō, for a fixed period of time, to develop its own sugar industry.[77]

With the Bakufu controlled by Sadanobu and his daimyo associates, it was not to be expected that official policy toward the daimyo class would be anything but tolerant. There were no attainders, and no fief reductions, save for that demanded of Tanuma Okitsugu on surrendering his office, nor were there any fief transfers. Personal misbehavior, or maladministration, on the part of any daimyo was greeted with a formal word of reproof, but no more. Naturally, there were no great impositions either.

Instead, when the Bakufu wanted money, it went to other sources. In 1806, 1809, and again in 1813, for example, large sums of money were collected from merchants in the big cities

<hr>

76. Ibid., p. 267.

77. Ibid., p. 241; Horie Yasuzō, *Kokusan shōrei to kokusan sembai*, p. 56, n. 3.

and from the peasants of Bakufu domains, so it neither hit
daimyo in their persons, nor poached on the economic resources
of their domains.[78] In 1805, it was finally decided that the costs
to the Bakufu (and to the daimyo who had hitherto done most
of the entertaining) of the Korean embassies were greater than
they warranted, and so the Koreans would thenceforth meet and
transact their business with Bakufu representatives in Tsu-
shima.[79] There are indications, too, that Matsudaira Sadanobu
considered the sankin kōtai system a useless drain and wanted to
change it to three years in Edo and three years in the han, something which would have immediately reduced traveling expenses.
He was known to be opposed to formal gifts, and said that "it
serves absolutely no purpose to order daimyo to do guard duty
at the castle," and also declared himself in favor of the total
abolition of Bakufu impositions upon the daimyo.[80]

In his autobiography, *Uge no hitokoto*, Matsudaira Sadanobu
left the following description of the way in which Bakufu decisions were taken during his years in office:

> As a matter of routine, I referred all plans and suggestions,
> and all official recommendations, to whomever was on duty.
> Matters of some complexity, however, were circulated among
> all the Senior Councilors, with my comments; after adding
> comments of their own, the Senior Councilors would all
> assemble in my chamber. With vital business, the Junior
> Councilors would also be included in the discussion, and
> enquiries would be made of officials like the Inspectors
> general (*ōmetsuke*) and the city magistrates (*sanbugyō*). If
> the matter was not decided after the initial consultation, it
> was referred to the shogun for his opinion . . . I disposed
> of nothing autocratically, no matter what it was.[81]

He was concerned to reestablish the Senior Councilors as a conciliar group in a way that had been neglected since Yoshimune's
lifetime,[82] and more than this, he was insistent that other daimyo,

78. Kitajima, *Seiji shi*, 2, pp. 348–49; Kitajima Masamoto, "Kasei-ki no seiji
to minshū," in *Iwanami kōza Nihon rekishi* 12 : 306, 307.

79. *Ōgaki-shi shi*, p. 513.

80. Matsudaira Tarō, (*Kōtei*) *Edo jidai seido no kenkyū*, p. 330.

81. Quoted in Tsuda, "Kansei kaikaku," p. 242.

82. Tsuda Hideo, "Matsudaira Sadanobu," in *Edo Bakufu—sono jitsuryoku monotachi*, ed. Kitajima Masamoto, 2 : 130–31.

like the sanke, the sankyō, and the *tamarizume,* be formally consulted.[83]

Here, just as in his insistence that restrictions be placed upon the power of the shogun and his personal companions, we can detect Sadanobu's concern that the combination of circumstances which had produced a Tanuma Okitsugu should not arise again. As long as government by daimyo, through discussion and general consultation, was maintained, and the shogun kept firmly in his place, it hardly mattered who was responsible for day-to-day administration. It may be that Sadanobu's resignation in 1793 arose from personal difficulties with Ienari, but there was no open rift between them. The fears of the daimyo who signed a petition asking Sadanobu to remain in office proved groundless; Bakufu policy continued as before. Until his death in 1817, Matsudaira Nobuaki, a friend and disciple of Sadanobu, was the dominant figure in decision-making, and his policies on this issue of central authority were no less passive than those of his master.[84]

Ienari and Mizuno Tadaakira

When Matsudaira Nobuaki died in 1817, the eleventh shogun was no longer the obedient boy to whom Sadanobu had given his tumid advice in the 1780s. In his forty-fifth year, Ienari was of an age to know his own mind, and of a temperament sufficiently willful and self-indulgent to demand the obedience of others; what is more, he had at his disposal the personal advisers to help him. Ever since his youth, even under Sadanobu's tutelage, the institutional groundwork for the return of "new men" had been laid, despite all the care with which his companions were to have been selected. All that was needed to complete the reversal was an opportunity, and this was provided in 1817 by the fatal illness of Matsudaira Nobuaki. On the day Nobuaki resigned his office as Senior Councilor, Ienari appointed to the vacancy a man who had been a friend and companion since childhood—Mizuno Tadaakira.

It was an appointment from which the shogun had every right to expect selfless service. By birth, as well as by the pattern of his career, Mizuno Tadaakira belonged unmistakeably on the

83. Shibusawa, p. 117.
84. For the circumstances of Sadanobu's resignation, see ibid., pp. 218ff., and for daimyo reaction, see *Tokugawa jūgodai shi,* 5 : 2507.

side of the new men. Like Iemitsu's advisers, and like Makino
Narisada, Yanagisawa Yoshiyasu, Manabe Akifusa, Ōoka Tadamitsu, and Tanuma Okitsugu, Mizuno Tadaakira was far from
what Arai Hakuseki had scornfully called "a daimyo's son." Born
into the family of a hatamoto who held a modest enfeoffment of
3,000 koku, he was subsequently adopted into another, the
Mizuno, who had even less. From here he entered Ienari's service
as a page, and like most other "new men" in this same position,
he became a close personal friend of the child, ten years his
junior, who was to be shogun.

It was at this point that his career began to deviate a little from
the model, for in late 1786, when Mizuno Tadaakira was already
in his early twenties, and well established in Ienari's household,
he was adopted for a second time. This time he entered a daimyo
household as heir apparent, his new father being Mizuno Tadatomo, a Senior Councilor and political ally of Tanuma Okitsugu.
No doubt, in the unsettled political atmosphere of that year
(Tanuma had just been dismissed), Mizuno Tadatomo thought it
discreet to have as heir to his 30,000 koku domain at Numazu
someone with friends at court. When Tadatomo died in 1802,
therefore, Tadaakira, as a daimyo in his own right, could be
promoted through the normal routes to Bakufu office. Instead
of receiving promotion to Senior Councilor from the post of
Grand Chamberlain, as had been the case with Tanuma,
Tadaakira was able to follow the standard progression from
Master of Shogunal Ceremony, Superintendent of Temples and
Shrines, and Junior Councilor before reaching the highest rank.[85]

His career in office, then, was orthodox to this extent, but,
if to the casual eye it might seem he was more a daimyo than a
"new man," there is no doubt that in his personal ties with the
shogun, and in the hostility these aroused among his contemporaries, he resembled Tanuma far more than he did Matsudaira
Nobuaki. Nobuaki had received no fief increases in office, but
Tadaakira's fief was to increase to 80,000 koku by the end of his
career.[86] So close was the resemblance to Tanuma that contem-

85. Kanai Madoka and Aoki Ryōko, eds., (Mizuno-ke kiroku) Kōtokuben
tsuketari han'piroku, p. 110.

86. Kitajima Masamoto, "Kasei-ki no seiji to minshū," in Iwanami kōza
Nihon rekishi 12 : 228.

poraries saw the period of Mizuno Tadaakira's ascendancy as a new Tanuma period. A jingle of the day went further, to include Yanagisawa Yoshiyasu's Genroku period in the comparison;

> Mizuno dete moto no tanuma ni nari ni keru
> Soro soro to yanagi ni utsuru mizu no kage

> [With the coming of the waters, the fields return
>   to marshes,
> And soon their reflection bathes the willow tree.] [87]

As with all such snatches depending entirely upon wordplays for their effect, virtually all the meaning is lost in translation; here, however, the symbolism is reasonably clear. *Mizuno de,* the coming of the waters, is a transparent reference to Mizuno *Dewa no kami* Tadaakira; with his appearance, the lines say, conditions are returning to that of the Tanuma period—*tanuma* meaning a marsh—and gradually coming to resemble the willow tree, or *yanagi,* the first character in the name of Yanagisawa Yoshiyasu.

Like Tanuma, Mizuno Tadaakira was to be accused of corruption; years after his death, Tokugawa Nariaki, the daimyo of Mito, who never forgave an injury, bitterly condemned the bribery of his years in office, comparing Tadaakira to the servile Chinese eunuchs and to vermin battening on the carcass of the state. The quotation with which this chapter begins is a pointed reference to Tadaakira's government, and Nariaki was later to make explicit the warning it contains, that such men are dangerous to political health. In 1838, when the shogun was about to appoint a new Senior Councilor, Nariaki wrote to warn him that "it will be of great harm to the state if you appoint another man like Mizuno Dewa no kami." [88] But there were other allegations as well—that Tadaakira had managed to win the approval of the eleventh shogun by means which were either unnatural (homosexual passion) or diabolical (he was believed to possess a secret cure for the headaches with which Ienari was much afflicted). Neither theme was new, as we have seen. The first allegation he shared with both Yanagisawa Yoshiyasu and Manabe Akifusa— and the Duke of Buckingham, for that matter. However such an hypothesis does not sit very well with the fact that Ienari is

87. Quoted in Kitajima, *Bakuhan-sei no kumon,* p. 226.
88. *Mito han shiryō (bekki jō),* pp. 114–15.

208   TREASURES AMONG MEN

known to have maintained a stable of forty concubines, siring
fifty-eight children by sixteen of them. The second allegation,
which recalls Rasputin's magic touch with Romanov headaches,
belongs to the same category as the arcane skills attributed to
Ōoka Tadamitsu, reputed the only man able to interpret Ieshige's
mouthings to the world outside.[89]

That Mizuno Tadaakira was disliked and distrusted by his
most influential contemporaries is clear; otherwise, he would have
a better image. What is not apparent is why he should have
suffered such a reception. His antecedents resembled those of
Tanuma, and his background—as well as his close friendship
with Tanuma's son—seemed to identify him as a sympathizer of
the old form of government,[90] but his policies, while more assertive of central power than those of Matsudaira Sadanobu, were
no more than a wan reflection of those of the Tanuma period.

There was a cautious reversal of some of the policies of the
Sadanobu-Nobuaki era of daimyo dominance, and certainly there
were no fresh gains for independence, but Mizuno Tadaakira was
able to produce little to restore Bakufu authority.[91] Rather than
attempting to bring the Bakufu back into commercial competition, Tadaakira resorted to the more orthodox policy of currency
debasement to keep the government solvent. Only seldom did he
interfere in the commercial process, but, when he did, it was to
show where his sympathies lay. Tokugawa Nariaki's hatred of
him, despite the Confucian moralism in which it was couched,
was not unrelated to just such a piece of interference in 1824.
One of the few commercially viable products of Nariaki's domain
at Mito was konnyaku, and in 1824 the Bakufu awarded a patent
of monopoly for this to a group of Edo merchants, whose rights
to its purchase and sale thus took priority over those of the
daimyo, the samurai, or the merchants of Mito. Nearly twenty
years later, Tokugawa Nariaki was still complaining about it.[92]

89. For allegations of homosexuality, see Kitajima, *Mizuno Tadakuni*,
pp. 211–12; for the treatment of headaches, see Kitajima, *Bakuhan-sei no
kumon*, p. 223, and for concubines, see p. 295. Information on his children
is from Saiki Kazuma, "Tokugawa shōgun seibo narabini saishō kō," in
Rekishi to jimbutsu, ed. Nihon Rekishi Gakkai, pp. 439–43.

90. Kitajima, *Bakuhan-sei no kumon*, pp. 225–26.

91. Kitajima, "Kasei-ki," passim.

92. Kitajima, *Mizuno Tadakuni*, p. 364; *Mito han shiryō (bekki jō)*, p. 140.

There were other indications of central control, also. Where Matsudaira Sadanobu had neglected Osaka, Tadaakira attempted to shore up its increasingly precarious position by commanding the provinces of western and central Japan to send their rapeseed crops directly to Osaka for processing, at the same time prohibiting any commercial pressing elsewhere. A similar attempt was to be made with cotton, but in each case the resistance of the peasant producers, aware of the profits to be made outside the established market system, proved too great.[93] In the Kantō, too, there was a move to rationalize the protection of the area from swelling bands of robbers and other dispossessed by forming villages into administrative units on the basis of contiguity. Each unit, although composed of villages which may all have paid their taxes to different authorities, whether daimyo, hatamoto, or Bakufu intendants, was to have its resident police force, directed by Edo.[94]

While significant, such measures hardly represent a turning point in Bakufu-daimyo relations. Given the cumulative deterioration of Bakufu powers, they may indeed have marked the limit to which the Tokugawa government could now assert itself without open confrontation of some kind. When Mizuno Tadaakira died in 1834, such a compromise was still feasible; but events in the world outside were soon to confront the Japanese with issues on which this would no longer be possible.

Ienari and Ieyoshi

From the beginning of the nineteenth century the first cracks began to be made in the seclusion Japan had enjoyed for nearly two hundred years, as the nations of Europe once again turned their attention to the Far East. Adam Laksman had arrived in Hokkaido in 1792 in an attempt to establish formal relations between Russia and Japan; twenty years later his countryman, Vasilii Golownin, was to spend two years in a Japanese prison. In 1808 the British frigate *Phaeton* took the Napoleonic Wars to Japan by sailing into Nagasaki Harbor and capturing the manager of the Dutch factory; twenty years later, other Englishmen were to claim the Ogasawara Islands, southwest of Japan,

93. Kitajima, *Mizuno Tadakuni*, pp. 241–42.
94. Ibid., p. 246.

for the greater glory of His Majesty George IV. In between, with
ominous frequency, came sightings of foreign vessels in Japanese
waters, as whalers, merchantmen and men-of-war found their way
into the northwest Pacific.

Such sightings, disturbing though they were to Tokugawa
Japanese, were not nearly as menacing as the news from China,
where the merchants, missionaries, officials, and soldiers of the
Western world were assisting the Ch'ing dynasty on its road to
ruin. In mid-1840 came a Dutch vessel with the most disturbing
news of all; hostilities had broken out between China and
Britain over the issue of the opium trade. Deeply disturbed,
Bakufu officials were able to verify this by interrogating the
Chinese community in Nagasaki, and three months later, they
could report nervously that the British had won with consum-
mate ease, inflicting considerable damage on the Chinese, while
losing not a single man of their own.[95]

The Japanese, who believed their own country to be the best
and most desirable of lands, considered it obvious that the
rapacious foreigners would soon bend their attention to Japan.
Only a step lay between this fear and the realization that Japan
was confronted with a dilemma of prodigious, and perhaps in-
surmountable, magnitude. How were they to cope with the
threat from abroad? The Bakufu, the central government, which
had once taken upon itself the duty of ordering Spaniards and
Portuguese from Japanese shores, was hamstrung through lack of
money, lacking even the military strength to preserve Edo, its
own center of government. How could the Bakufu be expected
to protect the daimyo domains of a nation which, as they were
only too well aware, seemed to consist mostly of coastline? If the
Bakufu could not offer such protection, who could? Certainly
no domain was in any position to guarantee its own defense—two
hundred years of the sankin kōtai system had seen to that.[96]
Therefore, if Japan was to continue to enjoy her independence,
some reorganization of power relationships was essential. If the

95. Ibid., p. 251.
96. In 1834, Sendai's debts amounted to 700,000 ryō, while in 1830, Satsuma
was five million ryō in debt. In the mid-1830s, Tosa domain expenditure was
twenty-five percent above its income. See Tanaka Akira, *Bakumatsu no hansei
kaikaku*, p. 126.

Bakufu was to fulfill its responsibilities and repel the barbarians, it would require the total subjection and assistance of the barons; it would have to transform itself into an absolute monarchy, as many states did when threatened from abroad. Should the daimyo reject the notion of surrendering their rights, then the only alternative course was a total reassertion of regional independence; the status quo, which weakened them without benefiting anybody, was untenable. The time of the centaur was past; whether for centralization or decentralization, a choice had to be made.

The issue was to be a vital one for the daimyo domains, since ultimately it would demand either their disappearance or their commitment to a course of total independence. But this was in the future. Ostrichlike, most daimyo preferred to ignore the appearance of foreign ships and to discount the rumors of British might on the China coast, pretending that nothing had happened, or would happen. For them, the status quo, while not ideal, had the advantage of familiarity; who could tell the hazards of a different form of political organization? Not until the arrival of Commodore Perry, when the threat was upon them and could be ignored no longer, did they come reluctantly to the threshold of decision.

Some were more perceptive. It is possible, even as early as the 1830s, to see party lines being drawn in preparation for the issue which was to emerge in 1853, as a few daimyo began to range themselves on the side of centralization or decentralization. Both had their risks; the logical end of a policy aimed at strengthening the Tokugawa Bakufu was the dismantling of the whole domain structure, and even if any particular daimyo could bring himself to accept this, he could expect nothing but implacable opposition from his vassals. By contrast, to espouse the cause of independence too openly could only provoke the Tokugawa Bakufu to act against the daimyo and his domain, something equally unacceptable to any group of vassals.

It needed a high degree of personal authority within the domain, and considerable force of character, to take a definite stand even after 1853; to do so in the 1830s, the daimyo had to be a most exceptional man. This is a tribute which, whatever his other failings, could never be denied Tokugawa Nariaki, the daimyo of Mito. For more than twenty years he was the most vocal and vigorous of the advocates of decentralization, playing his part to the full, despite danger to himself and his domain. Appalled at the prospect of interference from foreign powers, and at the turmoil which would erupt within Japan as an inevitable consequence, he embarked during the 1830s on a program of political action aimed at reform of a system which he considered incapable of meeting any new challenge. With his own considerable personal influence, and the intellectual reputations of the scholars he employed, to help him, Nariaki set out on his political career, attracting other daimyo to his cause, interfering in the appointment of Bakufu officials, peppering shogun and Senior Councilors with unsolicited letters of advice and memorials.

The daimyo of Mito was no unctuous Confucian reformer; in his hands even the most hackneyed proposals contained an obdurate kernel of hostile and partisan criticism. His call for government of men of talent, an obligatory cliché, carried far less conviction than the spirited attack on Mizuno Tadaakira (and by extension Ienari) that accompanied it.[97] His condemnation of commercialization, another Confucian reflex, was less than thorough; brushing aside his own commercial aspirations and those of his fellow daimyo, he reserved his most trenchant criticism for those merchants to whom the Bakufu had granted monopolistic privileges. Because of their stranglehold, he claimed, "even in a little village like Mito people complain, and all daimyo . . . are sorely afflicted"; better, surely, to abolish their privileges, and throw the Japanese key markets of Edo and Osaka open to free passage of goods.[98]

In two areas of policy, in particular, Tokugawa Nariaki made his position clear, showing beyond any doubt where his sympathies lay in the struggle between centralization and decentralization. The first was on the subject of Hokkaido—then called Ezochi—which Nariaki regarded as "the back door to Japan"; seeing it as too important to be left in the charge of the minor daimyo who held it, Nariaki suggested first that it be placed under direct Bakufu control, and then, more forcefully, in 1834,

97. *Mito han shiryō (bekki jō)*, pp. 83, 115.
98. Ibid., p. 140.

that it should be given to him as part of his personal domain, so that he might give it the care it needed.[99] His anxiety over the foreign threat was undeniable, but his reaction was to demand more power for himself, not less. "Twenty years ago," he was to complain to the Bakufu in 1855, "I predicted what has now come to pass. On numerous occasions from 1834 onwards I asked that I be given all of Matsumae and Ezo, but this was not granted. Had I been given what I then requested, matters would not now have reached the present state, where Russians can come to our country and be allowed to establish themselves here." [100]

Shipbuilding was the other issue over which Nariaki felt sufficiently strongly to show his hand. It seemed patently obvious to him that the foreigners could not be resisted by coastal batteries alone; they had to be met on equal terms, and that meant in ships as swift, as maneuverable and as well armed as those the foreigners had themselves. Therefore, he repeatedly urged that the 1635 prohibition against the construction of large ships be abandoned. "If you give permission to daimyo and shipmasters to build stout ships," he wrote, "it will not cost you a farthing. . . . If daimyo . . . have strong ships they can be assembled in time of emergency and will prove a remarkable defense." [101] Once again his sympathies were directed towards decentralization of military power; under no circumstances was he prepared to advocate that the Bakufu relax the prohibition on its own behalf alone.

The Bakufu, however, was unenthusiastic, and in its reply to Nariaki said so in unambiguous terms: "In particular, if we allow everybody to build warships, who can tell what evils will follow? The great daimyo of the west country and elsewhere may begin to conspire, and manufacture unconventional ships, and this would have grave effects on our administration of the law." [102] It was a strangely prescient answer, in view of what was to take place when the prohibition finally was repealed, but it failed to convince Tokugawa Nariaki, who had already rejected the argument, comparing it to "forcing everybody to wear

99. Ibid., pp. 110–12, 263–64, 274.
100. Quoted in "Hotta kafu."
101. *Mito han shiryō (bekki jō)*, p. 173.
102. Ibid., p. 182.

wooden swords because one madman has unsheathed his in the palace." [103] If not to all daimyo, he writes, why not give special permission to the sanke (of whom he is one) and the daimyo of the Tamarinoma (a handful of the larger fudai and ichimon daimyo)? In any case, he continues, "leaving aside the possibility of the Bakufu's possessing such ships while nobody else does"— a possibility which he was reluctant to consider—"if neither Bakufu nor anyone else has them, then it is exactly as if both had them, except that while there are no ships we are unprepared to protect ourselves against foreign vessels." [104]

Such was Tokugawa Nariaki's reaction to the impending crisis, to press as hard as he could, within the existing system, for a greater diffusion of power in preference to its concentration in the hands of the Tokugawa Bakufu. Other daimyo agreed with him. But there were still some who, equally conscious of the danger from abroad, were prepared to commit themselves to the cause of a central government. One of them was Mizuno Tada-kuni, the fudai daimyo of Hamamatsu, who, as Senior Councilor, was the leading figure within the Bakufu from his promotion to that post in 1834 to his dismissal in 1843.[105] In almost every respect he was as single-mindedly concerned with the welfare of his domain, and of the daimyo class in general, as were any of his peers. To cope with the problem of his domain debts, his advice to his vassals was that they should repudiate all debts owing outside the domain (except those they owed the Bakufu) and repay only what was due to their own merchants; even when holding Bakufu office, as Keeper of Osaka Castle, he did not hesitate, in his alternative capacity as daimyo of Hamamatsu, to repudiate his debts to leading Osaka merchant houses, which were entitled to his official protection as Keeper of Osaka Castle. His very reason for seeking Bakufu office seems to have been determination to make some money from it; in working his way up the ladder he maintained a special fund for bribes, and then, once in office, apparently took bribes himself. He had no greater love for the shogun's personal followers than any other daimyo,

103. Ibid., p. 178.
104. Ibid., p. 184.
105. He was subsequently reappointed the following year, but retired in 1845, after only eight months in office.

and, as Senior Councilor in 1841, he ruthlessly purged those with whom the former shogun, Ienari, had surrounded himself. In a memorial to Ienari's successor, Tadakuni made his position quite clear: of late, he wrote,

> the cabinet would confer with the shogun, and then communicate their decision to the other officials; whereupon members of the shogun's household would inform the officials that the decision was against the shogun's wishes, and would have to be reconfirmed. In consequence it became common for officials to show communications from the Senior Councilors to the shogun's personal attendants. I would like you to prohibit this, as it makes nonsense of administrative procedures; . . . it is curious that mere secretaries should be aware of the shogun's opinions before the Senior Councilors know of them, . . . and I would like it stopped.[106]

Nevertheless, on the matter of the foreign threat, and the reorganization necessary to cope with it, Tadakuni stood apart from the daimyo whom in other respects he resembled so closely. Beginning his career as a daimyo not long after the *Phaeton* incident, he paid two visits to Nagasaki, in 1812 and 1816, interviewing the head of the Dutch factory while he was there, and he maintained his interest in foreign relations and defense matters thereafter. Later, as Senior Councilor at the time of the Opium War he launched a program to reform the coastal defenses around Edo, and to have the samurai acquainted with the principles of Western gunnery; in his own domain at Hamamatsu he embarked on a scheme of coastal fortification overriding all objections from his vassals.[107]

Both Tadakuni's background and his career in office stamped him as a conventional official from the fudai daimyo class. He was most emphatically a fudai daimyo by birth, born into one of the more notable families, and by his previous career in

106. For debt repudiation, see Kitajima, *Mizuno Tadakuni*, pp. 115–16, 138, 148, and for bribes, see pp. 144–46, 283–84. Information on the purge is found on pp. 253–54 of the same work, while part of the text of Tadakuni's memorial appears on p. 275.

107. See ibid., p. 226 for Nagasaki, p. 456 for Hamamatsu, and pp. 436ff. for Edo defense and gunnery.

domain administration, he was no stranger to the difficulties of
han government and its needs. His career in Bakufu office, which
he had entered in 1815, passing slowly and nervously through the
prescribed promotions until he became Senior Councilor in 1834,
owed nothing to the favor of Ienari and little to the interest of
Mizuno Tadaakira, who, despite the common surname was no
relation and who needed to be bribed in various ways as Tadakuni rose in stature. Therefore he had nothing in common with
previous spokesmen for increased Bakufu power and, as we have
seen, approved of the traditional instruments of the shogun's
personal government as little as did Tokugawa Nariaki.

Background and career notwithstanding, Mizuno Tadakuni's
policy stamps him as a convinced supporter of shogunal absolutism in the face of the dilemma to come. In his first years in office
he was overshadowed by the eleventh shogun, Ienari, who, despite his retirement in 1837 nevertheless continued to dominate
the Bakufu until his death in 1841, and the years 1834–41 produced little in the way of dramatic proof of Tadakuni's leanings.
Once Ienari was gone, however, and the twelfth shogun, Ieyoshi,
aged forty-two, was installed in his place, Tadakuni had a free
hand.

Apart from the purge of Bakufu officials following Ienari's
death, the first sign of change in Bakufu policy appeared in mid-
1841, when Ieyoshi, the twelfth shogun, announced to his assembled officials his wish for a new period of reform, modeled
upon the Kyōhō and Kansei eras. Immediately, the machinery of
the traditional Confucian reform was set into motion; economy
was urged on all, from officials down to peasants, and stringent
and detailed instructions were issued to make sure that nobody
ate, dressed, got married or buried in a manner above his station;
once more prices were lowered by fiat and migrants to the cities
ordered back to their native villages. This much was common
to all reform movements, and need cause no comment.

Other aspects of the Tempō Reforms, however, were frankly
more unorthodox and revealed much more in common with the
policies of the Genroku and Tanuma periods. Why should a
government committed to an economy campaign reintroduce the
formal shogunal progress to Nikkō? The last progress had been
ordered for Ieharu, the tenth Tokugawa shogun, by Tanuma

Okitsugu nearly seventy years before. Now, in 1843, with the foreigners about to pounce, the almost forgotten ritual was revived at great cost and inconvenience to all the daimyo, who had to participate in it and contribute men and money. This progress was to occupy as many as 150,000 men for almost a week, as the shogun made his elaborate and stately journey to worship at the tombs of Ieyasu and Iemitsu amongst the cryptomerias at Nikkō. It did not pass without unfavorable comment. "The shogunal progress to Nikkō is a most welcome example of filial piety," Tokugawa Nariaki was to write in one of his regular letters of complaint to the Bakufu, "however the daimyo . . . will be impoverished by the vast cost. . . . I am sorry, but I feel that, although it is difficult to divine the will of the gods, you should fully restrict all useless ostentation" [108] The only reason for reviving such an ancient ritual, and it must surely have been apparent to all who were forced to participate, was to reemphasize, in a form all could see, the unique role of the Tokugawa house and of the Bakufu, its organ of government, in unifying Japan. By providing armed men to guard the shogun along his way, each daimyo was giving symbolic reaffirmation of his subservience to the Tokugawa and was therefore indicating to himself and his peers that he knew where his duty lay in the crisis to come.

The progress to Nikkō was hardly over when the Bakufu added fresh fuel to daimyo suspicion. Bakufu impositions on the daimyo are seen by Yoshizumi Mieko—who has traced their rise and fall —as being revived in greater numbers in the Tempō period than at any time over the previous hundred years or so.[109] This time, it was a large-scale civil engineering project, the drainage of the Imbanuma, the large marsh to the northeast of the city of Edo. The very name carried echoes of Tanuma, who had attempted to drain it back in 1785, but where he at least used merchant capital to help him, Mizuno Tadakuni thrust the entire cost onto the shoulders of five individual daimyo, who together were to spend on it more than 230,000 ryō they could ill afford. Once again the past glories of the Tokugawa were being revived; it had been sixty-seven years since the previous progress to Nikkō, but even

108. *Mito han shiryō (bekki jō)*, p. 144.
109. Yoshizumi, "Tetsudai bushin," p. 99.

longer since any daimyo had been forced to shoulder such a civil engineering burden as this. Furthermore, the very nature of the project itself was ominous. It had been calculated that, if the project were successful, the reclaimed land would produce as much as 100,000 koku a year. This would go to the Bakufu, as the reclaiming agent, not to any of the daimyo who had owned the marsh. Also, since the process of drainage involved deepening the Kemi River and linking it to the Tone River, largest of the Kantō rivers, it would give Edo easy access to the goods of the Tōhoku and simplify communications both to the Tōhoku and to the Pacific coast at Kasumigaura. In this way, the commercial and military position of Edo would be enhanced; perhaps this reason lay behind the opposition to the scheme expressed by Tokugawa Nariaki in yet another letter of complaint to the Bakufu.[110]

Even as the daimyo absorbed the implications of the Imban-uma project, some among them were already reeling from an onslaught of a different sort, although equally damaging and dangerous. On the first day of the sixth month of the year 1843, several daimyo—among them Mizuno Tadakuni, himself, and two other leading Bakufu officials—received an official notification which read as follows: "A measure has now been announced by which, for the purposes of better control, all land adjacent to Edo Castle is to become Bakufu land. Therefore you are ordered to surrender, from your fief in X Province, Y County, land productive of more than Z koku. You will shortly be given land in exchange for this." [111] This was the famous agechi-rei, by which the Bakufu sought to consolidate its central landholdings at daimyo expense. Nine daimyo were forced to give up pockets of land they held within a ten-mile radius of Edo Castle, and two weeks later, sixteen daimyo with similar tracts around Osaka Castle were required to do the same.[112]

The agechi-rei (Order to Surrender Land) was yet another example of Tadakuni's willingness to provoke a confrontation with the daimyo by attacking their traditional rights—this time their

110. *Mito han shiryō* (*bekki jō*), p. 173; for Imbanuma, see Kitajima, *Mizuno Tadakuni*, pp. 412ff.
111. Ibid., p. 424.
112. Ibid., pp. 423ff.

right of land tenure. For many, substantial amounts of land were involved; in the case of the Senior Councilor, Doi Toshitsura, it was a matter of a quarter of his entire enfeoffment of 80,000 koku. For many, too, the lands surrendered were the most productive sections of their entire domain, and what is more, in each case, the land they were to be given in exchange was among the least productive in the Bakufu's possession. In consequence, what seemed on the surface to be a simple exchange of land was in reality a fief reduction to a greater or lesser extent for each man involved.[113] Tadakuni knew what risks he ran; his reasons are clear. Kitajima Masamoto has listed three: first, to increase Bakufu income by exchanging its low yield land for land with a higher productivity; second, to remind the daimyo of the Bakufu right to order their fiefs however it saw fit, without reference to them; and third, to have Edo and Osaka under unified military control in the face of the foreign threat. If the daimyo themselves did not perceive this, then they certainly resisted as if they did, as we shall see.[114]

In one further area, Mizuno Tadakuni's Bakufu asserted its control over the daimyo and, in so doing, touched a particularly sensitive nerve. At the end of 1841 the Bakufu announced an end to all specially privileged merchant groups, thus, effectively opening up commerce to free competition. In this sense it was a new withdrawal from commercial competition but aimed not so much at pacifying those who opposed special merchant privileges, like Tokugawa Nariaki, as experimenting to see whether, as Nariaki had claimed, prices would decrease in consequence. Tadakuni, if prepared to withdraw the Bakufu from commerce, was not willing to do so unilaterally. Where Nariaki had requested the dissolution simply of that privileged group of Bakufu-sponsored merchants who controlled the commerce of the Kantō, Tadakuni went on to make clear, early the following year, that he intended the dissolution order to apply equally to all specially privileged merchants, no matter where they conducted their business and no matter who awarded them their special privileges. Even those groups which were tied to various do-

113. Ibid., p. 431.
114. For Kitajima's list, see ibid., p. 432.

mains, and paid to the daimyo a fee and a proportion of their profits, were ordered dissolved.[115]

This was followed by a further order, late in 1842, specifically prohibiting all domain monopolies on the grounds that daimyo had been abusing their powers by buying up goods from other domains and cornering the market in various products, selling only when the price was highest.[116] As we have seen, many domains were profiting by their formal monopolies, and they therefore viewed this latest Bakufu intrusion, which meant the end of their special rights, with as much displeasure as their grandfathers had regarded Tanuma's decision to bring the Bakufu into competition with them. Each threatened a form of income and a way of life that was coming to mean more and more to their financial health. For this reason, neither the abolition of the privileged merchant groups nor of domain monopolies was accepted readily by han which had grown dependent upon either form of commercial activity. The dissolution of the merchant groups provoked more or less open defiance from domains like Hikone, Hiroshima, Owari, Fukui, Aizu, Matsue, and Awa, and there is no evidence to suggest that domain monopolies were influenced at all by their formal proscription.[117]

As a fudai daimyo playing a role in Bakufu politics previously limited to new men, Mizuno Tadakuni represents an anomaly, and for explanation one has to resort to his perception of the foreign threat. There is no such difficulty in explaining his downfall. His daimyo colleagues in the Bakufu, many of whom stood to lose, as he did, by the agechi-rei, came to dislike him very quickly. His peers outside the Bakufu, afflicted by more demands, more threats, and more central presumptions to power than they had ever previously encountered, disliked him no less. Had he been the shogun's creature, Tadakuni's position would nevertheless have been secure as long as Ieyoshi lived, no matter who else opposed him, but, as a fudai daimyo in the Bakufu, imposing his policy on the shogun, regardless of how atypical that policy was in itself, he had no claim to the patronage of the shogun

115. Ibid., p. 369.

116. Horie, Kokusan shōrei, p. 149.

117. Kitajima, ed., Seiji shi, 2, pp. 417–18; Hikone-shi shi, 2 : 395; Yamamoto Tomio, "Awa han no shakai to keizai," in Rekishi kyōiku, vol. 6, pt. 1, p. 30.

either. Therefore, once Tadakuni's allies within the Bakufu were alienated, as they all were, one by one, the twelfth shogun could accept the fact and call for Tadakuni's resignation with as little personal involvement as had been the case when the reformer first assumed office.[118]

Tadakuni's successor in office was another fudai daimyo, of a notable family, and with an impressive, though brief, record in Bakufu office behind him. This was Abe Masahiro, daimyo of Fukuyama, who was to remain the leading figure in the Bakufu for the rest of Ieyoshi's life. There is nothing to suggest that he was any more, or any less, a personal favorite of the shogun than Tadakuni had been; under Abe Masahiro, Ieyoshi remained as shadowy as he had been under his father, Ienari, and subsequently under Mizuno Tadakuni. However, although the conditions were the same, the policy differed, and this was only to be expected from a man who had come to power as leader of a group of officials who had rejected his predecessor and his policies. Abe Masahiro's most aggressive moves consisted of strangling all of Mizuno Tadakuni's most ambitious measures as quickly as possible. Even as Tadakuni was tottering on the edge of dismissal, the agechi-rei, which had been designed to enrich and strengthen the Bakufu, and enhance its authority, was rescinded. Within a matter of days of its planner's departure from office, the Imbanuma project, as close as it was to completion, was scrapped, and with it disappeared the Bakufu's prospects of land reclamation and increased military and commercial influence.[119] The prohibition of domain monopolies was never enforced, which might be anticipated from a Senior Councilor whose own domain at Fukuyama maintained its own monopoly of tatami rush matting, and the dissolution of the merchant organizations was retained without great enthusiasm until 1851, when it, too, was repealed. All that remained of Mizuno Tadakuni's attempt to confront the issue before it arrived was the memory of the shogunal progress to Nikkō in 1843; having become a matter of historical record, it alone was inviolable.

The prospect of a crisis from abroad did not vanish, however,

---

118. For erosion of Tadakuni's support, see Kitajima, *Mizuno Tadakuni*, pp. 473ff.

119. For agechi-rei, see ibid., pp. 483ff., and p. 423 for the Imbanuma.

and it was to be thrust directly upon Abe Masahiro in 1853; long
before this time, however, he had shown where his allegiance
lay. Like his predecessor, Abe was to show reserve at first towards
Tokugawa Nariaki, but, as Conrad Totman has shown, this was
soon to develop into a "limited cooperation," in the course of
which the Senior Councilor was prepared to show the daimyo of
Mito secret correspondence with the Dutch and the Americans,
and was prepared to tell him, in 1846, of Bakufu plans to begin
building large ships, and also, "depending on the situation," of
allowing others to build them too.[120] Abe Masahiro had already
made up his mind on the issue of more or less central government for Japan, and could, therefore, in 1853, throw away two
of the Bakufu's greatest prerogatives—the right to decide on
foreign policy, and the right to restrict the armaments of the
daimyo domains—with the serene confidence of one who does
what is best.

120. Conrad Totman, "Political Reconciliation in the Tokugawa Bakufu:
Abe Masahiro and Tokugawa Nariaki, 1844–1852," in *Personality in Japanese
History,* ed. Craig and Shively, pp. 186–93.

6. Epilogue

Bestowing gold, silver and jewels upon the daimyo of Japan
is like casting them into the sea. Why? Because the daimyo
. . . will bend as grass in the wind to whomever is strongest. This will happen one day.

Ōkubo Hikozaemon, 1622 [1]

In the summer of 1853, four vessels of the United States Navy
anchored at the mouth of Edo Bay. They brought with them a
document, signed by President Fillmore, calling upon the Japanese to abandon those restrictions by which, for two centuries,
the rest of the world had been kept at arm's length. The request
was politely phrased, but there was no mistaking the menace
behind Commodore Perry's announced intention to return, with
more ships, for a favorable answer the following year. On this
second visit, early in 1854, he received the anticipated assent,
and Japan, slowly and painfully at first, dragging her feet, moved
out unwillingly to meet the world. Within five years, intercourse
with the West had become a reality, and, within fifteen, a commonplace.

To the Japanese, these years seemed charged with great peril.
They were conscious of their weakness and disunity and very
sharply aware of the opportunities such disarray presented to
enemies. Perhaps in their apprehension they exaggerated the sinister intentions of the four powers most immediately involved—
Britain, France, the United States, and Russia—and the allure-
ments Japan offered to imperialist activity, but this was understandable. What had happened to India, and was already under
way in China, gave the Japanese little confidence in the self-
restraint of the great powers; their own country, smaller and
more accessible, could be dismembered with even less ceremony.

Only a government capable of arousing and coordinating an
effective national response could hope to meet such a crisis; thus
the problem faced previously only by a few had now to be met by
all. If a stronger form of government was needed, what shape

1. *Mikawa monogatari*, p. 415.

was it to take? Should the daimyo surrender all their independence to the Tokugawa Bakufu, or should the Bakufu, abandoning all pretensions to central authority, renounce its prerogatives and share them with all daimyo? Much of the political dissension of the years 1853–68 (the Bakumatsu period), although
dissembled behind a variety of moralistic slogans, was generated
by this issue. So, too, in the end, was the fall of the Bakufu itself.
Had it not been necessary to confront this particular problem of
government reorganization decisively, had no Perry injected any
urgency, the Tokugawa Bakufu might very well have survived,
continuing its gentle decline just as the Muromachi Bakufu had
done, until a stronger feudal body replaced it. Instead, the decay
of Tokugawa power, already pronounced, was accelerated by
Perry's visit. The tension between regionalism and centralism,
between daimyo prerogatives and Bakufu authority, unresolved
since the foundation of the Tokugawa state, could remain so no
longer if Japan wished to preserve her independence. It is in the
Bakumatsu that the stresses inherent in centralized feudalism
come to a head, in a process by which the daimyo of Japan—or
men speaking in their name—first extort from the Bakufu privileges not enjoyed since the early seventeenth century, and finally
overthrow it.

Erosion was to appear first in that area in which authority had
been claimed so successfully by Iemitsu in the 1630s—the right to
determine Japanese foreign policy and to negotiate with foreign
powers, without reference to any other source of influence in
Japan. As we have observed, Abe Masahiro had been content to
see this principle undermined during the 1840s and saw no
objection to relinquishing it altogether in the summer of 1853,
when he forwarded to the daimyo and hatamoto of Japan a request for their opinions on this most pressing of foreign policy
decisions. Thereafter, daimyo participation in the formulation
of foreign policy became a matter of course. No sooner had Perry
departed for the Ryukyus and Hong Kong than Abe was to invite
his old friend Tokugawa Nariaki to official conferences on coastal
defense, and the former Mito daimyo was the first to be consulted when Sir James Stirling requested British use of Japanese
harbors the following year. By 1855 he was sufficiently influential
to force the dismissal of two uncongenial Senior Councilors,

marking him indisputably as a figure of power—if indeed he had not been so before. It must be added, however, that not even this degree of eminence satisfied so restless an ambition; he is to be seen later in his career demanding to be sent to the United States to negotiate on Japan's behalf. Other daimyo too, were to attain positions of prominence, whether formal or otherwise, in the determination of Bakufu policy—among them Matsudaira Yoshinaga and Shimazu Nariakira.[2]

So frank a retreat from authority served only to multiply the difficulties of a period already difficult enough. More people to consult meant more time wasted, more indecision, and more bruised feelings, since nobody proffering advice was content to have it rejected. Rather more disturbing in its implications, however, was the development of private and uncoordinated relations between some domains and foreign diplomatic and mercantile interests, along lines independent of, and frequently antipathetic to, Bakufu activity. By 1864, both Satsuma and Chōshū, for example, while proclaiming their irreconcilable hatred and mistrust of the foreigner, were beginning to reach private agreements with the intruders, a form of daimyo activity not seen in Japan for over two hundred years.[3]

Restrictions on the right to build large sailing vessels, another notable feature of Iemitsu's *sakoku* legislation, was also to be abandoned in Perry's wake. Tokugawa Nariaki had recommended it long before 1853, and Shimazu Nariakira, daimyo of Satsuma, had already sent retainers to learn the elements of shipbuilding from the Dutch at Nagasaki, establishing at Sakurajima a naval yard in which they could employ their new skills. Both men were to greet the news of Perry's arrival with formal demands for freedom to build warships, and in the autumn of that year Abe Masahiro complied, lifting the prohibition which had been effective since 1635. It was a concession which held the gravest consequences for the Tokugawa, as one after another the most powerful daimyo embarked on an internecine arms race, the wealthiest of them acquiring in this manner considerable military strength, sometimes building their own vessels and casting

2. Imaizumi Shōzō, *Nagaoka no rekishi*, 1 : 115; W. G. Beasley, *Select Documents on Japanese Foreign Policy 1853–1868*, p. 169.
3. Ishii Takashi, *Meiji ishin no butai ura*, chaps. 1, 2.

their own cannon, sometimes buying them from foreign merchants.[4] Nor were ships and cannon the only objects of this arms race. Guns and ammunition were also very much in demand among those daimyo domains with the resources to afford them. Ernest Satow, while in Nagasaki, noted that the retainers of great daimyo "came into frequent contact with foreigners, whose houses they visited for the purchase of arms, gunpowder and steamers." Such a development, long urged by those impatient of Bakufu control, could not fail to damage a military position already attenuated.[5]

The increased physical strength of many Japanese domains was a function of their newfound wealth, built up, in most cases, by monopoly activities since the beginning of the nineteenth century. Profits derived from her monopoly in ginseng enabled Matsue Han to enter the arms race with the purchase of ships and arms overseas, for example, and Kii, similarly successful, was able to do the same. Both Satsuma and Chōshū, overwhelming in their military presence during the Bakumatsu, were so simply because of their buoyant economies. Having resisted Mizuno Tadakuni's attempt to strangle the monopolies, increasingly an important source of domain income, a large number of han entered the Bakumatsu with money to spend on armaments (something the Bakufu lacked), and also with a full knowledge of the benefits of commercial activity. Contact with foreign nations was to transmute this into an interest in foreign trade. In the case of Satsuma, in fact, such an interest was already present, nourished by long experience of foreign trade carried on, via the Ryukyu Islands, with China. Other domains, while lacking this background, were nonetheless prompt to recognize the advantages foreign trade could bring. Even such a chauvinist as Tokugawa Nariaki, when demanding to be sent to America, added the request "that you should let me act as middleman for the goods in which Americans want to trade." [6]

However, in the 1860s, when even those most vociferous in

4. Iwata Masakazu, *Okubo Toshimichi*, pp. 3–34; Imaizumi, 1 : 112; Ishizuka Hiromichi, "Bakuhan-ei gunji kōgyō no keisei," *Shigaku zasshi*, vol. 80, nos, 8–9 passim.

5. Ernest Satow, *A Diplomat in Japan*, p. 22.

6. For Matsue and Kii, see Horie Yasuzō, *Kokusan shōrei to kokusan sembai*, pp. 88, 141; for the Satsuma trade, see Ishii Takashi, *Meiji ishin no butai ura*, p. 16. The Nariaki quotation is from Beasley, p. 169.

their hatred of the foreign nations were beginning to profess interest in trading with them, the only ports at which foreign vessels were permitted to land were those nominated by the Bakufu, all of them under the control of the Bakufu itself— Nagasaki, Hakodate, Yokohama, Niigata, Edo, Osaka, and Kobe. This was increasingly resented as Satow was to discover after a private meeting with some Chōshū men in 1864. "They spoke with great bitterness of the Tycoon's dynasty," the English diplomat wrote, and "accused them of keeping all the trade, both foreign and native, in their own hands, by taking possession of every place where trade was likely to develop." [7]

Such resentment, growing out of the new international situation, merged easily into more general and increasingly overt criticisms of the Bakufu, now amenable to such attacks as never before. Already, before Perry's arrival, members of the Mito school had deplored the general tenor of Bakufu policy towards the daimyo domains. One writer expressed the Bakufu's aim as "to strengthen the base and weaken the ends," rendering Bakufu more powerful and daimyo weaker. Nishimura Shigeki, as vassal to a fudai daimyo currently holding high office, could not afford to be so outspoken, but one can detect a similar concern behind his plea for the strengthening of the daimyo class. Both Matsudaira Yoshinaga and his adviser Yokoi Shōnan also joined the critics eagerly, the former in a memorial written in 1857, in which he reproved the "evil practices by which the daimyo and lesser lords have been impoverished," while the latter was to deplore the way in which the Bakufu had forced daimyo to "isolate their own provinces, not considering the harm so long as there was gain for themselves." Wherever the Bakufu turned it found little cause for comfort. A censor's report on the Sendai domain in 1859, for example, claimed that "the domain officials, . . . and those residing there, hold the Bakufu in contempt. On the surface they proclaim the highest regard for the special favors they have received from . . . [Tokugawa Ieyasu] and his successors, but the vassals and the people of the domain mutter their hope that the Tokugawa house will not be strong enough to prevail over the northern daimyo, or even over the foreigners." [8]

7. Satow, p. 99.
8. The quotations from the Mito school and Yokoi Shōnan are from H. D. Harootunian, *Toward Restoration: The Growth of Political Consciousness in*

The criticism, and the admission of the major critics to official or semiofficial positions within the Bakufu, had its effect. The daimyo class increased its independence, even to winning the relaxation of that most distinctive element of Bakufu control, the sankin kōtai system, which in the past had cost the domains so dearly.[9] But none of these measures—the admission to Bakufu counsel of daimyo previously deemed unacceptable, the freedom to build and buy ships and other weapons of war, virtual abolition of alternate attendance and the hostage system which was an essential part of it—appeased anybody. The criticism continued, and as the Bakufu, jettisoning its traditional prerogatives one by one, grew still weaker, that criticism developed first into rivalry, and then, from 1864 onward, into rebellion, the first since the Shimabara incident of 1637.

The Chōshū domain, as is well known, was the first to throw down the challenge to Tokugawa control, claiming a higher loyalty to justify a stance in which the considerations of self-interest were perhaps not wholly absent. A military campaign mounted by the Bakufu against Chōshū in 1864 resulted only in a brief capitulation, and in 1865 it was decided that a more convincing expression of Bakufu authority would be needed to bring the rebels to heel. Under the influence of its "conservatives," the Bakufu decided to call to Edo both the former daimyo and the present daimyo of Chōshū, together with the daimyo of a branch domain at Tokuyama, to receive sentence. The sentence, which imposed resignations, house arrest, and a 100,000 koku fief reduction for the Chōshū domain, was generally unpopular amongst the daimyo, who saw it as an unwarranted intrusion on the prerogatives of a colleague. Those involved, naturally, cared for it even less and refused to go either to Edo or Osaka to submit, leading to the announcement of a second campaign against them.

Tokugawa Japan, pp. 109, 367; the quotation from Matsudaira Yoshinaga is in W. G. Beasley, *The Modern History of Japan*, p. 66; Nishimura Shigeki's attitude is expressed in Kojima Shigeo, "Bakuhan-sei hōkai-ki ni okeru kaimei-ha kanryō no keisei," in *Nihonshi ronkyū*, p. 454. The report from Sendai is to be found in (*Ii-ke shiryō*) *Bakumatsu fūbun tansaku sho*, 2 : 295.

9. In fact, the sankin kōtai system was not formally abolished. However, it was altered drastically, demanding only 100 days of residence in Edo every three years—see *ZTJ* 51 : 369ff. for details—and even in its altered form seems not to have been insisted upon after 1862.

This time, however, the difficulties were more pronounced, for the habit of defiance had spread. Satsuma, having secretly negotiated an agreement with Chōshū, was already supplying her with arms. Many domains, suspicious of the Bakufu's motives, and mortally afraid of increased expenses, refused their assistance when the Bakufu commanded it. The daimyo of Nagoya, Wakayama, Satsuma, Tosa, Fukui, Okayama, Tottori, Hiroshima, Kumamoto, and Fukuoka all voiced their dissent. Satsuma and Hiroshima refused outright to lend their support, while others complied only with reluctance.

Consequently, when the Bakufu troops moved out of Osaka in 1866, on their way to selected points on the Chōshū border, they were already well on the way to defeat. Many had spent over a year at Osaka and had grown stale waiting for the order to march. Others were disturbed at the general lack of enthusiasm, particularly that of Satsuma, which, it was well known, had no reason to love Chōshū, an old, and recently bitter, rival. Still others, bearing no affection for Chōshū themselves, were even less enthusiastic about the severity of the policy they were pledged to support. Their opponents were, by contrast, fighting for the integrity of their domain, a cause in which they had aroused general enthusiasm from the common people, peasants and merchants, who participated willingly in its defense, fighting beside their samurai superiors. The outcome was defeat for the Bakufu forces and an uneasy truce, occasioned by the timely death of the fourteenth shogun, Iemochi, in the autumn of 1866.

The Bakufu, as a united, viable political institution, had reached the end of its road, weakened to the point of impotence and split among several factions, almost all of them prepared to accept, even to welcome, an end to the burden of autocratic rule. Its only hope of survival lay in resigning all claims to political supremacy and sharing its powers with any daimyo interested enough to accept. This the Bakufu prepared to do throughout the year 1867, led by Tokugawa Yoshinobu, last of the Tokugawa shogun, whose own political record as an enemy of shogunal absolutism made him an ideal leader for a government preparing to bend its head to the decree of the furies from the southwest. When the blow fell, in the shape of the Tosa proposal, and the subsequent Satsuma-Chōshū coup, it was far more severe than even the most conciliatory of Bakufu politicians had anticipated. Instead of a council of daimyo in which the Tokugawa house, by virtue of landholdings far greater than those of any other member, would still be prominent, the southwestern domains insisted that Yoshinobu restore to the emperor not only the government of Japan, but the Tokugawa lands as well. It was a sentence of banishment from the political world, and Yoshinobu, at last, despite the readiness of some of his subordinates to fight, was content to accept it.

The Fudai Daimyo in the Bakumatsu

What role did the fudai daimyo play in the decay of the Bakufu during its last years, and what was their position during its overthrow and the brief flurries of resistance that followed? As men who owed their positions and privileges to the favor of the Tokugawa house, who boasted of their loyalty to the Tokugawa line, cherishing the memory of ancestors who had fought bravely in the service of Ieyasu and his forebears, treasuring in their storehouses all manner of gifts from Tokugawa shogun— swords, daggers, scrolls, specimens of calligraphy, and other bric-a-brac—what was their reaction to a process which robbed these hallowed associations of any meaning? The fudai myth, and the greater one which spawned it, that of the survival of the allegiances of 1600 throughout the Tokugawa period, have combined to keep attention away from this question. Assuming total fudai subordination to, and dependence upon, the Tokugawa Bakufu, and exaggerating the effects of want of stature, the habit of unquestioning loyalty, and the enticements of Bakufu office, there has been little temptation to examine the fudai daimyo. After all, if the movement by which the Bakufu was brought to the ground happened to be led by two tozama domains defeated at Sekigahara, what could be more natural than to assume that the fudai domains, no less than Chōshū and Satsuma, chose sides on the issues of the 1860s along lines determined at Sekigahara, two hundred and more years earlier? Almost without exception, historians of the period have explained the daimyo politics of the early Bakumatsu solely in terms of those who wished to participate in the making of Bakufu decisions—namely the tozama and ichimon daimyo—and those who tried to prevent them, that is, the fudai daimyo.[10]

In fact, no such clear and decisive characterization of fudai daimyo activity during the Bakumatsu years is possible. At no stage did the varying members of the fudai class ever come together upon anything like a common policy; for the most part they were content to see the Tokugawa Bakufu come to an end rather than face the alternative, which was to place themselves and their domains in jeopardy by attempting to save it. Of the two warring elements within every fudai daimyo, it was most often the daimyo element—the independent baron, not the Tokugawa vassal—which spoke with the loudest voice, prompting them to the very course of action Ōkubo Hikozaemon had predicted, namely, bowing to the wind. The Bakumatsu years, in fact, represent the sudden maturation and unambiguous display of all the fudai attributes discussed in earlier chapters. There was no unanimity in their response to this final crisis: they were often personally preoccupied with the welfare of their domains; when they were not, they were frequently overruled by their vassals; they did not, in choosing sides, hesitate to ally themselves with tozama; they did not care deeply for their traditional rights to Bakufu office; they continued to work, on the whole, as they had always done, against shogunal absolutism, and for a greater relaxation of central constraints upon the daimyo class. Nishimura Shigeki was to observe that, "if the shimpan and fudai could effectively combine into one group and appeal to the nation, it would not be very difficult to counter the Satsuma-Chōshū-Tosa plot," thereby drawing attention to the traditional role of the fudai in the military support of the Tokugawa house.[11] The balance of power relied on fudai support, but in fact, in the final crisis, support was given partially, grudgingly—and often not at all. The combination of Tokugawa forces—spearheaded by

10. Examples of this view are to be seen in Beasley, *Documents*, p. 18; Marius B. Jansen, *Sakamoto Ryoma and the Meiji Restoration*, chap. 2; and Albert M. Craig, *Choshu in the Meiji Restoration*, p. 91. It has been expressed as recently as 1970 in George M. Wilson, "The Bakumatsu Intellectual in Action: Hashimoto Sanai in the Political Crisis of 1858," in *Personality in Japanese History*, ed. Craig and Shively, p. 243.

11. Nishimura's statement is quoted in Kojima, "Kaimei-ha kanryō," p. 457.

the fudai daimyo—which had been successful in 1600 in defeating the enemies of the Tokugawa house, was never to materialize again, not even when it was needed most, and not even when it became plain that without it the Tokugawa and their Bakufu could no longer survive.

It would be misleading, however, to suggest that the increasingly abrupt degeneration of the Bakufu and its authority after 1853 was part of an unrelieved downward slide to impotence. As had been the case throughout the history of the Tokugawa Bakufu, there were, in these last fifteen years, periods in which the slide was halted and some sort of rally made. The period of the Ansei purge, and its brief aftermath, represent one such small recovery, and signs of another are to be detected after 1864; the fudai reaction to each of these is of some interest.

The Ansei purge, which takes its name from the Ansei period (1854–60), was in fact led by a fudai daimyo, Ii Naosuke, head of that most eminent of fudai houses, the Ii of Hikone. Appointed to the position of Grand Councilor (*tairō*) early in 1858, Naosuke set about restoring the Bakufu to a position of strength in Japanese affairs that it had not filled since the resignation of Mizuno Tadakuni. Ignoring the wishes of many Japanese daimyo, he determined the shogunal succession, choosing the malleable Iemochi in preference to Tokugawa Yoshinobu, already politically compromised by close association with those attempting to reduce Bakufu authority. Reverting to a more traditional attitude to the Imperial Court, he ignored its expressed wishes by ordering the ratification of a commercial treaty with the United States in 1858. His critics, daimyo or no, were treated without compunction; Tokugawa Nariaki was ordered into close confinement, and Matsudaira Yoshinaga of Fukui and Tokugawa Yoshikatsu of Owari were forced to retire. Some members of the opposition, of lesser rank, were brusquely forced from office, and others, like Yoshida Shōin and Hashimoto Sanai, were thrust abruptly into eternity.

There is no doubt that Ii Naosuke, like Mizuno Tadakuni before him, was a fudai daimyo to whom, in the drastically altered world of the mid-nineteenth century, the choice for increased central authority represented Japan's only guarantee of

safety. Long before assuming office, Naosuke was to use his influence in helping remove the ever-placatory Abe Masahiro from
the post of leading Senior Councilor. But like Mizuno Tadakuni,
although a fudai daimyo, Ii Naosuke hardly spoke for all his
fellows. True, he had his supporters in office, among them such
daimyo as Wakizaka Yasuori, who resigned within a month of
his leader's death, and Andō Nobumasa, who remained in office
for awhile, attempting to continue the Ii policy. His support,
however, is less impressive than the hostility he evoked, not only
from those he had chastised, but even from the very fudai daimyo
whose champion he is often claimed to have been.[12]

How else is one to explain the resignations during Naosuke's
period of dominance? Kuze Hirochika, leaving his position as
Senior Councilor after the tairō had been six months in office,
was to return to claim his former position within a month of
Naosuke's death. Another Senior Councilor, Manabe Akikatsu,
resigned to express his opposition to Naosuke's policies, just as
he had done years before when confronted with the no less uncongenial policies of Mizuno Tadakuni. Matsudaira Tadakata,
another Senior Councilor, also resigned. Itakura Katsukiyo, no
less a fudai daimyo than the other three, was to be dismissed
from his office as Superintendent of Temples and Shrines, partly
because of his lack of enthusiasm for controversial political matters (for Naosuke was nothing if not controversial) and, no
doubt, partly because of a secret report identifying him as a
supporter of the disgraced Tokugawa Nariaki. He too was to
reenter the Bakufu after Naosuke's death, becoming a Senior
Councilor in 1862.[13]

Ii Naosuke's personal career came to an abrupt end outside
the Sakurada Gate of Edo Castle, where he was assassinated by
a group of samurai, all but one of them from Mito. As if his
life were not payment enough for so bold a policy, further punishment was demanded even in death. His domain was reduced, as

12. Imaizumi, 1 : 115–16.
13. This information comes largely from Takayanagi Mitsuhisa and Takeuchi Rizō, eds., *Nihonshi jiten;* from the Index of *Kyōto shugōshoku shimatsu,* and from Asamori Kaname, "Ansei no taigoku o megutte," *Nihon
rekishi* 243 : 88, and also from *Ii-ke shiryō,* 2 : 75.

Mizuno Tadakuni's had been; in this case, 100,000 koku were taken from a 350,000 koku fief for alleged dishonesty in office, an accusation evoking echoes of Yanagisawa Yoshiyasu and Tanuma Okitsugu, earlier champions of shogunal authority.[14] Yet, although Naosuke died immediately, his policy was to survive for a period in the hands of Andō Nobumasa, who also did his best, under mounting difficulties, to shore up the Bakufu.

Realizing that as long as the Bakufu lagged behind the daimyo in the arms race it could never speak from a position of strength, Andō Nobumasa was responsible for drafting plans to restore Tokugawa military preponderance. They included the projected purchase of a fleet of over four hundred warships, and the provision of a well-equipped standing army—responsible to the Bakufu alone—of ten thousand men. The money for such an ambitious program was to come from commercial enterprises, in which the Bakufu would take advantage of its still commanding position in the nascent foreign trade. Andō was responsible for an attempt to reorganize Japan's foreign trade, under which the products most popular abroad would be concentrated into the hands of specially licensed merchants under Bakufu supervision. In 1861, too, a *kaisho* was established in Edo, run with merchant cooperation, to collect the products of the Kantō and adjacent provinces for sale overseas.

Such policies proved no more popular than those of Ii Naosuke, and ultimately Andō Nobumasa was to pay the price. Once again, as in the case of the tairō, there was an assassination attempt by Mito samurai, this time outside the Sakashita Gate. When Andō survived it, sustaining only a slight wound, the attack moved to the political sphere, culminating in 1862 with a letter from Shimazu Hisamitsu, father and guardian to the young daimyo of Satsuma, to an influential courtier in Kyoto, urging that Andō be dismissed. A few days later he was, and shortly after, like Ii Naosuke, Mizuno Tadakuni, and Tanuma Okitsugu before him, he too was to be punished, forfeiting 20,000 koku of his fief, and placed under long-term house arrest.[15]

14. *Hikone-shi shi*, 3 : 9.
15. See Tanaka Akira, "Andō Nobumasa," in *Edo Bakufu—sono jitsuryoku monotachi*, ed. Kitajima Masamoto, 2 : passim.

Toward the end of 1864, after the four-nation attack on Chō-shū, came a further attempt to reassert Bakufu authority, this time, as if in desperation, one far more ambitious than had ever been seen before, and one which, if successful, would quite un-ambiguously have placed the Tokugawa in the position of abso-lute monarchs. The form resembled the stance taken by Andō Nobumasa, being concerned mainly with two aspects of power; military strength, and the money with which to provide for it. The announcement, early in 1865, of a second campaign against Chōshū, destined to be so unpopular with the daimyo, was made as part of a show of Bakufu strength. There was much pressure, too, within the Bakufu, to ask for foreign assistance in carrying this out. To this end, the years 1865–66 saw the growth of very close relations between elements of the Bakufu, and the French, whose minister to Japan, Léon Roches, had shown himself sym-pathetic to Bakufu ambitions. In 1865 France agreed to provide technical and financial assistance toward building a shipyard for the Bakufu at Yokosuka and sent, the following year, a special envoy for the purpose of drawing up the contract, involving a loan of six million dollars. Even the Bakufu's own internal mili-tary structure showed signs of impending change, notably a draft plan to call on all fudai daimyo and hatamoto to contribute not men, but money, to the Bakufu military machine, thus making possible the recruitment, equipment for, and maintenance of a force of fighting men in every way more efficient—and more steadfastly loyal—than any feudal army.

To pay for the refurbishing of its military machine, the Bakufu was also forced, as under Andō Nobumasa, to consider commer-cial activities of various sorts. The French, motivated neither by charity nor dispassionate belief in the principles of absolute monarchy, were eager to win commercial privileges in return for their assistance. In particular, they wanted access to Japan's sup-plies of raw silk, but Coullet, the special envoy, while proffering six million dollars with one hand, was with the other, also urg-ing upon the Bakufu a new mining policy, involving an aggres-sive search for mines of all kinds, particularly coal mines, thereby uncovering again, although the Frenchman was not to know it, a very ancient bone of contention in centrally feudal Japan. At

home, too, the Bakufu had begun to give renewed attention to
the possibilities of commercial control, with plans for a central
bank and for moneylending in cooperation with merchant houses
like the Mitsui, all financed by the customs revenue gained from
the opening of the ports.[16]

The association of fudai daimyo with this new and unprece-
dentedly ambitious policy is by no means clear. The Bakufu as
an institution was already beginning to crumble, split between
a group centered on Kyoto, where Hitotsubashi Yoshinobu, Matsudaira Katamori, and Matsudaira Sadataka occupied all the
major Bakufu posts, following the line of compromise favored
by all; another, grouped around the shogun, Ieyoshi, at Osaka,
where he had taken up temporary residence; and a third, which remained in Edo, growing progressively more restive at the collapse of Tokugawa authority. It was this latter group which
took the initiative in negotiating with the French and in drawing up plans for a Tokugawa monarchy.

Significantly, it was a policy which owed little or nothing to
the fudai daimyo. If Abe Masatō and Matsumae Takahiro (who,
incidentally, was hardly a fudai) cooperated, then others did not;
two of them resigned from the post of Senior Councilor on the
day the second campaign against Chōshū was announced. Rather,
reflecting the extent to which fudai had begun to disassociate
themselves from the Bakufu and all its works, this final reassertion of shogunal authority is linked with members of the hatamoto class, the direct vassals of the Tokugawa who filled the
lower positions in the official hierarchy. Unlike the fudai daimyo,
they maintained no domains of their own, being paid for the
most part in stipends from the Tokugawa treasury. They had no
independent power base and no source of income other than
their salaries and whatever extra could be won through Bakufu
office. Consequently, they were tied to the Tokugawa house, and
its organ of government, in a way which was altogether less ambivalent than was the case with the fudai daimyo, and their dependence on the Tokugawa was far more absolute. Were the
Bakufu to vanish, the hatamoto, unlike the fudai daimyo, would

16. Ishii Takashi, *Meiji ishin no kokusai-teki kankyō*, pp. 535ff., and also
Ishii Takashi, "Oguri Tadamasa," in *Edo Bakufu—sono jitsuryoku monotachi*, ed. Kitajima Masamoto, 2 : passim.

have nothing else to sustain them; perhaps it is for this reason that at the very last the Tokugawa were to find among them their most committed and ambitious supporters.

Most closely associated with this policy was Oguri Tadamasa, a hatamoto with an annual stipend of 2,500 koku, who, in the course of a successful career, had been a member of the first group of Japanese to travel abroad. His sympathies are apparent in a complaint, voiced in 1862, about daimyo interference in the Bakufu and the resulting "unconscionable alterations to policies already settled," in defiance, he believed, of the form of government under which Japan had been ruled since the Kamakura period. Later Oguri was to go beyond mere complaint to envisage a system in which there would be no more daimyo. If the Bakufu managed to obtain ships from France, he was later to say, then such ships would first be used to crush Chōshū, and then turned upon Satsuma, producing a situation in which "not one great daimyo in the whole country will dare argue. Then, with such strength, we will cut the daimyo down to size, and form a centralized government (*gunken no sei*)." It is hardly surprising that so outspoken a supporter of so unpopular a policy should have been one of the first political victims of the Meiji Restoration. In 1868 he was to be beheaded by Imperial troops as "a great criminal who should no longer be allowed on the face of the earth." [17]

Although the leader of this group of hatamoto, Oguri was by no means the only one of his kind to advocate a strong line. Kurimoto Kon, Ikeda Yorikata, and Enomoto Takeaki were all of the same mind. So too was Fukuzawa Yukichi, at this time a minor Bakufu official. Despite his more famous later recriminations against the Bakufu, expressed at a time when such sentiments had become both safe and fashionable. Fukuzawa was at this time sufficiently alarmed at the prospect of its overthrow to write a memorial on the subject, calling for the use of foreign troops against Chōshū in an attempt to bring about what he called *"Taikun no monarukii,"* or shogunal monarchy.[18]

17. The quotations are to be found in Ishii, "Oguri Tadamasa," p. 250, and Ishii Takashi, *Kokusai-teki kankyō*, pp. 548–49.

18. Fukuzawa's opinion appears in Tōyama Shigeki, "Ishin tōji no Fukuzawa no shisō," in *Sekai ni okeru Nihon no bunka*, ed. Saegusa Hirōto Kinen

If there is little to indicate convincing fudai support for the Bakufu in the politics of its years of crisis, what was their attitude to the opposition? Were they any more committed to the movement by which the Bakufu was progressively stripped of its powers? Such would seem closer to the truth, although a precise weighing of the impact of fudai politicians on either side would be difficult to achieve. During the years from 1853 to the beginning of the ascendancy of Ii Naosuke, control of the Bakufu lay with two men, Abe Masahiro and Hotta Masayoshi, both fudai daimyo, well supported by the other Senior Councilors, and both committed to reducing the range of Bakufu authority. Abe Masahiro's position on this issue had already been established before the arrival of the black ships. He had deferred to Tokugawa Nariaki, and he continued to do so; other daimyo found him equally complaisant, and were disturbed at his resignation from the position of leading Senior Councilor in 1855. His successor, Hotta Masayoshi, however, gave them nothing to fear. As Shimazu Nariakira, tozama daimyo of Satsuma, wrote to Matsudaira Yoshinaga, ichimon daimyo of Fukui, "It seems that with the emergence of Hotta all our worries are lessened." [19] Indeed, it seemed they were, for Hotta had established his credentials by his opposition to Mizuno Tadakuni over a decade before, and, until 1858, he was to prove himself as solicitous of the interests of the larger daimyo as Abe Masahiro had been. That he was not without fudai support may be judged by the extent of his following, among them Makino Tadamasa, and those who were later to clash with Ii Naosuke—Kuze Hirochika, Matsudaira Tadakata, and Itakura Katsukiyo.

A similar point can be made about the fudai politicians during 1862–64, the years of greatest *kōbu gattai* influence. By tradition the fudai daimyo are regarded as distinct from the daimyo supporters of the kōbu gattai movement, the one seen as gripping desperately to their formal monopoly of Bakufu office, supposedly

Rombun-shū Hensei-kai. It should be noted that not all hatamoto were as favorably disposed to the Bakufu; Katsu Rintarō, never fond of the Oguri group, whom he called "sinister little people," worked for the *kōbu-gattai* group and finally made his own accommodation with the successful anti-Bakufu forces. On this point, see Handa Yoshiko, "Dai ni-ji sei-Chō o meguru Bakufu no dōkō—Yoshinobu seiken no seiritsu to sono seikaku," *Shisō* 8 : 37.

19. Imaizumi, 1 : 115–16.

the only form of distinction left to them, and the other as determined, for the best possible motives, to throw the affairs of
government open to men of talent, a term which, although used
widely, was interpreted narrowly, usually meaning only oneself
and a few intimate friends. In fact, however, although one of
the aims of the kōbu gattai movement lay in stripping the fudai
of their role in government, there is no compelling evidence of
fudai antipathy or opposition. Some, like Ii Naosuke and Andō
Nobumasa, may have stood out in defiance, but they were the
exceptions. The kōbu gattai daimyo, for all their stated aims of
bringing court and Bakufu together, and despite the new scope
of the demands, fitted snugly into a very old tradition of Tokugawa politics. They, too, were opponents of big government and
wanted the utmost room to maneuver both within their own
domains and in their relations with the foreign nations at the
door; thus, the appeal of this policy to fudai daimyo cannot be
discounted. The men who dominated the kōbu gattai movement were undeniably tozama and ichimon daimyo—Matsudaira
Yoshinaga, Yamanouchi Toyoshige, Date Munenari, Matsudaira
Katamori, Tokugawa Yoshinobu—but, for their successes after
1862, they had the support of fudai politicians like Itakura Katsukiyo, Makino Tadayuki, Suwa Tadamasa, Ogasawara Nagamichi, and Mizuno Tadayuki.

It seems likely, then, that during the Bakumatsu the politically active fudai daimyo, although far from united, were on
the whole as ready to encourage the diminution of central power
and, therefore, by extension, the enhancement of their own security, as they had ever been. The attitude of those who took
no part in politics is more difficult to evaluate, until the time
comes, in 1866, and again in 1867–68, to put armies into the
field. There is, however, at least one other way of gauging their
position during these years of great turmoil. Had they been concerned at the political trend of the Bakumatsu years, which was
to belittle the dynasty their ancestors had served for over two
centuries, part of the remedy lay in their own hands. They could
have proved their concern by joining in the struggle for Bakufu
office. But they did not. True, there was a remarkable turnover
of Bakufu officials after 1853, involving more people than was
usual, but a glance at official appointments shows the Bakufu

often forced to scrape the bottom of the administrative barrel. Some Senior Councilors were not fudai daimyo, among them Arima Michizumi, Matsumae Munehiro, and Tachibana Tanemasa. Others, while from fudai families, were not themselves daimyo, as was the case with Ogasawara Nagamichi, who was only heir apparent to the daimyo of Karatsu, and also Inaba Masami, who had retired and taken the tonsure before being dragged unwillingly back into politics, his desperate excuses of deafness and stomach pains notwithstanding.[20] At least four Senior Councilors were still in their twenties when appointed, while others were drawn into high political office without any prior experience. Only seven of the twenty-two newly appointed Senior Councilors after 1860 could be said to have reached their posts by the regular course—that is, the route leading from Superintendent of Temples and Shrines to either Keeper of Osaka Castle or Kyoto Deputy—before their final promotion. Indeed, one of those seven, Ōkōchi Masatada, having passed through all these stages before his twenty-fourth birthday, could hardly be called a seasoned administrator. The remaining fifteen had all followed abnormal careers, three coming from the post of Junior Councilor, another eight being promoted directly from the position of Superintendent of Temples and Shrines, and four being made Senior Councilor without previous experience of any sort.[21]

Although this suggests a lack of fudai determination to preserve the Bakufu through its darkest hour, such evidence is far from decisive. For more telling indications, we must turn to the behavior of the fudai daimyo at large during the military crises of 1866 and 1867–68, when even the most inarticulate and administratively untalented had the chance to give their loyalty tangible expression. But even here there are no convincing signs of fudai commitment.

There is no reason to believe that the significance of the second Chōshū campaign had escaped the fudai daimyo. Makino Tadayuki, daimyo of Nagaoka, at least summed up the situation accurately in an address to his troops at the beginning of the campaign. "This is the gravest crisis in the history of the Toku-

20. For Inaba Masami, see Kojima Shigeo, "Bakumatsu ishin ni okeru fudai Ōtaki han no dōkō," *Juntendō Daigaku Taiikugakubu kiyō* 1 : 112.

21. Calculated from Takayanagi and Takeuchi, pp. 1042–55.

gawa dynasty," he said, "and the fate of the government depends upon its outcome." [22] Yet, despite this, in a situation where concerted and enthusiastic fudai support might have salvaged matters, the traditional supporters of the Tokugawa house avoided total involvement.

The record of Hikone Han during this campaign is probably representative of those fudai domains ordered to provide troops. Certainly the requisite numbers were assembled and duly forwarded to Hiroshima. However, as a measure of their tepid approach to the fighting in which they were engaged, after three months of action in the van of the Bakufu forces at Iwakuni, where the bulk of the Chōshū men were concentrated, Hikone could show a casualty list of only twenty-one dead and forty-one wounded. For a domain having a samurai roster of more than thirteen thousand, these losses were rather less than spectacular.[23]

Fukuyama Han, too, fought with comparable absence of desperation. In mid-1866 some eight hundred Fukuyama samurai crossed the mountains to set up camp at Masuda, on the Japan Sea coast, in preparation for an attack on the Chōshū flank in conjunction with troops from the Bakufu and the adjacent Hamada Han. After their first engagement with the enemy, the Fukuyama men lost fifteen dead and twenty wounded; this apparently so crippled the other 765 that they began a withdrawal, ultimately permitting the Chōshū army to take Hamada Castle. Then came three weeks of retreat, after which the Fukuyama daimyo, Abe Masakata, last of a long line of fudai stalwarts, withdrew his men, apparently without first consulting the Bakufu. He promptly brought them back to Fukuyama and set them to work at a task which was obviously more important to them—preparing domain defense against a possible invasion by the boisterous Chōshū men, who had already moved outside their own borders to take Kokura and Hamada.[24]

Of all the fudai domains caught up in the second Chōshū campaign, the most determined fighting came from the forces of Kokura Han, who struggled for four months, despite the deser-

22. Imaizumi, 1 : 133.

23. Nishida Shūhei, "Meiji ishin ni okeru Hikone han," *Nihon rekishi* 203 : 76; Konishi Shirō, *Kindai 1*, p. 138.

24. *Fukuyama-shi shi*, 2 : 1142–45.

tion of their allies and the prudent withdrawal of Ogasawara
Nagamichi, who, as Senior Councilor, had been placed in charge
of the Kyushu attack. The Kokura troops fought bravely, even
desperately, refusing to submit until brought to their knees by
lack of ammunition.

Such spirited resistance, however, was not intended for the
preservation of the Bakufu, which had proved itself so weak a
reed. No less than the samurai of Fukuyama, those who continued to fight against Chōshū in Kokura were concerned primarily with the integrity of their domain. At Fukuyama they
hoped to prevent an invasion; at Kokura that invasion had already come. The Kiku Peninsula, which covers the eastern approach to the Straits of Shimonoseki, was part of the Kokura
domain, and it was a part which Chōshū coveted. Its position,
and its gun emplacements at Moji and Tanoura, were of peculiar strategic importance, since any vessel approaching Shimonoseki from the east would pass within easy gunshot. Chōshū,
fresh from its encounter with foreign vessels in 1864, and well
aware of its vulnerability from the sea, knew that control of
these gun emplacements was indispensable and so struck its first
blow in the second Chōshū campaign by launching an attack on
Kokura to get them. Thus the Kokura troops were, from the
first, fighting on their own soil for their own sake, and this alone
lent them the energy. When their Kumamoto allies abandoned
the struggle, as they could, for their own domain was not threatened, the reaction at Kokura was bitter, one contemporary account observing with emotion that "the Hosokawa men, till now
trusted like gods, like blood relations, left like the scattering of
a spider's brood"; yet had the positions been reversed, no doubt
Kokura would have done the same. Their recriminations were
reserved for the shabby treatment they—not the Tokugawa—
had received. Their hot—and vain—pursuit of Ogasawara Nagamichi, who had crept away disguised as one of his own servants,
was not for the sake of the Bakufu, whose representative he was,
but for their own, since they sought from him some assurance
that they would not be abandoned. Similarly, after setting their
castle to the torch rather than allowing it to fall into Chōshū
hands, they continued to fight well after the Bakufu had made

its own humiliating peace and ordered all domains to do like-
wise. When Kokura finally ceased fighting, it was not at the
behest of the Bakufu but, rather, of two other Kyushu domains,
Satsuma and Kumamoto.[25]

The Bakufu's defeat in the second Chōshū campaign changed
the complexion of the political struggle within Japan from one
in which it ran the risk of losing many of its remaining powers,
to one in which it faced the possibility of total overthrow. Yet,
although many daimyo—fudai among them—may have had reservations about the new form of government Satsuma and Chōshū were preparing for them in the emperor's name, few made
any effort to preserve the Bakufu. The fudai, together with most
daimyo, refrained from committing themselves for as long as
possible. When they finally chose the Imperial side, as discretion commanded, they had lost all chance of gaining prominence
in the new government, but then so had the majority of tozama
domains, which had been equally reluctant to commit themselves
selves. As is the case with most issues in the Tokugawa period,
to see the fall of the Bakufu in fudai-tozama terms is a gross
oversimplification.

Toward the end of 1867, Yoshinobu, the last of the Tokugawa
shogun, sure no longer of his position, his policy, or his support,
surrendered his right to rule to the emperor. Before long, however, he began to regret it, for an Imperial order promptly deprived him of his domains, rather more than he had bargained
for. To his support came a handful of daimyo, who, on his behalf, engaged the Imperial forces at the beginning of 1868 in the
battles of Toba and Fushimi, and lost. Of all the Japanese
daimyo who had reservations about the new regime—almost
certainly the majority of them—only ten fought here to defend
the Tokugawa from the depredations of Satsuma and Chōshū.[26]
Of those ten, four were ichimon, the remainder were fudai—
from Ōgaki, Hamada, Obama, Miyazu, Toba, and Nobeoka. If

25. An'ura Teruhiko, "Keiō ninen heiin no yaku ni okeru Kibi-tōge,
Tanuki-yama fujin no senjutsu-teki igi," *Kiroku* 11 : 38–40, 53; *Buzen sōsho*,
21 : 123–24. The quotation is from *Buzen sōsho*, p. 119.

26. Kojima Shigeo, "Bakumatsu, ishin ni okeru fudai han no dōkō," *Nihon
rekishi* 221 : 64–65.

it is argued that their presence in this last-ditch battle was due to their fudai status, which demanded their loyalty to the Tokugawa cause, one might ask where the other 120-odd fudai daimyo were; and if it is argued that these six fudai joined together to protect their privileged position within the Bakufu, it should be asked why they previously had not valued it more. Of the six, only the Sakai of Obama had shown any particular interest in Bakufu office throughout the Edo period. Two others, the Matsudaira branches at Hamada and Miyazu, had shown little Bakufu activity prior to the Bakumatsu. As for the other three— the Naitō of Nobeoka, the Inagaki of Toba, and the Toda of Ōgaki, it would be difficult to find fudai families who had participated less in the official life of the Bakufu throughout the Tokugawa period.

It may well be that the presence of forces from these six fudai han is no token of inflexible devotion to the Tokugawa but, instead, an unhappy result of having been caught in the wrong place at the wrong time. Perhaps the presence of the Inagaki of Toba can be explained by the fact that one of the battles took place on their doorstep. Ōgaki Han was involved simply because three months earlier, in return for having between 20,000–30,000 koku of its domain moved from Ōgaki to a more productive area, it had volunteered troops for guard duty at Osaka. Certainly it was not prompted by feudal obligation or attachment to the Bakufu cause, for while part of the han forces were thus engaged as Osaka, negotiations were afoot to bring Ōgaki Han over to the Imperial side, and forces at Ōgaki Castle were under instruction to surrender to the Imperial troops without resistance if the need arose.[27]

Meanwhile, most of the other fudai domains lay very low. Hikone actually fought on the Imperial side in these engagements, but it was the only fudai domain to commit itself so early to the Imperial cause. The Inaba of Yodo Han, who, in terms of Bakufu service, had more reason to fight on the Tokugawa side than any of those who actually did so, save the Obama Sakai, remained neutral during the nearby Fushimi battle. Then, as the defeated Bakufu forces straggled off towards Osaka, the Inaba

27. Hosokawa Michio, "Bakumatsu, ishin-ki ni okeru Ōgaki han no dōkō," *Nihon rekishi* 221 : 64–65.

refused them the use of Yodo Castle as a center around which to regroup.[28]

Once the defeat at Toba and Fushimi had made it certain that neither the Tokugawa nor the Bakufu could be revived, there was a torrent of conversions, as daimyo of all complexions suddenly found themselves gripped by the sublime logic of the Imperial cause. Ōgaki Han, which just days before had fought on the Tokugawa side, joined the spearhead of the Imperial army which was setting off up the Tōzandō, and informed the former shogun that "if you should ever again raise a great army in an unrighteous cause, even though you win each of one hundred battles, there is no way to restore the Bakufu's authority." [29] Other fudai domains of western and central Japan also promptly pledged allegiance to a cause they had previously kept at arm's length. On their way through the fudai strongholds of the Tōkai and the Kantō, the Imperial forces met little or no resistance from fudai daimyo, unconvinced that their destinies and that of their Tokugawa master were so closely intertwined that the fall of the one would inevitably bring down the other. They were not unconcerned at the prospect of Satsuma-Chōshū domination, and they found evident cause for alarm in the severe treatment accorded the last of the Tokugawa shogun, but most fudai domains elected to approach the matter pragmatically. By his resignation, and his steadfast refusal to fight for his heritage, Tokugawa Yoshinobu had given the fudai domains a perfect face-saving device. Not only was resistance an offense to the emperor, but it could also be portrayed as contrary to the wishes of the head of the Tokugawa house himself—an argument used effectively in various fudai domains at the time.[30] Nevertheless, while submitting willingly enough to the Imperial forces, the fudai domains of eastern Japan were not above covering their bets in order to keep their domains secure, no matter which way the wind blew. Tateyama Han, for example, in the hands of the fudai house of Inaba, declared for the Imperial side when the

28. Kojima, "Fudai han no dōkō," p. 18.

29. Hosokawa, "Ōgaki han no dōkō," p. 67.

30. An example of this is to be found in Sakura Han, where Nishimura Shigeki made use of just this point to dampen an embryonic resistance movement amongst the younger samurai of the domain. See Kojima, "Kaimei-ha kanryō," p. 461.

time came but kept a door open by thereafter allowing the rebellious Enomoto Takeaki and his fleet of ships to land and buy
fuel and water.[31] On the whole, the fudai daimyo at the very
beginning of the Meiji period had every expectation that, given
good behavior and enthusiastic cooperation, their holdings—
which ranked largest in their scale of values—would be no whit
diminished under a new and gentler regime; had the course of
events turned the other way, and Oguri Tadamasa been successful in his plan to turn the Bakufu into a centralized monarchy,
they could not have been nearly so confident. Paradoxically, of
course, within three years, the very fate Oguri had sketched out
for the daimyo was brought into being by the new government,
but in 1868 no one was to foresee this, except perhaps the men
who were later to introduce it, and they wisely kept their own
counsel.

The only resistance the Imperial forces were to meet during
their triumphal sweep was in the northeast, where almost all of
the Tōhoku domains formed an alliance against them and fought
an extended campaign which finally ended with the fall of Aizu
Castle some eight months later. Yet, the simple fact that these
twenty-six Tōhoku han (only a handful of them fudai) fought
against the Imperial army does not necessarily make their leaders,
as one prominent scholar has dubbed them, "Tokugawa parti-
sans." [32] There is little to support a claim that they were working toward a Tokugawa restoration. They procured their own
Imperial pretender, Prince Rin'ōji, proclaimed him the Emperor
Tōbu (with the era name Taisei), and assigned themselves prominent positions in his government. It seems far more likely that
this vast regional alliance of heterogeneous domains either expected to prevail, and win for themselves the power which was
about to go to Satsuma and Chōshū, or else anticipated proving
such a thorn in the Imperial side that they could be bought off
with assurances that their autonomy would not be molested.

So the Bakufu vanished, without complaint from those most
closely associated with it. The Tokugawa fell, ignored by those
who for so long had trumpeted their loyalty. It has been my
theme that the employment of the servants helped bring the
master to the ground, yet, beyond suggesting that the loyalties

31. Kojima, "Ōtaki han no dōkō," p. 113.
32. M. B. Jansen, *Sakamoto Ryoma and the Meiji Restoration*, p. 334.

of men are not always what they proclaim them to be, it is not my intention to berate the fudai daimyo for horrid duplicity. There were, after all, limits to what any daimyo could do. Even at the best of times, as we have seen, there was a silent struggle between the daimyo and his vassals for control of the domain. This struggle was to intensify during the Bakumatsu, when risks were greater and stakes higher. Too forceful a move in either direction could bring fearful consequences, a truth brought home to the Ii vassals when one-third of their domain was taken from them in consequence of the errors of their former daimyo. The result in many domains was the virtual disappearance of the daimyo as a political figure. Ernest Satow, personally acquainted with many daimyo at the time, described the situation as one in which "power nominally exercised by the chief daimiōs came to be wielded by the more energetic and intelligent of their retainers, most of whom were samurai of no rank or position. These men it was who really ruled the clan, determined the policy of its head and dictated to him the language he should use on public occasions." [33] In the Bakumatsu, more so than at any other time in the Tokugawa period, domain policy was the subject of fierce and widespread debate among the samurai, and under such circumstances no daimyo could easily override those dependent upon him.

In any case, the course of Bakumatsu events conspired to rob the daimyo of his individual authority, since they moved so quickly and in so many different directions. At Oshi Han, for example, the domain of the fudai Okudaira Matsudaira branch, there were three distinct centers of power by 1867: one at Gyōda, the castle town, where the retired daimyo, Matsudaira Tadakuni, was in residence; a second at Edo, home of Matsudaira Tadazane, the incumbent; and a third in Kyoto, where the domain had sent its own officials to keep it informed of developments there. It was no longer possible for one man to keep control; even had the daimyo wished to, been capable of, and been allowed to direct the affairs of his domain himself, geography was against him.[34]

As the Bakumatsu political crisis reached its peak, in 1867, it

33. Satow, p. 37.
34. Kojima Shigeo, "Bakumatsu ishin ni okeru fudai Bushū Oshi han no dōkō," *Juntendō Daigaku Taiikugakubu kiyō* 6 : passim.

was quite common for daimyo to take a further step into obscurity; deprived of their right to make their own decisions, for
the most part, many of them were soon to be robbed even of
the luxury of appearing to have made those decisions, since their
vassals postponed any irrevocable decision for as long as possible.
On occasion it was feigned illness, which reached epidemic proportions among the Bakumatsu daimyo, as one by one they took
to their beds to avoid going anywhere or saying anything. Sometimes an institutionalized lightning rod was employed, that is,
someone of comparable eminence in the domain who could balance a contrary opinion against whatever stand the daimyo finally
took, making sure that, with either side fully represented, the
domain itself would be preserved, with at least one figurehead
untainted by an association with the losing side. Sometimes the
lightning rod was the retired daimyo, sometimes the heir apparent. At Nagaoka, for example, Makino Tadamasa retired in
1867, turning the succession over to an adopted son, rather than
his real son. Therefore, when the adopted son chose the losing
side in 1868, and was punished for it, the domain could pass
automatically to Tadamasa's real son.

There was an even more obvious assignment of roles at Oshi,
involving the retired daimyo, Matsudaira Tadakuni, and the current daimyo, Matsudaira Tadazane. In early 1868, when the Oshi
samurai had their full-scale conference to determine just where
the domain should place its allegiance, Tadakuni urged support
for the Imperial side in these words: "Our house has always acknowledged the Tokugawa as head, but nevertheless it is difficult to resist the majority; we should accept the Imperial cause
completely." By contrast, Tadazane insisted on support for the
Tokugawa, saying: "The Tokugawa family established the lesser
domains for just such an eventuality as this. We must accept that
obligation. I am no enemy of the Imperial court, but Satsuma
and Chōshū must be resisted." No matter what the outcome, the
domain was fully insured, but later, still uneasy, the domain was
to introduce yet another institutional device to acquit the domain of responsibility in any circumstances. This was the figure
of the scapegoat senior vassal, not uncommon in domain history,
who emerged later in 1868 when, the Imperial army just outside
the town, a decision had to be made immediately. Reluctantly,

the domain declared allegiance to the Imperial side, but, to guard against the eventuality of a Tokugawa revival, the oath of allegiance was signed only by a senior samurai, who promised to atone with his life if the domain should later alter its position. While not a comfortable position for the man concerned, the domain could thereby survive under any circumstances, if necessary repudiating the Imperial cause simply by repudiating him.[35]

In such ways, the daimyo of the Bakumatsu, fudai as well as tozama, made sure of the greatest possible flexibility at any given moment. The security of their domains was at stake, and this was far too important to sacrifice for the simple pleasure of total commitment to a cause which could easily lose. All options were kept open as long as possible. The Matsudaira of Oshi Han, linked by marriage to a family of Kyoto nobles, the Shijō, preserved friendly connections with Shijō Takauta throughout the 1860s, despite the fact that for most of that time the courtier was under Bakufu interdiction, hiding in Chōshū. Even after having presented a force of ninety samurai to the Imperial side, that domain was still agonizing over the safest course to take. Notable instances of fudai loyalty to the Imperial side were not uncommonly linked with a simpler, less exalted urge to keep the domain free from harm. The Hikone *ashigaru* who swung the tide of the domain argument over to the Imperial side did so because they felt any other course was gambling with the safety of the domain. At Sakura, the Imperial loyalist, Hirano Shigehisa, could urge acceptance of the Imperial cause on his fellows by warning them that further vacillation could bring on Sakura a fate already suffered by Odawara, which had been deprived of some of its domain in punishment.[36]

35. There is an interesting example of vassal scapeboats in the ichimon domain of Takamatsu. After fighting for the Bakufu at Toba-Fushimi, Takamatsu promptly reversed its allegiance, and in token of its new loyalty, sent to the Imperial headquarters the heads of two such scapegoats. See Kimura Motoi and Sugimoto Toshio, eds., *Fudai hansei no tenkai to Meiji ishin,* p. 308.

36. The material on Oshi comes from Kojima, "Oshi han," pp. 163, 169, while that on Hikone is from *Hikone-shi shi,* 3 : 163. The information on Sakura is from Kimura and Sugimoto, p. 314, and also Kojima Shigeo, "Fudai Sakura han no kyōjun to Satō Taizen," p. 58.

Under such circumstances it was inevitable that the old fudai
virtues of self-sacrifice and dedication to the Tokugawa house
should vanish. Only in the rhetoric of the period did it survive,
and then only briefly. Late in 1867, Sakura Han could announce:
"We think it is incumbent upon fudai to fulfill their obligation
as vassals, no matter what the consequences . . . this is no time
for the shimpan and fudai houses to sit back with indifference."
Within a year, however, its tune had changed; in response to a
plea for aid from the rebels at Aizu, the Sakura daimyo replied:
"It is well known that my house has received the grace and favor
of the Tokugawa family ever since the time of my ancestors; but
nevertheless it is now an established fact that we support the Imperial cause—despite the respect we have for the wishes of the
Lord Tokugawa; no matter who urges us, and no matter how
strongly we are urged, to change this, I believe we must not." [37]

The fudai daimyo chose, as they had to, the path which guaranteed them, and those dependent on them, the greatest measure
of security. No daimyo who played a part in the Meiji Restoration was to know that he and his kind would soon be consigned
to obscurity. The social revolution had thrust into prominence
men of undistinguished origin who, with only talent and vigor
to sustain them, were to guide the new Meiji government along
lines which, within three short years, were to sever the daimyo
class from lands and vassals. Had the daimyo known, it is very
likely that they, and the vassals themselves, would not have wandered so obligingly into the Restoration.

The Meiji government was gradually to acquire for itself the
very powers which the daimyo had resisted under the Bakufu.
By 1871 the institution of the daimyo was no more, and those
who filled it were pensioned off with money—amounting to a
solid personal income—and fobbed off with illusory political
duties. In their place, as provincial governors, were administrators appointed by the central government and kept in the provinces at the government's pleasure, a major step toward ending
the regionalism characteristic of Japan since long before the
Nara period. Foreign affairs, and the guidance of trade and industry were placed under undisputed central control. The armed
forces, although at first dominated by Satsuma and Chōshū, were

37. Kojima, "Satō Taizen," pp. 56–58.

never again to reveal regional sectionalism, even though they remained notoriously the least integrated part of the Meiji settlement.

By resisting the temptation to persevere with the decentralization and regionalism which lay implicit in the functions of the daimyo of the Tokugawa period, the Meiji administrators, no matter how precarious their government in its early years, had taken the one step the Tokugawa Bakufu could never take, and so assured for Japan a truly national government, despite its *hanbatsu* overtones, at a time when Japan stood most in need of it.

Much has been made of the Tokugawa Bakufu's success in maintaining itself for so long. It lasted for 265 years, but it is hard to say that the Tokugawa earned this immunity from civil turmoil. Beneath the veneer of centralized government lay all the ancient traditions of regionalism, reinforced by the daimyo institution, strong enough to keep a distant government at bay, sufficiently diffuse to prevent under normal circumstances the emergence of new coalitions. An earlier visit by an earlier Perry, posing the same problem, would have evoked from the Bakufu the same response, which, provoking the daimyo into resistance, would have brought with it an earlier resolution. Whether it would also have brought into being a government of new men capable of replacing the daimyo so adroitly, so gradually, by broaching from the side the walls of a regionalism impregnable to frontal assault, is another question.

The Role of the Fudai Daimyo

Of all the virtues most emphasized by a feudal nobility, that of loyalty is the most important. The personal bond between man and master, lord and vassal, is the most characteristic sign of feudalism in action, whether in Europe or Japan. The vassal who, loyal to his lord above all things, is prepared to sacrifice prosperity, wife, children, and finally life itself in his master's service, is a stock character in traditional Japanese theater, and shows little signs of losing popularity. Although exaggerated, frequently to the point of caricature, it cannot be shrugged off entirely, for, beyond the protestations of loyalty unto death of the Tokugawa samurai class, the majority of whom were staid civil servants, and the fantasies woven around those sentiments by dramatists whose own loyalties were directed to the box office, lie two facts. The first is that, for the men of the warrior generation, like Ōkubo Hikozaemon, there was a great emotional appeal in those bonds between master and man which could only be forged in time of war. The second is that, even in peacetime, for the samurai civil servants and the society they built up, it was this loyalty, or its polite counterfeit, which kept society working so smoothly. The samurai worked hard for his daimyo, who worked hard for his shogun, who in turn worked hard to build a proper society in obedience to his mandate from the emperor— and it was loyalty which cemented every one of the joins. The social contract of feudal Japan was phrased not in terms of rights, but of obligations, which were themselves nothing other than the expression of loyalty.

Therefore, of necessity, in a society in which the landed class transferred its property by inheritance, it was essential to accept the pretense that the fierce battlefield loyalties could be transmitted from father to son in the same manner as physical characteristics. It was, of course, impossible, but society depended upon the fiction being sustained. In this way the special myth of the fudai daimyo arose, and with it a form of institutionalized loyalty, which condemned the Tokugawa Bakufu to finding its senior civil administrators from one class of men, judged more loyal than others by virtue of the deeds of their ancestors. It was a fiction in which the shogun, for the most part, acquiesced, and in praise of which the fudai daimyo themselves lifted their voices aloud.

But it was a fiction, nothing more, and ultimately the Tokugawa house was to pay dearly for its acquiescence. Because of it, the Bakufu was obliged to seek its administrators from among a group of men, who, like the form of government for which they worked, stood somewhere in the penumbra between the poles of feudalism and centralized monarchy, sharing in the dualism which pulled outward to regionalism and inward to centralization. For a government which once had the opportunity of becoming a centralized monarchy, as the Tokugawa Bakufu did, the fudai daimyo represented a pool of civil servants that was far from ideal. All of them, within their own domains, were beneficiaries of a process which had forced their vassals into castle towns, separated them completely from the land, and freed them of all temptations to serve particular interests at the expense of the whole. True, the fudai daimyo were no more free than were other daimyo from power struggles centered around the domain's administration, but, in such battles, both sides invariably worked for the whole domain; the vassals, since they drew their rewards from the domain storehouses at an agreed rate, instead of cultivating gardens of their own, had no incentive other than to strive for the prosperity of the whole domain, no matter how much they may also have worked to increase their own share of those resources. As servants of the Bakufu, however, the fudai daimyo resisted, without stepping outside the accepted framework of government, and resisted successfully, any attempt by the Tokugawa house to win the battle for centralization in which they themselves, on a smaller scale, were already victors.

For this reason they made poor servants of autocracy. As other governments, more successful in the movement toward national monarchy, had discovered, the only possible servants were those who had no competing claims upon their allegiance. Self-interest, yes, but of a sort that contributed to the whole, instead of detracting from it. The Tudors, for example, who used low born counselors, rewarded them well, and changed them often, avoided the risk the Tokugawa were forced to take, and managed to make their government one which has become synonymous with successful despotism. This is not to say that the Tudors were completely effective as absolute monarchs. They were not, as their Stuart successors were to discover when confronted by a Parliament which, growing increasingly restive under Elizabeth, was to erupt under James, bursting into open rebellion under Charles. Nevertheless, although the Tudors and the Tokugawa began their careers under similar circumstances, the Tudors within three generations had achieved measures of control over national taxation, military strength, and local government which, while not without weaknesses, were not to be equaled in Japan until the Meiji period.

Where the Tudors had taken care to avoid being saddled with a fudai class of advisers, the Tokugawa seemed unable to do so. Keeping the daimyo institution as a form of local government, and creating new daimyo rather than allowing the institution to die out, the Tokugawa Bakufu in effect committed itself to the preservation of feudalism and continued to choose its servants from among that class. Perhaps the Tokugawa were seduced by the concept of loyalty itself, unable to believe that those most vociferous in their professions of loyalty might interpret that elusive concept rather differently from themselves. Perhaps, as some scholars have claimed, in the absence of any relevant model for centralization, the Tokugawa saw no alternative to the system that had developed—although it seems unlikely that they could be ignorant of the process of centralization in microcosm which had already been so effective in the daimyo domains. Perhaps they were the victims of historical consequences, prevented at first by military weakness from putting an end to the daimyo who had helped them into position, and later, under more complaisant shogun, politely barred by the fudai daimyo from choosing any such path. Perhaps, too, the obliging disappearance of the threat of foreign invasion after the 1630s helped the Tokugawa remain in their position of titular power. The Tudors, threatened from over the Channel by France and Spain, could not afford the luxury of regionalism. Not until they received news of the Opium War were the Japanese to find themselves in such a position, where an uncomfortable choice had to be made. No matter how weakened they were as a government, the Tokugawa did at least have inertia, a very powerful force, on their side, helping them remain in nominal authority until the problem of foreign affairs was to present itself finally in an inescapable form.

The fudai daimyo were the custodians of that inertia, and the Tokugawa, by submitting so often to their declarations of monopoly over administrative positions, did little to alter the balance of power. The Tokugawa failed in what has always been one of the chief problems confronting any dynasty, the problem of counsel. At the beginning of the Tokugawa period, the lesser fudai were in fact ideal servants of government, but as the daimyo element in their duality gained strength, they gradually hardened into a pressure group, nonetheless effective for its refusal to declare itself as such, from which only a handful of individuals, most notably Mizuno Tadakuni and Ii Naosuke, were ever to disassociate themselves. It was a process in which the Tokugawa themselves were unwitting accomplices, trapped no doubt by the initial quandary of a government too weak to stand alone. In the domains, few samurai households were to keep their enfeoffments intact without assuming, from time to time, the responsibilities of domain office. It was not so with the Bakufu, which countenanced automatic inheritance of fudai domains even when no service had been given. This was one mistake which helped keep the fudai daimyo aware of their independence of the Tokugawa house. The other major error, also doubtless attributable to the restricted strategic situation in which the first Tokugawa found themselves, was to assign to the fudai large numbers of vassals for whose well-being they were made responsible. This of its own was sufficient to make the daimyo responsive to the demands of his vassals, to increase their hold over him, and ultimately to reduce his capacity for anything approaching the selfless devotion which was the fudai ideal.

It is not surprising then, that, in the end, all of these secondary claims for the attention of the fudai daimyo should have become of primary importance, leading the majority of the fudai to make their final gesture of allegiance away from the Tokugawa. It is significant that, in almost all cases, that gesture, when it finally came, was no gesture of loyalty to the emperor, whom none of them knew, nor of adherence to the glorious principle of *taigi meibun,* although they recognized a bandwagon when they saw one, nor of admiration for the righteous leadership of Satsuma and Choshu, whose motives were all too transparent, but rather a gesture of loyalty to their domains. They were ultimately to be disappointed, when the social revolution rolled across them, as it did over all their peers, but having elected to bend with the wind, as Ōkubo Hikozaemon saw they would, there was no way to resist when that wind became a tempest, sweeping away all that remained of their world.

Appendix: Fudai Daimyo, 1853

(Based on the list in Tokyo Daigaku Shiryō Hensanjo, eds., *Dokushi biyō*, pp. 475ff., and amended where necessary by reference to Takayanagi and Takeuchi, eds., *Nihonshi jiten*, and Fujino, *Bakuhan*, pp. 721ff.).

Daimyo	Domain	Province	Kokudaka
Ii	Hikone	Ōmi	350,000
Yanagisawa	Kōriyama	Yamato	151,200
Ogasawara	Kokura	Buzen	150,000
Sakai	Himeji	Harima	150,000
Sakakibara	Takada	Echigo	150,000
Sakai	Shōnai	Dewa	140,000
Ōkubo	Odawara	Sagami	113,129
Abe	Fukuyama	Bingo	110,000
Hotta	Sakura	Shimoosa	110,000
Sakai	Obama	Wakasa	103,558
Inaba	Yodo	Yamashiro	102,000
Abe	Shirakawa	Mutsu	100,000
Okudaira	Nakatsu	Buzen	100,000
Toda	Ōgaki	Mino	100,000
Tsuchiya	Tsuchiura	Hitachi	95,000
Matsudaira (Nagasawa Ōkochi)	Takasaki	Kozuke	82,000
Doi	Koga	Shimoosa	80,000
Makino	Kasama	Hitachi	80,000
Toda	Utsunomiya	Shimotsuke	77,800
Makino	Nagaoka	Echigo	74,000
Matsudaira (Matsui)	Tanakura	Mutsu	73,000
Honjō	Miyazu	Tango	70,000
Matsudaira (Fukōzu)	Shimabara	Hizen	70,000
Matsudaira (Nagasawa Ōkōchi)	Yoshida	Mikawa	70,000
Naitō	Nobeoka	Hyūga	70,000
Akimoto	Tatebayashi	Kōzuke	60,000
Aoyama	Sasayama	Tamba	60,000
Inoue	Hamamatsu	Tōtōmi	60,000
Honda	Zeze	Ōmi	60,000

Daimyo	Domain	Province	Kokudaka
Ishikawa	Kameyama	Ise	60,000
Matsudaira (Toda)	Matsumoto	Shinano	60,000
Matsudaira (Ogyū)	Nishio	Mikawa	60,000
Ogasawara	Karatsu	Hizen	60,000
Kuze	Sekiyado	Shimoosa	58,000
Matsudaira (Fujii)	Ueda	Shinano	53,000
Okabe	Kishiwada	Izumi	53,000
Ōta	Kakegawa	Tōtōmi	50,370
Naitō	Murakami	Echigo	50,090
Andō	Iwakitaira	Mutsu	50,000
Honda	Okazaki	Mikawa	50,000
Itakura	Matsuyama	Bitchū	50,000
Manabe	Sabae	Echizen	50,000
Matsudaira (Katahara)	Kameyama	Tamba	50,000
Mizuno	Numazu	Suruga	50,000
Mizuno	Yamagata	Dewa	50,000
Aoyama	Gujō	Mino	48,000
Doi	Ōno	Echizen	40,000
Honda	Tanaka	Suruga	40,000
Matsudaira (Sakurai)	Amagasaki	Settsu	40,000
Nagai	Takatsuki	Settsu	36,000
Makino	Tanabe	Tango	35,000
Nishio	Yokosuka	Tōtōmi	35,000
Toki	Numata	Kōzuke	35,000
Naitō	Takatō	Shinano	33,000
Kutsuki	Fukuchiyama	Tamba	32,000
Matsudaira (Nōmi)	Kitsuki	Bungo	32,000
Nagai	Kanō	Mino	32,000
Inagaki	Toba	Shima	30,000
Itakura	Annaka	Kōzuke	30,000
Itakura	Fukushima	Mutsu	30,000
Kuroda	Kururi	Kazusa	30,000
Matsudaira (Ogyū Ishikawa)	Iwamura	Mino	30,000
Matsudaira (Fujii)	Kaminoyama	Dewa	30,000
Ōkubo	Karasuyama	Shimotsuke	30,000
Suwa	Takashima	Shinano	30,000
Torii	Mibu	Shimotsuke	30,000
Sakai	Matsuyama	Dewa	25,000
Uemura	Takatori	Yamato	25,000
Doi	Kariya	Mikawa	23,000

Daimyo	Domain	Province	Kokudaka
Miura	Katsuyama	Mimasaka	23,000
Ōoka	Iwatsuki	Musashi	23,000
Ogasawara	Katsuyama	Echizen	22,777
Matsudaira (Ogyū)	Funai	Bungo	21,200
Anbe	Okabe	Musashi	20,250
Honda	Iiyama	Shinano	20,000
Honda	Izumi	Mutsu	20,000
Hoshina	Iino	Kazusa	20,000
Ii	Yoita	Echigo	20,000
Ishikawa	Shimodate	Hitachi	20,000
Itakura	Niwase	Bitchū	20,000
Masuyama	Nagashima	Ise	20,000
Matsudaira (Okudaira)	Obata	Kōzuke	20,000
Matsudaira (Nagasawa Ōkōchi)	Ōtaki	Kazusa	20,000
Naitō	Koromo	Mikawa	20,000
Sakai	Isezaki	Kōzuke	20,000
Mizuno	Yūki	Shimoosa	18,000
Abe	Sanuki	Kazusa	16,000
Hotta	Sanō	Shimotsuke	16,000
Matsudaira (Ogyū)	Okudono	Mikawa	16,000
Honda	Kambe	Ise	15,000
Makino	Komoro	Shinano	15,000
Mizuno	Tsurumaki	Kazusa	15,000
Naitō	Iwamurata	Shinano	15,000
Naitō	Yūnagaya	Mutsu	15,000
Watanabe	Hakata	Izumi	13,500
Inagaki	Yamagami	Ōmi	13,043
Hotta	Miyagawa	Ōmi	13,000
Kanō	Ichinomiya	Kazusa	13,000
Ōkubo	Oginosanchū	Sagami	13,000
Matsudaira (Hisamatsu)	Tako	Shimoosa	12,000
Miyake	Tawara	Mikawa	12,000
Sakai	Kachiyama	Awa	12,000
Yonekura	Kanazawa	Musashi	12,000
Toda	Ashikaga	Shimotsuke	11,000
Yonezu	Nagatoro	Mutsu	11,000
Yamaguchi	Ushiku	Hitachi	10,017
Arima	Fukiage	Shimotsuke	10,000
Inoue	Takaoka	Shimoosa	10,000
Hayashi	Jōzai	Kazusa	10,000

Daimyo	Domain	Province	Kokudaka
Honda	Yamazaki	Harima	10,000
Honjō	Takatomi	Mino	10,000
Hori	Shiiya	Echigo	10,000
Inaba	Tateyama	Awa	10,000
Inoue	Shimozuma	Hitachi	10,000
Matsudaira (Takiwaki),	Ojima	Suruga	10,000
Matsudaira (Yoshii)	Yoshii	Kōzuke	10,000
Morikawa	Oimi	Shimoosa	10,000
Nagai	Shinjō	Yamato	10,000
Niwa	Mikusa	Harima	10,000
Ogasawara	Anji	Harima	10,000
Ogasawara	Kokura Shinden	Buzen	10,000
Ōoka	Nishiōhira	Mikawa	10,000
Sakai	Kikuyama	Echizen	10,000
Takagi	Tannan	Kawachi	10,000
Tanuma	Sagara	Tōtōmi	10,000
Toda	Ōgaki Shinden	Mino	10,000
Uchida	Omigawa	Shimoosa	10,000
Yanagisawa	Kurokawa	Echigo	10,000
Yanagisawa	Mikkaichi	Echigo	10,000
Yagyū	Yagyū	Yamato	10,000

Glossary

The following Japanese words may be either singular or plural, according to context, and they have been used in this way throughout the book.

ashigaru   Foot soldiers, the lowest section of the warrior class.

baishin   A rear-vassal.

Bakufu   A military government; specifically, in the context of Tokugawa Japan, the administrative organ of the Tokugawa house.

daikan   In the Tokugawa period, a local official employed by the Bakufu to supervise regional administration and the collection of taxes within the Tokugawa domains.

daimyō   A territorial magnate; specifically, in the Tokugawa period, a baron whose domain produced an annual 10,000 koku or more of rice or some equivalent crop.

han   A feudal principality, or domain.

hatamoto   Those of the shogun's personal retainers whose enfeoffments were below the 10,000 koku required for daimyo status, but who nevertheless retained the privilege of direct audience with their lord.

hyō   A bale; specifically, in the context of this work, a bale of rice.

kabu nakama   Officially licensed associations of merchants or craftsmen.

kan   A unit of weight, corresponding to 3.75 kilograms; alternately, a term meaning 1,000 copper cash.

kashin   The personal retainers of a feudal lord, whether daimyo or shogun; referred to, in a group, as *kashindan*.

kōbu gattai   The Bakumatsu movement aimed at uniting Court and Bakufu by effecting various compromises between them.

koku   A unit of capacity, measuring a little under five bushels.

konnyaku   A tuber containing an edible starch.

ri   A unit of length, measuring a little less than four kilometers.

ryō   The standard gold coin of the Tokugawa period, sometimes called a *koban.*

sakoku   The official isolation of Japan from all but minimal foreign contact between 1639 and 1853.

shijimi   A small shellfish.

shōgun   A military commander; in the context of Tokugawa Japan, the head of the Tokugawa house, and of the Bakufu, its administrative arm.

tawaramono   One of the chief exports of Tokugawa Japan; bundles of dried sea slugs, dried abalone, and sharks' fins.

Bibliography

A. *Unpublished sources*

Cabinet Library, Tokyo
  Shōnai kemmon roku
Shiryō Hensanjo, Tokyo
  (Tanakura) Abe kafu
  (Echizen Maruoka) Arima kafu
  Hotta kafu
  Inaba kafu
  (Kazusa Tsurumai) Inoue kafu
  (Mikawa Toyohashi) Ōkōchi kafu
  Ogyū Matsudaira kafu
  Ōkubo kafu
  (Harima Himeji) Sakai kafu
  (Wakasa Obama) Sakai kafu
  Tsuchiya kafu
Tokyo Municipal University
  Hiyōroku, from the archives of the Mizuno family
Ministry of Education Archives, Tokyo
  (Tsuchiura han) Edo sumai goke-chū sekijun
  (————) Kantō kawagawa gofushin gotetsudai ikken
  (————) Onari nikki
  (————) Shoshi nempu
  (————) Tsuchiura sumai goke-chū sekijun

B. *Published sources*

Beasley, W. G. *Select Documents on Japanese Foreign Policy 1853–1868.* London, 1967
Buzen sōsho. 22 vols. Kita Kyushu, 1962–67
Cocks, Richard. *Diary of Richard Cocks, Cape-Merchant in the English Factory in Japan, 1615–1622.* Hakluyt Society Series, vols. 66, 67. London, 1883.
Cooper, Michael. *They Came to Japan: An Anthology of European Reports on Japan, 1543–1640.* Berkeley, 1965.
Dokai kōshūki. Edited and annotated by Kanai Madoka. Edo shiryō sōsho Series. Tokyo, 1967.
Hankampu, by Arai Hakuseki. 5 vols. Tokyo, 1967–68.

(*Ii-ke shiryō*) *Bakumatsu fūbun tansaku sho*. Edited by Ii Masahiro. 3 vols. Tokyo, 1967.

Kaempfer, Engelbert. *The History of Japan, Together with a Description of the Kingdom of Siam, 1609–1692*. 3 vols. Glasgow, 1906.

Kanai Madoka and Aoki Ryōko, eds. (*Mizuno-ke kiroku*) *Kōtoku-ben tsuketari han'piroku*. Waseda Daigaku Toshokan Kiyō, 4.

Kansei chōshū shokafu. 9 vols. Tokyo, 1917–18.

Keiroku hen. Vols. 5, 6 of Yamagata-ken shi (shiryō hen). Tokyo, 1961.

Kyōto shugōshoku shimatsu. Edited and annotated by Tōyama Shigeki. 2 vols. Tokyo, 1968.

Mikawa monogatari, by Ōkubo Hikozaemon. In Ieyasu shiryō shū Sengoku shiryō sōsho Series, edited by Ono Shinji. vol. 6, Tokyo, 1965.

Mito han shiryō. 5 vols. Tokyo, 1917.

Nakamura Kōya. *Tokugawa Ieyasu monjo no kenkyū*. 4 vols. Tokyo, 1958.

Ochibo shū. Edited and annotated by Hagiwara Tatsuo and Mizue Renko. Edo shiryō sōsho Series. Tokyo, 1967.

Ofuregaki Kampō shūsei, Edited by Takayanagi Shinzō and Ishii Ryōsuke. Tokyo, 1958.

Ōkubo Toshiaki, Kodama Kōta, Yauchi Kenji, Inoue Mitsusada, eds. *Shiryō ni yoru Nihon no ayumi*. 4 vols. Tokyo, 1957.

Ono Kiyoshi, ed. (*Shiryō*) *Tokugawa Bakufu no seido*. Tokyo, 1968.

Oritaku shiba no ki, by Arai Hakuseki. Edited and annotated by Miyazaki Michio, under the title *Teihon 'Oritaku shiba no ki' shakugi*. Tokyo, 1964.

Ryūeibunin. Edited by Tokyo Daigaku Shiryō Hensanjo. Dai Nihon kinsei shiryō Series. 5 vols. Tokyo, 1963–65.

Saiyū zakki, by Furukawa Koshōken. In Kinsei shakai keizai sōsho, vol. 9. Tokyo, 1927.

Satow, Sir Ernest. *A Diplomat in Japan*, London, 1968.

Tokugawa jikki. Vols. 38–47 of (Shintei zōhō) Kokushi taikei. edited by Kuroita Katsumi. Tokyo, 1964–66.

Tokugawa jūgodai shi, by Naitō Chisō. 6 vols. Tokyo, 1968–69.

Tokugawa kinreikō. Edited by Hōseishi Gakkai. 11 vols. Tokyo, 1958–61.

Tōyū zakki, by Furukawa Koshōken. Edited and annotated by Ōtō Tokihiko. Tokyo, 1964.

Zoku Tokugawa jikki. Vols. 48–52 of (Shintei zōhō) Kokushi taikei, edited by Kuroita Katsumi. Tokyo, 1966–67.

C. *Reference works*

Chihōshi Kenkyū Kyōgi-kai, eds. *Chihōshi kenkyū hikkei.* Tokyo, 1961.
Endō Motoo and Ōmori Shirō, eds. *Nihonshi handobukku.* Tokyo, 1963.
Kanno Michiaki. *Jigen.* Tokyo, 1955.
Mitamura Engyō. *Buke jiten.* Tokyo, 1963.
Takayanagi Mitsuhisa and Takeuchi Rizō, eds. *Nihonshi jiten.* Tokyo, 1968.
Tokyo Daigaku Shiryō Hensanjo, eds. *Dokushi biyō.* Tokyo, 1966.

D. *Official local histories*

Aichi-ken shi. 5 vols. Tokyo, 1939.
Chiyoda-ku shi. 3 vols. Tokyo, 1960.
Fukui-ken shi. 5 vols. Tokyo, 1921.
Fukuoka-ken shi. 8 vols. Kita Kyushu, 1962–66.
Fukuyama-shi shi. 2 vols. Hiroshima, 1963–67.
Gumma-ken shi. 4 vols. Tokyo, 1927.
Gyōda-shi shi. 2 vols. Tokyo, 1963–64.
Hikone-shi shi. 3 vols. Kyoto, 1960.
Karatsu-shi shi. Karatsu, 1962.
Kuwana-shi shi. 2 vols. Nagoya, 1959.
Nagaoka-shi shi. Nagaoka, 1931.
Ōgaki-shi shi. 3 vols. Ōgaki, 1930.
Ōsaka-shi shi. 8 vols. Osaka, 1911–13.
Saitama-ken shi. 7 vols. Tokyo, 1936.
Tsuruoka-shi shi. Tokyo, 1962.

E. *Books*

Beasley, W. G. *The Modern History of Japan.* New York, 1967.
Craig, Albert M. *Choshu in the Meiji Restoration.* Cambridge, Mass., 1961.
Eisenstadt, S. N. *Modernization—Protest and Change.* Englewood Cliffs, N. J., 1966.
Fujino Tamotsu. *Bakuhan taisei shi no kenkyū.* Tokyo, 1961.
Hall, John W. *Government and Local Power in Japan, 500–1700: A Study Based on Bizen Province.* Princeton, 1966.
———. *Tanuma Okitsugu, 1719–1788: Forerunner of Modern Japan.* Cambridge, Mass., 1955.
Harootunian, H. D. *Toward Restoration: The Growth of Political Consciousness in Tokugawa Japan.* Berkeley, 1970.
Hanseishi Kenkyūkai, eds. *Hansei seiritsu shi no sōgō kenkyū— Yonezawa han.* Tokyo, 1963.

Hirao Michio. *Tosa han.* Tokyo, 1965.
Hirono Saburō. *Tokugawa Iemitsu kō den.* Nikkō, 1961.
Horie Yasuzō. *Kinsei Nihon no keizai seisaku.* Tokyo, 1942.
———. *Kokusan shōrei to kokusan sembai.* Tokyo, 1963.
Imai Rintarō. *Ishida Mitsunari.* Tokyo, 1961.
Imaizumi Shōzō. *Nagaoka no rekishi.* 6 vols. Sanjō, 1968–69.
Ishii Takashi. *(Gakusetsu hihan) Meiji ishin ron.* Tokyo, 1968.
———. *Meiji ishin no butai ura.* Tokyo, 1970.
———. *Meiji ishin no kokusai-teki kankyō.* Tokyo, 1957.
Iwata Masakazu *Okubo Toshimichi, The Bismarck of Japan.* Berkeley, 1964.
Jansen, M. B. *Sakamoto Ryoma and the Meiji Restoration.* Princeton, 1961.
Kanai Madoka. *Hansei.* Tokyo, 1962.
Keene, D. *The Japanese Discovery of Europe.* London, 1952.
Kimura Motoi and Sugimoto Toshio, eds. *Fudai hansei no tenkai to Meiji ishin.* Tokyo, 1963.
Kishi Dembei. *Kawagoe hansei to bunkyō.* Tokyo, 1958.
Kitajima Masamoto. *Bakuhan–sei no kumon.* Vol. 18 of Chūō Kōron Nihon no rekishi. Tokyo, 1967.
———. *Edo Bakufu no kenryoku kōzō.* Tokyo, 1964.
———, ed. *Edo Bakufu—sono jitsuryoku monotachi.* 2 vols. Tokyo, 1964.
———. *Edo jidai.* Tokyo, 1958.
———. *Mizuno Tadakuni.* Tokyo, 1969.
———, ed. *Oiesōdō.* Tokyo, 1965.
———, ed. *Seiji shi, 2.* (Taikei Nihon-shi sōsho, 2). Tokyo, 1967.
Kobata Atsushi. *Kinsei shakai.* (Shin Nihon-shi taikei, 4). Tokyo, 1952.
———. *Nihon kōzan no rekishi.* Tokyo, 1968.
Kobayashi Seiji. *Date Masamune.* Tokyo, 1960.
Kodama Kōta. *Genroku jidai.* Vol. 16 of Chūō Kōron Nihon no rekishi. Tokyo, 1967.
——— and Kitajima Masamoto, eds. *Monogatari han shi.* 8 vols. Tokyo, 1964–65.
——— and ———, eds. *Dai ni ki monogatari han shi.* 7 vols. Tokyo, 1966.
Konishi Shirō. *Kindai I.* Vol. 8 of Nihon zenshi. Tokyo, 1959.
Kurita Motoji. *Edo jidai shi, jō.* Vol. 9 of Sōgō Nihon shi taikei. Tokyo, 1935.
Kuroya Naofusa. *Nakatsu han shi.* Tokyo, 1940.
McEwan, J. R. *The Political Writings of Ogyū Sorai.* Cambridge, 1962.
Matsudaira Tarō. *(Kōtei) Edo jidai seido no kenkyū.* Tokyo, 1964.
Matsuyoshi Sadao. *Kanemochi daimyō binbō daimyō.* Tokyo, 1964.

Murai Masuo. *Edo-jō.* Tokyo, 1964.

Murdoch, James. *A History of Japan.* 3 vols. London, 1926.

Nakajima Kurō. *Satō Nobuhiro no shisō.* Tokyo, 1941.

Nakai Nobuhiko. *Bakuhan shakai to shōhin ryūtsū.* Tokyo, 1961.

Nakamura Kōya. *Tokugawa Ieyasu kō den.* Nikkō, 1965.

———. *Tokugawa-ke.* Tokyo, 1961.

Ochiai. Tamotsu. *Kishiwada han shi kō.* Kishiwada, 1945.

Ōrui Noboru. *Nihon jōkaku zenshū.* 15 vols. Tokyo, 1967.

Ōsaka Rekishi Gakkai, eds. *Hōken shakai no mura to machi—Kinai senshin chiiki no shi-teki kenkyū.* Tokyo, 1960.

Sansom, Sir G. B. *The Western World and Japan.* New York, 1958.

Sasaki Junnosuke. *Daimyō to hyakushō.* Vol. 15 of Chūō Kōron *Nihon no rekishi.* Tokyo, 1967.

Shibusawa Eiichi. *Rakuō kō den.* Tokyo, 1936.

Shinji Yoshimoto. *Edo jidai no buke no seikatsu.* Tokyo, 1961.

Takahashi Kamekichi. *Tokugawa hōken keizai no kenkyū.* Tokyo, 1941.

Takigawa Seijirō, ed. *Nijō jinya no kenkyū. (Kujiyado no kenkyū—zoku).* No. 21 of *Waseda daigaku hikō-hō kenkyū-jo kiyō.* Tokyo, 1962.

Tanaka Akira. *Bakumatsu no hansei kaikaku.* Tokyo, 1965.

Taniguchi Sumio. *Ikeda Mitsumasa.* Tokyo, 1961.

———. *Okayama han.* Tokyo, 1964.

Tejima Masuo. *Aki Bingo ryōkoku idaijin den.* Tokyo, 1937.

Totman, Conrad. *Politics in the Tokugawa Bakufu, 1600–1843.* Cambridge, Mass., 1967.

Tsukahira, T. G. *Feudal Control in Tokugawa Japan: The Sankin Kotai System.* Cambridge, Mass., 1966.

Tsuji Tatsuya. *Edo kaifu.* Vol. 13 of Chūō Kōron Nihon no rekishi. Tokyo, 1967.

———. *Kyōhō kaikaku no kenkyū.* Tokyo, 1963.

———. *Tokugawa Yoshimune.* Tokyo, 1958.

———. *Tokugawa Yoshimune kō den.* Nikkō, 1962.

Wakabayashi Kisaburō. *Maeda Tsunanori.* Tokyo, 1961.

Wakamori Tarō. *Sumō ima mukashi.* Tokyo, 1963.

F. *Articles*

Andō Seiichi. "Kinsei jōkamachi no shōgyō tōsei—Harima Tatsuno han no baai." *Kokugakuin zasshi,* vol. 63, nos. 10–11.

An'ura Teruhiko. "Keiō ninen heiin no yaku ni okeru Kibi-tōge, Tanuki-yama fujin no senjutsu-teki igi." *Kiroku,* no. 11.

Asamori Kaname. "Ansei no taigoku o megutte." *Nihon rekishi,* no. 243.

Doi Akitaka. "Tanuma Okitsugu, Okitomo fushi." In *Edo Bakufu—*

sono jitsuryoku monotachi, edited by Kitajima Masamoto, vol. 2. Tokyo, 1964.

Endō Shinnosuke. "Boshin Tōhoku sensō no bunseki." In *Tōhoku-shi no shin kenkyū*, edited by Furuta Ryōichi Hakase Kanreki Kinenkai. Sendai, 1963.

Fujino Tamotsu. "Edo Bakufu." In *Iwanami kōza Nihon rekishi*, vol. 10. Tokyo, 1963.

———. "Kongo no hansei-shi kenkyū no kadai." *Chihōshi kenkyū* 44 : 10.

Fukushima Kimiko. "Edo Bakufu shoki no seiji seido ni tsuite—Shōgun to sono sokkin." *Shisō*, no. 8.

Furushima Toshio. "Bakufu zaisei shūnyū no dōkō to nōmin shūdatsu no kakki." In *Nihon keizai-shi taikei*, edited by Furushima Toshio, vol. 4. Tokyo, 1965.

Handa Yoshiko. "Dai ni-ji sei-Chō o meguru Bakufu no dōkō—Yoshinobu seiken no seiritsu to sono seikaku." *Shisō*, no. 8.

Harafuji Hiroshi. "Kaga han kahō no seikagu." *Kanazawa Daigaku Hō-Bungakubu ronshū (Hōkei hen, 5)*.

Hosokawa Michio. "Bakumatsu, ishin-ki ni okeru Ōgaki han no dōkō." *Nihon rekishi*, no. 221.

Ishii Takashi. "Oguri Tadamasa." In *Edo Bakufu—sono jitsuryoku monotachi*, edited by Kitajima Masamoto, vol. 2. Tokyo, 1964.

Ishizuka Hiromichi. "Bakuhan-ei gunji kōgyō no keisei." *Shigaku zasshi* vol. 80 nos. 8–9.

Kitajima Masamoto. "Kasei-ki no seiji to minshū." In *Iwanami kōza Nihon rekishi*, vol. 12. Tokyo, 1963.

———. "Makino Narisada to Yanagisawa Yoshiyasu." In *Edo Bakufu— sono jitsuryoku monotachi*, edited by Kitajima Masamoto, vol. 2. Tokyo, 1964.

———. "Meikun no higeki", In *Kokumin seikatsu-shi kenkyū*, edited by Itō Tasaburō. Tokyo, 1957.

———. "Mizuno Tadayuki", In *Edo Bakufu—sono jitsuryoku monotachi*, edited by Kitajima Masamoto, vol. 2. Tokyo, 1964.

Kojima Shigeo. "Bakuhan-sei hōkai-ki ni okeru kaimei-ha kanryō no keisei." In *Nihonshi ronkyū*. Tokyo, 1961.

———. "Bakumatsu ishin ni okeru fudai han no dōkō." *Rekishi kyōiku*, 1968, nos. 1–2.

———. "Bakumatsu ishin ni okeru fudai Ōtaki han no dōkō." *Juntendō Daigaku Taiikugakubu kiyō*, no. 10.

———. "Bakumatsu ishin ni okeru fudai Bushū Oshi han no dōkō." *Juntendō Daigaku Taiikugakubu kiyō*, no. 6.

———. "Fudai Sakura han no kyōjun to Satō Taizen." *Juntendō Daigaku Taiikugakubu kiyō*, no. 5.

Miyazaki Michio. "Arai Hakuseki to Manabe Akifusa." In *Edo Bakufu*

—*sono jitsuryoku monotachi,* edited by Kitajima Masamoto, vol. 2. Tokyo, 1964.

Murakami Tadashi. "Shoki Bakufu seiji no dōkō—Ōkubo Iwami no kami Nagayasu jiken o chūshin ni." *Nihon rekishi,* no. 205.

Nakabe Yoshiko. "Bunsei Tempō-ki hansei kaikaku to Ōsaka shōnin shihon (ge)—Bungo Funai han to Kōnoike Izuke—." *Hyōgo shigaku,* no. 18.

Nishida Shūhei. "Meiji ishin ni okeru Hikone han." *Nihon rekishi,* no. 203.

Ōishi Shinzaburō. "Genroku, Kyōhō-ki no keizai dankai." In *Nihon keizai-shi taikei,* edited by Furushima Toshio, vol. 4. Tokyo, 1965.

———. "Kyōhō kaikaku." In *Iwanami kōza Nihon rekishi,* vol. 11. Tokyo, 1963.

———. "Tanuma Okitsugu ni kansuru jūrai no shiryō no shimpyōsei ni tsuite." *Nihon rekishi,* no. 237.

Okamoto Ryōichi. "Tempō kaikaku." In *Iwanami kōza Nihon rekishi,* vol. 13. Tokyo, 1963.

Ono Masao. "Kambun, Empō-ki no ryūtsū kikō." In *Nihon keizai-shi taikei,* edited by Furushima Toshio, vol. 3. Tokyo, 1965.

Reischauer, E. O. "Japanese Feudalism." In *Feudalism in History,* edited by Rushton Coulborn. Princeton, 1956.

Saiki Kazuma. "Tokugawa shōgun seibō narabini saishō kō." In *Rekishi to jimbutsu,* edited by Nihon Rekishi Gakkai. Tokyo, 1964.

Saitō Toshio. "Sendai han no kashindan kōsei—seiritsu-ki no kōsatsu." *Nihon rekishi,* 219.

Sasaki Junnosuke. "Bakuhan kankei ni okeru fudai daimyō no chii." *Nihonshi kenkyū,* no. 58.

Shindō Mitsuyuki. "Hansei kaikaku no kenkyū—jōkamachi shōgyō no kiki o tsūjite mita Nakatsu han hōken kōzō no hōkai katei—." *Keizaigaku kenkyu,* vol. 2, no. 2.

Shinji Yoshimoto. "Tokugawa Tsunayoshi." In *Buke no sekai* (vol. 6 of *Nihonshi no jimbutsuzō*), edited by Okada Akio. Tokyo, 1968.

Shively, D. H. "Tokugawa Tsunayoshi, the Genroku Shogun." In *Personality in Japanese History,* edited by Albert M. Craig and Donald H. Shively. Berkeley, 1970.

Takahashi Shin'ichi. "Tanuma Okitsugu." In *Buke no sekai* (vol. 6 of *Nihonshi no jimbutsuzō*), edited by Okada Akio. Tokyo, 1968.

Tanawa Akira. "Andō Nobumasa." In *Edo Bakufu—sono jitsuryoku monotachi,* edited by Kitajima Masamoto, vol. 2. Tokyo, 1964.

Totman, Conrad. "Political Reconciliation in the Tokugawa Bakufu: Abe Masahiro and Tokugawa Nariaki, 1844–1852." In *Personality in Japanese History,* edited by Albert M. Craig and Donald H. Shively. Berkeley, 1970.

———. "Political Succession in the Tokugawa Bakufu: Abe Masahiro's

rise to power, 1843–1845." *Harvard Journal of Asiatic Studies* 26.
Tōyama Shigeki. "Ishin tōji no Fukuzawa no shisō." In *Sekai ni okeru
Nihon no bunka,* edited by Saegusa Hirōto Kinen Rombun-shū
Hensei-kai. Tokyo, 1965.
————. "Kindai-shi gaisetsu." In *Iwanami kōza Nihon rekishi,* vol. 14.
Tokyo, 1963.
Toyoda Takeshi. "Eiyū to densetsu." In *Rekishi to jimbutsu,* edited by
Nihon Rekishi Gakkai. Tokyo, 1964.
Tsuda Hideo. "Kansei kaikaku." In *Iwanami kōza Nihon rekishi,* vol.
12. Tokyo, 1963.
————. "Matsudaira Sadanobu." In *Edo Bakufu—sono jitsuryoku
monotachi,* edited by Kitajima Masamoto, vol. 2. Tokyo, 1964.
————. "Tempō kaikaku no keizai-shi-teki igi." In *Nihon keizai-shi
taikei,* edited by Furushima Toshio, vol. 4. Tokyo, 1965.
————. "Tempō no kaikaku." In *Nihon rekishi kōza,* vol. 4. Tokyo,
1956.
————. "Tokugawa Yoshimune to Tanuma Okitsugu." In *Nihon
jimbutsu-shi taikei,* edited by Hayashi Motoi, vol. 4. Tokyo, 1963.
Watanabe Sansei. "Bakuryō azukaridokoro ni okeru shihai no seikaku—
Echigo-kuni Ojiya-machi no baai—." *Chihōshi kenkyū,* no. 96.
Wilson, G. M. "The Bakumatsu Intellectual in Action: Hashimoto
Sanai in the Political Crisis of 1858." In *Personality in Japanese
History,* edited by Albert M. Craig and Donald H. Shively. Berkeley,
1970.
Yagi Akihiro. "Ōsaka shūhen no shoryō haichi ni tsuite." *Nihon rekishi,*
no. 231.
Yamamoto Tomio. "Awa han no shakai to keizai." *Rekishi kyōiku,* vol.
6, no. 1.
Yoshinaga Akira. "Han sembai seido no kiban to kōzō." In *Nihon
keizai-shi taikei,* edited by Furushima Toshio, vol. 4. Tokyo, 1965.
Yoshizumi Mieko. "Edo Bakufu no kansatsu seido." *Nihon Rekishi,* no.
244.
————. "Tetsudai bushin ni tsuite." *Gakushūin Daigaku Bungakubu
kenkyū nempō,* no. 14.

Index

Abe family, Fukuyama branch: domain, 54, 66; finances, 60; marriages, 98–99; in Bakufu office, 98, 136, 141, 143, 145
Abe family, Shirakawa branch, 143, 145
Abe Masaharu, 53
Abe Masahiro, 98, 238; rewards from office, 126; domain, 151; policy, 221–22, 224, 225; resignation, 233
Abe Masakata, 241
Abe Masakiyo, 60, 136
Abe Masakuni, 63, 147
Abe Masakura, 26, 63
Abe Masamoto, 60
Abe Masasuke, 99, 137
Abe Masatake, 174
Abe Masatō, 150, 236
Abe Masatomo, 130, 137–38
Abe Masatsugu, 126, 146–47, 162
Abe Shigetsugu, 98, 147, 162–63
Abe Tadaaki, 53, 150, 162, 163, 166
Agechi-rei, 103, 218-19, 221
Agemai-rei, 37, 129, 188
Aizu Han, 46; and Bakufu land, 25; monopolies in, 61; wax-making in, 195; fall of, 246
Akimoto Takafusa, 130
Akimoto Takatomo, 174
Akita Han, 15–16, 26
Andō Nobumasa, 233–34
Andō Shigekata, 53
Ansei purge, 232-33
Aoyama family, 47
Aoyama Tadatoshi, 146
Aoyama Yoshimasa, 120
Arai Hakuseki, 89, 181–83, 188, 189, 198; on Bakufu finances, 25, 177; opinions of various contemporaries, 47, 158, 164, 171, 173, 182–83, 187; describes Mt. Fuji eruption, 109

views on rōjū, 117, 151, 181–82; disliked by daimyo, 157; policy of, 184; resigns, 186
Arima family, 90, 97, 98, 107
Arima Toyouji, 103
Asano family, 93, 95–97
Awa Han, 26, 92
Azukaridokoro, 184–85, 188

Bakufu: as seen by others, 1, 18, 38, 39, 86, 227; established, 3; strategic situation of, 4, 10–15, 28–30, 39, 51, 218, 235; landholdings of, 25–26, 34, 177, 184–85, 188, 218; finances of, 25–27, 188, 201–02; administration of, 118–25; fall of, 229–30
Bakufu authority: extent of, 6–19, 21, 27–28, 39, 91–94, 106, 191, 228–29; decline of, 19–36, 159–60, 227–29, 232, 237; limitations upon, 21, 30, 33, 36–37, 58, 133, 149–53, 251
Bakufu office: cost of, 80, 134–38; relation to influence, 125; advantages of, 129–134; rotation of, 132; competition for, 138–46, 239–40
Bakufu policy: inspection system, 9–10, 30–33, 164, 169; shipbuilding, 10, 30, 213–14, 222, 225–26; impositions on daimyo, 11–13, 28–30, 164, 168, 177–78, 184, 194, 203–04; foreign trade, 15, 226–27, 234–36; currency, 15–16, 22, 178; commerce, 15–16, 24–25, 66, 194–96, 218; mining, 16, 23–24, 222–26, 235; foreign policy, 16–17, 36, 210–11, 223; aid to daimyo, 29, 34, 104, 109, 113–16, 178, 189; fief transfers, 34–36, 54–55, 91, 131, 151, 163, 168, 176; attainders, 102–03, 163, 166–67, 174–76, 184, 193–94, 203

271

Ogasawara family, 48, 54, 73, 90, 102, 141, 143
Ogasawara Nagahiro, 147
Ogasawara Nagamaru, 80
Ogasawara Nagamichi, 239, 240, 242
Ogasawara Nagashige, 147
Ogasawara Nagatane, 176
Ogasawara Nagatsugu, 50
Ogasawara Tadakata, 127, 134
Ogasawara Tadatomo, 50
Ogasawara Tadayū, 128
Ogasawara Tadazane, 50, 90, 101
Oguri Tadamasa, 237, 246
Ogyū Sorai, 37, 86, 89, 91, 101, 132
Oie-sōdō, 69–73, 69, 73, 168, 175, 176, 197
Okabe family, 107, 141, 143
Okabe Nagachika, 112
Okabe Nagakazu, 119
Okabe Nagamoto, 112
Okabe Nagayasu, 112
Okabe Nagayori, 113
Okayama Han, 30, 57, 110–11, 113, 229
Okazaki Han, 54, 75, 79, 82, 94, 138, 178
Ōkubo family, 47, 149
Ōkubo Hikozaemon, 116, 150, 231, 252, 255; on fudai identity, 87–88, 89; on new men, 160–61; on daimyo, 223
Ōkubo Tadachika, 5–6, 87, 136
Ōkubo Tadatomo, 137
Ōkubo Tadazane, 144
Okudaira family, 48, 102, 107, 194
Okudaira Nobumasa, 104
Ōoka Tadakata, 130
Ōoka Tadamitsu, 148, 150, 191–92, 193–95, 206, 208
Opium War, 36, 210–11, 215, 254
Osaka campaigns, 5, 103, 105
Osaka Castle, 2, 11, 12
Osaka market, 15, 26–27, 64–65, 195, 202, 209
Oshi Han, 26, 53, 64–65, 247, 248–49
Owari Han, 26, 46, 100, 133, 161, 229

Peasant unrest, 30, 59, 112, 136, 167, 184; official attitude to, 164, 184, 189

Rin'ōji, Prince, 246
Roches, Léon, 235
Rōjū, 106, 117, 119–20, 121, 122–23, 134, 154, 240; rewards from office, 126–38; landholdings, 139, 140; under Tsunayoshi, 172, 174; under Ienobu, 180, 181, 183; under Yoshimune, 186; under Matsudaira Sadanobu, 200, 204; under Mizuno Tadakuni, 215
Rōnin, 44, 166–67

Sagara Han, 64–65, 66, 193
Sakai family, 47, 139–40, 141
Sakai family: Obama branch, 66, 98, 136; Shōnai branch, 70, 72, 79, 108, 109–10; Himeji branch, 71, 98, 115, 123
Sakai Tadakata, 35, 175
Sakai Tadakatsu, 9, 70, 148, 165, 166
Sakai Tadakiyo, 90–91, 124, 132, 165, 166, 168; dismissal, 171–72, 175, 186n
Sakai Tadamochi, 152
Sakai Tadanobu, 96, 152
Sakai Tadaoto, 129
Sakai Tadayasu, 133
Sakai Tadayo, 162
Sakai Tadayori, 133, 135
Sakai Tadayoshi, 133
Sakai Tadazane, 178–79
Sakakibara family, 47, 71
Sakura Han, 53, 82, 137, 145n, 147, 149, 176, 249; finances, 60, 64, 127, 135–36
Sakurajima shipyard, 225
Samurai: and Bakufu, 8, 14, 81–82; and daimyo, 20–21, 68–83, 247–49; stipends, 59, 72–73, 79; and domain office, 74–75
Sanada family, 47, 107